FOOL ME TWICE

FOOL ME TWICE

OBAMA'S SHOCKING PLANS FOR
THE NEXT FOUR YEARS EXPOSED

By

AARON KLEIN &
BRENDA J. ELLIOTT

WND Books

FOOL ME TWICE

WND Books
Washington, D.C.

Copyright © 2012
Aaron Klein and Brenda J. Elliott

Book designed by Mark Karis; edited by Benyamin Korn

WND Books are distributed to the trade by:
Midpoint Trade Books
27 West 20th Street, Suite 1102
New York, NY, 10011

WND Books are available at special discounts for bulk purchases. WND Books, Inc., also publishes books in electronic formats. For more information, call (541-474-1776) or visit www.wndbooks.com.

First Edition

Hardcover ISBN: 978–1–936488–57–5
eBook ISBN: 978–1–936488–93–3

Library of Congress information available

Printed in the United States of America
10 9 8 7 6 5 4 3 2 1

CONTENTS

INTRODUCTION

A MERICAN VOTERS HAVE often heard a presidential election called "the most important election of your lifetime." And surely the failure to defeat Barack Hussein Obama in November 2012 would be momentous. It would mean a continuation of his relentless expansion of federal government power; more explosive increases in his crushing, multitrillion-dollar intergenerational debt; a weak foreign policy coupled with his evisceration of America's military; and the likelihood that more Obama-appointed Supreme Court justices would assure a left-leaning majority on America's top court for at least a generation.

But these trends, insidious as they are, do not capture the real meaning of a second Obama term. These conventional concerns—which would normally be at least partly reversible under some future change in administration—do not encompass what is truly at stake for America in 2012. That risk is the progressive socialist takeover of our country, the "fundamental transformation of the United States of America" that Obama proclaimed just five days before the general election in 2008. The danger is that 2012 may not only be the most important election of our lifetimes, but that it will be the last chance we have to save liberty as Americans have known it since 1776.

The progressive socialists normally operate—to borrow a Fabian socialist term—by *stealth*. But Obama himself accidentally revealed his duplicitous program in a now notorious "open microphone" incident with Russian president Dmitry Medvedev. Americans were momentarily stunned to hear the two in private conversation on the sidelines of a March 26, 2012, Nuclear Security Summit in Seoul, South Korea:

> Obama: "On all these issues, but particularly missile defense, this, this can be solved but it's important for him to give me space."
> Medvedev: "Yeah, I understand. I understand your message about space. Space for you…"
> Obama: "This is my last election. After my election I have more flexibility."
> Medvedev: "I understand. I will transmit this information to Vladimir."

These deceitful remarks do not simply betray Obama's willingness to compromise American security interests. As we expose in this book's chapter on defense policy, a second Obama term would go far beyond caving in to Russia's objections to U.S. missile defenses for Europe or the Kremlin's longstanding goal of diminishing America's nuclear arsenal. What Obama's "open-mic moment" made stunningly clear is his strategy of concealing his true agenda from the American people by telling the leader of Russia that he will have more "flexibility" after his reelection to enact policies the American public would oppose—if only we knew. This begs the obvious question: What other unpopular policies is Obama hiding that he plans to foist on the country if he wins a second term?

This book reveals the blueprint for a second term that Obama and his progressive backers don't want you to know. Months of painstaking research into thousands of documents have enabled coauthor Brenda J. Elliott and me to expose the secret template for Obama's next four years—the one actually created by Obama's own top advisers and strategists.

Fool Me Twice is our third and most important book-length investigation into Obama and the progressive socialist movement. Here we lay out in great detail the progressive agenda for a second Obama term. All the main areas of domestic policy are covered—jobs, wages, health care, immigration, electoral "reform," as well as the "green scheme," or what passes in pro-gressive circles for a national energy policy. Each of these plans seeks to permanently remake America into a government-dominated socialist state.

The American public has a broad sense of the president's agenda, should he capture four more years. For example, Obama has been clear he would use another term to ensure the implementation of the legally challenged ObamaCare and the "reform" of our financial sector. Obama also stated recently he would attempt the central goal of progressive-style immigration reform, as well. But these generalized ambitions do not scratch the surface of the specific, radical assault that is planned upon our country and that we have labored to expose in this work. Here are just a few samples from dozens upon dozens of specific plans unveiled herein:

- detailed plans to enact single-payer health care legislation con-trolled by the federal government, regardless of any Supreme Court decision to overturn ObamaCare;
- the re-creation of a 21st-century version of FDR's Works Progress Administration (WPA) program within the Department of Labor that would oversee a massive new bureaucracy and millions of new federal jobs;
- further gutting of the U.S. military in shocking ways, while using the "savings" for a new "green" stimulus program and the found-ing of a federal "green" bank to fund so-called environmentally friendly projects;
- the spreading of already vastly reduced resources of the U.S. Armed Forces spread even thinner by using them to combat "global warm-ing," fight global poverty, remedy "injustice," bolster the United Nations, and step up use of "peacekeeping" deployments;
- an expansive new amnesty program for illegal aliens linked with a reduction in the capabilities of the U.S. Border Patrol and plans to bring in untold numbers of new immigrants with the removal of caps on H-1B visas and green cards.

And this is just the start.

How did we uncover this radical blueprint? Surprisingly, many of the plans are lying in plain sight but are in need of investigative energies and trained eyes. In our previous book, *Red Army*, Brenda and I copiously traced the origins of Obama's first-term signature policies, including ObamaCare, defense initiatives, and the massive "stimulus." In nearly every case, we found each plan was crafted and perfected over time by key progressive organizations and activists, usually first promoted in extensive research and policy papers. Many times, the plan at hand was only gradually introduced into legislation pushed by progressive Democrats. Progressive marketing strategists, we found, were then brought in to sell the plan to the American public, cloaking the most radical proposals in the guise of moderation, in the bland-sounding rhetoric of popular social ideals.

For example, we documented how ObamaCare was largely a rehashed version of legislation that first originated in progressive research in 2003 as something called Health Care for America, the centerpiece of the progressive Economic Policy Institute's Agenda for Shared Prosperity. Many of the major facets of the health care law, we showed, were attempted in earlier, less grandiose legislative efforts. We revealed how progressive marketing experts helped to sell ObamaCare to the public, even providing suggestions on exactly which words supporters should use to promote the bill.

We further documented how key progressive organizations served as the nerve center for formulating such White House initiatives as the "stimulus," defense strategy, and education reform. This same cast of characters has been busy plotting Obama's second-term agenda in exhaustive detail.

To be clear, we do not argue that every plan exposed in this book would be implemented by Obama exactly as outlined. But we have no doubt that we are presenting you with the detailed game plan that would form the basis of a second Obama term.

I have been investigating Barack Obama since December 2007 when the Democratic primary was getting into full swing and the largely unknown junior senator from Illinois emerged as a serious contender. At the time, I was a Jerusalem-based reporter primarily focused on the Middle East. From five thousand miles away, I was forced to involve myself in U.S. domestic affairs, since I found the Washington press corps to be mysteriously uninterested in doing any real vetting of Obama's background.

I am proud to have played a role in uncovering Obama's radical history.

My own Middle East investigations led me to first piece together Obama's extensive relationship with unrepentant Pentagon-bomber Bill Ayers, penning an article that broke into a major issue of the 2008 Presidential campaign. I also first documented Obama's close personal and professional ties to the PLO-connected, anti-Israel professor Rashid Khalidi, as well as a host of other nearly lifetime ties to radical groups and anti-American personalities, including the Nation of Islam; the Association of Community Organizations for Reform Now, or ACORN; and the Service Employees International Union (SEIU).

It was in a now-notorious April 2008, WABC Radio interview with myself and then cohost John Batchelor that a top official of the Palestinian terrorist organization Hamas "endorsed" Obama for president. Our interview made world headlines and became a prominent theme of the 2008 presidential campaign.

Later, as his presidency took shape, I teamed up with Brenda and together we researched Obama and White House officials. We were among the first to report that Obama's "Green Jobs Czar," Van Jones, had founded a communist organization—a theme later picked up by Fox News Channel's Glenn Beck leading to Jones' resignation. We also released a video, circulated nationwide, in which White House communications director Anita Dunn boasted that Obama's presidential campaign had focused on "making" the news media cover certain issues while rarely communicating anything to the press unless it was "controlled." Dunn stepped down weeks later, though she continues to this day to serve the White House in an advisory role. Together, we wrote both *Manchurian President*, documenting Obama's lifelong ties to radicals, and *Red Army*, which detailed how the progressive machine formulated the president's first-term White House strategy.

Of course, it is now our hope to contribute even further to the exposure of President Obama's radical policies, and of the progressives' deceptive designs for our country. America's failure to grasp—or unwillingness to confront—the grave threat we now face is not limited to liberal elites or to practitioners of what has become essentially the partisan news media. Even much of the "conservative" political class has not risen to this challenge. We despair, for example, to hear conservatives criticize Obama as being "either too naïve or too incompetent" to govern effectively. To the contrary, what we continue to document here is that he is a highly skilled political radical who has spent a lifetime preparing to reach the pinnacle of American power, and is for the most part succeeding in implementing the progressive socialist agenda.

But we realize, also, that the continued success of Barack Hussein Obama depends on concealing his true nature, his radical policies, and his second-term goals. We are about to blow the lid off all of that.

Obama is notorious for blaming his predecessor, President George W. Bush, for the current economic woes, as well as a host of other failures. One joke going around Washington after the rare earthquake of August 2011 was that Obama had proclaimed it: "Bush's fault." Yet it was Bush who must be credited with dusting off an old American saw that well applies to his White House successor: "Fool me once, shame on you. Fool me twice, shame on me."

Will we, the American public, allow ourselves to be fooled again? Let us pray, not. For even a politician most adroit at manipulating democratic elections (see Chapter 9) cannot succeed to "fool all of the people, all of the time."

Aaron Klein

U.S. ARMED FORCES TO
FIGHT "INJUSTICE," POVERTY,
AND "GLOBAL WARMING"

I MAGINE THE FUNDAMENTAL transformation of the U.S. Armed Forces into a
social work organization designed to combat "global warming," fight
global poverty, remedy "injustice," bolster the United Nations, and increase
"peacekeeping" forces worldwide.

This messianic fantasy of "swords into ploughshares" is to be implemented in our dangerous world, driven by the think tanks of '60s radicals
and their disciples who have infiltrated the highest levels of American—and
global—power.

The major leagues of progressive groups with deep ties to the Obama
administration got together to produce a comprehensive, ninety-six-page
report with these and other specific recommendations for how Obama
should reform the U.S. military during his second term in office. This
detailed blueprint, titled "A Report of the Task Force on a Unified Security
Budget for the United States" (or 2012 Unified Security Budget), lays out a
future Obama "defense" agenda.[1]

The Unified Security Budget is a joint product of the Center for American
Progress (CAP) and the Institute for Policy Studies (IPS). Throughout this
book, we will thoroughly examine CAP's deep influence in framing White
House policy under Obama, indeed in directing Obama's initial transition
into the White House, aiding in the selection of administration officials,

and crafting Obama's specific first- and second-term plans. It is fair to say CAP, led by John Podesta, is the de facto policy nerve center of the Obama administration. *Time* magazine called CAP Obama's "idea factory," noting that "not since the Heritage Foundation helped guide Ronald Reagan's transition in 1981 has a single outside group held so much sway."[2] *Time* reported it is "difficult to overstate the influence in Obamaland of CAP."

It is instructive that CAP got together with the IPS, a policy group infamous for its Cold War-era support of the Soviets and its long–standing crusade to diminish the U.S. military, all while pushing for the elimination of our nuclear arsenal. Later in this chapter we will detail Defense Secretary Leon Panetta's ties to the IPS, including his past advocacy for the group's specific military recommendations. We will also document how key members of other organizations sponsoring the Unified Security Budget, such as the Connect U.S. Fund, can now be found at the top level of the Obama administration. Another Unified Security Budget report sponsor deserving special attention is George Soros's Open Society Institute.

The 2012 Unified Security Budget itself recalls how the group's policy recommendations from some other of its recent defense papers have already been adopted by Obama's Sustainable Defense Taskforce, which has notoriously recommended $1 trillion in cuts over ten years.

> The Unified Security Budget project has contributed to this debate by outlining a set of cuts in unneeded military programs that formed the core of a proposal by the Sustainable Defense Task Force . . . A majority, though not a supermajority, of the members of the President's Commission on Fiscal Responsibility and Reform adopted the annualized figure of $100 billion, and many of the recommendations from this proposal.[3]

And it continues:

> These figures—the $100 billion annual benchmark and the 10-year accumulated total—were not invented by the Commission's staff. They aligned closely with the two major blueprints released during the Commission's deliberations that had given military spending a

role in deficit reduction commensurate with its dominant role in the discretionary budget. The first, the Sustainable Defense Task Force (SDTF), expanded on the recommendations for military cuts from the 2010 Unified Security Budget (USB) report.

The report revels in the overlapping membership between the two policy groups: the "Unified Security Budget and Sustainable Defense task forces share several members, including both USB principal authors."

We do not believe Obama would adopt every defense recommendation in the 2012 Unified Security Budget, including some shocking suggestions we will soon reveal. But what is certain—given these groups' influence within the administration until now—is that the report would serve as a defense policy wish list for a second Obama term and that its concepts will inform Obama's military approach if he wins reelection. We will even show how much of the report has already been incorporated into key progressive House and Senate legislation.

WHO NEEDS A STANDING ARMY, NUKES, MISSILES, OR SUBMARINES?

The Unified Security Budget proclaims its goal as the "rebalancing" of our country's security resources to "strengthen our capacity to prevent and resolve conflict by non-military means, and to constrain terrorist threats not by waging a 'war on terror' but by finding and isolating terrorists and bringing them to justice, protecting ourselves from future attacks, and strengthening the capacity of the United States and other nations to resist terrorism."

Of immediate concern is the stated objective of transforming our armed forces to stress conflict resolution and diplomacy. For most Americans, the entire purpose of military spending is to maintain the capability of using force when such action becomes necessary. The resolution of conflict by non-military means—diplomacy, economic aid, technical assistance—is the proper focus of other government (and nongovernment) agencies. In other words, the very premise of the report—minimizing defense capacity and redirection of resources—is deeply flawed and dangerous.

The report sets the tone of its lofty agenda by demanding immediate reductions in the military's already heavily slashed budget. But there is one interesting exception requiring massive *increases* in funding—any spending that funds "alternative energy" or that focuses Defense Department resources on combating "climate change as a security threat." The report authors recommend investing "the lion's share" of the few allotted increases in addressing the "threat" of so-called climate change.

Half of all savings from military cuts, the report recommends, should be used for investing in "job creation," while the other half is to be allocated to deficit reduction. The report does not spell out exactly how Obama should "invest" this money in "job creation." Perhaps this is an allusion to a future massive "stimulus" or to various other second-term progressive economic machinations and spread-the-wealth schemes to be exposed in our coming chapters.

The report takes issue with the use of forces on the ground in various countries to secure or influence the longer-term strategic position of other nations. And how to minimize that influence? For starters, by scaling back all U.S. ground forces by 20 percent; reducing the Navy's surface fleet by 20 percent (including two carriers and carrier combat air wings) and reducing the Air Force by two combat air wings—while cutting standing peacetime overseas deployments (Europe, East Asia) by up to 50,000 troops at a time.

The Unified authors are just getting warmed up. Another recommendation, which the report claims will save $21 billion, is to reduce the U.S. nuclear arsenal to no more than 292 deployed nuclear weapons and the complete elimination of the Trident II nuclear missile—a process President Obama already initiated in April 2010 when he signed a deal with Russia reducing stocks of weapons-grade plutonium. The accord was signed at a nuclear summit in Washington arranged by Obama, at which leaders of forty-seven nations committed to reducing the world's nuclear stockpiles even as Iran drives ever closer toward nuclear weaponization, a development likely to spark a multi-country Mideast nuclear arms race.[4] One week earlier, Russian president Dmitry Medvedev and Obama signed the new Strategic Arms Reduction Treaty, or START, committing both countries to reducing their deployed nuclear arsenals.

Obama had broadly proclaimed his disarmament intentions during a 2007 campaign speech: "Here's what I'll say as president: America seeks a world in which there are no nuclear weapons."[5] By 2010, as president, he was arguing: "We need to change our nuclear policy and our posture, which is still focused on deterring the Soviet Union—a country that doesn't exist."[6] Unfortunately, Obama's declaration came just as Russia was signing a major arms deal with Syria and began to revive its Cold War–era naval bases in the Middle East, including in the Syrian ports of Tartus and Latakia on the Mediterranean. Moscow had also maintained bases in Damascus during the Cold War, but post–Soviet Russia's military posture in the region weakened for a time. As of this writing, Moscow had resumed giving diplomatic cover, along with its military assistance, to the murderous Assad regime.

And just as Iran, North Korea, and other aggressor countries (e.g., Venezuela) aim to develop or enhance intercontinental missile capabilities, the IPS report next recommends the U.S. cease all further development of missile *defenses*. Yes, you read that correctly. The report goes through a list of current missile defense programs, including Ground-based Midcourse Defense, Airborne Laser, Kinetic Energy Interceptors, and a number of others, pushing for all programs to be cut. "It is unwise to fund more advanced systems for missile defense while current ones have yet to be proven effective against their targeted threats," complains the report. In other words, it is desirable for Obama to invest billions and billions in taxpayer funds on questionable solar and other "green energy" projects, even as many of those projects prove impracticable or go bankrupt, but investment in "unproven" national defense systems is to be slashed with abandon.

The military's vital Research, Development, Test, and Evaluation program is to be cut by $10 billion across the board. After all, why should the armed forces research, develop, test, or evaluate weapons or programs when the money can be better reinvested in wind turbines and "peacekeeping" forces? (We're not being sarcastic here—keep reading.)

Next on the chopping block: the complete cancelation of the second SSN-744 Virginia Class submarine. While the Unified Security Budget describes the new model as "unnecessary to address any of the threats facing the United States today" and "a weapon looking for an enemy," the SSN-774 is designed for covert collection of intelligence, transportation of special operations teams, and launching of tactical Tomahawk missiles— flexible capabilities tailored to rapid responses required by the 21st-century's conflicts with irregular combatants. Similarly targeted for cancelation are the V-22 Osprey helicopter and the Navy and Marine Corps versions of the F-35 Joint Strike Fighter. And, as mentioned earlier, the report calls for the massive reduction of active-duty personnel stationed in Europe and Asia as well as the cutting of two active component air wings and two carrier-battle groups along with their associated Air Force air wings.

And what to do with all these savings? The Unified Security Budget provides a helpful graph that shows how the money can be used to "meet the State Department's request of $2.14 billion for the Contributions to International Peacekeeping Activities account." The savings can also be used to "support Egypt's burgeoning democracy through economic and humanitarian assistance." Yes, the same Egyptian democracy currently seeing the Muslim Brotherhood, along with Islamist parties to the right of the Brotherhood, taking power. Another progressive recommendation: Use the savings to "increase the government's investment in renewable energy and energy efficiency to a level that would achieve the Obama administration's stated climate security goals."

REMOVE CONGRESSIONAL OVERSIGHT OF MILITARY SPENDING

For now, Congressional oversight serves as a check to some of Obama's ambitious calls for defense budget reductions. Some would even give Congress more power in this realm. The progressive groups, however, have concocted a plan to wrest budgetary control from Congress—where it is vested by the U.S. Constitution—and instead place our military's purse strings in the hands of an "independent panel." "Congressional power isn't the solution," contends the report, which then offers a range of options that "think outside the box of existing structures." How "outside the box" is their thinking? The report first endorses a recommendation, from the Straus Military Reform Project at the Center for Defense Information, for an "independent panel to review the military's procurement budget every year." Membership would exclude both current and retired military officers who "have any financial ties to defense corporations or reserve the right to forge such ties in the future." Another option for bypassing Congressional oversight would be a "Select Committee on National Security and International Affairs" to examine our overall security needs and the best balance of available tools to achieve them. And it could be empowered with making changes to the committee's own structure. Congress—especially one under the control of progressive Democrats—could also authorize a "Commission on Budgeting for National Security and International Affairs" made up of "similarly committed members, to examine the current balkanized budget process, and recommend a restructuring that would enable decision-making on security that more effectively considers the overall balance of security tools and puts the national interest over parochial interests."

The report recommends that the State Department and the ever-effective Department of Homeland Security have more authority over the Defense Department's budget.

MILITARY TO FIGHT POVERTY, SO-CALLED GLOBAL WARMING

After massively slashing the military and its funding, and wresting control of the funding process from Congress, the 2012 Unified Security Budget seeks no less than to change the very role and mission of our Armed Forces. It complains that, after the 9/11 Islamic terror attacks, the U.S. military's "mission objectives have grown much more ambitious." And what do the report authors recommend? Of course! Using the military to combat "global warming," fight global poverty, remedy "injustice," bolster the United Nations, and increase "peacekeeping" forces worldwide.

As poverty is a key contributor to state weakness, it is imperative for the United States to be actively engaged in the fight to end global poverty as a primary focus of our national security strategy. Effective U.S. global development policy can support countries and people to manage their own way forward from poverty and injustice. As this helps improve the livelihoods of millions, it reduces the sources of discontent and disenfranchisement that fuel global security threats.

In other words, if only the polar ice caps weren't melting and our country's wealth was only redistributed to the developing world, Iran would simply stop seeking nuclear weapons, North Korea would quit being an aggressor, those al-Qaida pests would just leave us alone, Russia and China would become partners for peace, and the bloated and corrupt bureaucracy that is today's UN would become a kind of global Mother Teresa, dispensing charity and goodness to all in need.

The CAP and Institute for Policy Studies are plotting to take billions of dollars from the U.S. military and instead use them for a "green stimulus." These groups also envision the military as a tool to fight so-called global warming. In 2011, the IPS released a forty-page CAP-endorsed report titled "The Green Dividend," a term the IPS defines as "a major shift of resources from the military budget to sustainable energy."[7]

The report complains of an excess of military spending:

> The obvious solution is to reduce military spending and apply those savings to a green technology initiative that reduces our dependency on fossil fuels, shrinks our carbon footprint, and creates jobs. Such a "green stimulus" could pull our economy out of recession.

IPS acknowledges the Obama administration made funding of "green initiatives" a significant part of his original stimulus package, but the spending of over $1 billion on risky ventures over which the private sector is highly skeptical is simply not enough for the progressive elite. The IPS now wants to shift jobs from the military sector to the "green growth" sector. It seeks to "play matchmaker and marry defense sector workers to green technology jobs." The IPS research paper identifies the Pentagon as the "largest institutional energy user—and greenhouse gas emitter—on the planet," arguing that if it undertook a "crash program" to convert to renewable energy sources and clean vehicles, it could make a significant impact on global emissions. It recommends redirecting much of the U.S. military budget from defense towards creating a Pentagon that is energy efficient; a military that stresses "designing and implementing a U.S. transition to a low-emissions future." Astonishingly, the IPS calls on the Pentagon to contribute to a green world "by simply getting out of the way, by handing over unneeded military installations to be converted into green job incubators."

The ever-resourceful IPS goes on to present five full pages of color-coded charts showing exactly which military programs can be converted to incubators for our country's "green" future.

The IPS's most recent "Green Dividend" report makes no bones about the progressive group's ultimate agenda—the virtual disarmament of much of the U.S. military, while transferring defense resources to fund alterative energy causes. With so many bloated government agencies that could be defunded, it is telling that the IPS only focuses on the Pentagon—the purveyor and protector of American strength, the key bastion of our country's exceptionalism, the sustainer of our superpower status. It seems the IPS is attempting to use environmental activism as a guise for a far more sinister aim, namely disarming the country.

The report lauds Obama's first ever U.S. Global Development Policy, which was issued in September 2010, and declares that the primary purpose of our development aid is to pursue broad-based economic growth as the means to fight global poverty.[8]

Unsurprisingly, the report goes on to recommend that massive funds be sent to combat global woes, including an increase of $3.5 billion to "Global Health" investment, and $2.14 billion to support United Nations peacekeeping and ensure that the United States does not fall behind in UN payments. Also outlined is a growing international consensus on "the need for rich countries, including the United States, to provide compensatory funding to developing countries to help them adapt to the impacts of climate change that are already underway." Such U.S. funding should make up for "reductions in food production caused by increases in droughts and flooding, greater climate variability leading to increased disease, decreased access to water and, in some cases, a need to relocate entire communities. These funds must be added to traditional streams of development assistance."

U.S. MILITARY FOR "GLOBAL WARMING" AID TO THIRD WORLD

A major progressive aim is the transfer of American wealth to the developing world. To borrow a battle cry from erstwhile "Green Czar" Van Jones,

"Give them the wealth! Give them the wealth!" Now we shall see plans to use the military to do just that if Obama is reelected.

The White House's most favored think tank, Podesta's Center for American Progress (CAP), released a fifty-two-page proposal, from January 2012, in which authors Michael Werz and Laura Conley lay out a plan for the U.S. military to be used as the delivery vehicle of aid to developing countries purportedly ravaged by so-called global warming.[9]

Within the general schema of using the "green agenda" to redirect defense funding to dubious environmental causes, the paper "Climate Change, Migration, and Conflict: Addressing Complex Crisis Scenarios in the 21st Century" contains a specific initiative to redistribute America's wealth and resources to developing countries, and to "revisit traditional divisions of labor between diplomacy, defense, and economic, social, and environmental development policy abroad." The CAP plan ridiculously blames "climate change" for such varied world events as the so-called Arab Spring and mass migrations, while pushing the transfer of enormous U.S. assets to the developing world. Nevertheless, a close reading of the report shows it concedes in several instances that there is zero proof for its contentions about climate change being responsible for dramatic world events. Yet CAP urges massive transfers of U.S. wealth anyway. In one section, the report admits:

> Climate change is among these newly visible issues sparking conflict. But because the direct link between conflict and climate change is unclear, awareness of the indirect links has yet to lead to substantial and sustained action to address its security implications.

On migration and climate change, CAP cites United Nations data to warn:

> In the 21st Century the world could see substantial numbers of climate migrants—people displaced by either the slow or sudden onset of the effects of climate change.

In that same section, the report concedes:

In fact there is major disagreement among experts about how to identify climate as a causal factor in internal and international migration. But even though the root causes of human mobility are not always easy to decipher, the policy challenges posed by that movement are real.

Likewise, the "Arab Spring"—really a series of Islamist coups brought to power through short-lived democratic uprisings—is viewed by CAP through the lens of . . . climate change!

The Arab Spring can be at least partly credited to climate change. Rising food prices and efforts by authoritarian regimes to crush political protests were linked first to food and then to political repression—two important motivators in the Arab makeover this past year.

Using the "science" of global warming, which will be dissected in the next chapter, CAP utilizes its unproved claims about world events to call for the United States, its allies, and key regional players to "work together to create a sustainable security situation to deal with climate change, migration, and conflict." In other words, the U.S. should provide lots and lots of money to fight climate change overseas. For starters, recommendations include an increase in funding for the Global Climate Change Initiative efforts, and more money for the Climate Adaptation Fund established by the parties to the Kyoto Protocol, as well as the United Nations Framework Convention on Climate Change to counter global warming, adopted by over 190 countries. The U.S. is singled out as one "of the few global powers capable and willing to act in the common interest." The report complains developing nations and small islands

will not only need adequate funding (no funds are allocated for migration so far), but also the expertise to carry out adaptation and mitigation efforts. These tasks could range from education or establishing early-warning systems, to implementing insurance for property and business owners, to altering crop mixtures and substantially modifying traditional land-use patterns. Assistance may also be required to help countries aggregate accurate nationwide data to identify mitigation needs and target relief to the most vulnerable communities.

There is little doubt the Obama White House is ready to embrace CAP's recommendation of filtering world conflict through the lens of climate change and transformative global engagement, in part, based on this peculiar worldview. Already, the Obama White House Interagency Taskforce on adapting to climate change recommended the government develop a strategy to help poor countries contend with purportedly climate-induced challenges.[10]

The Obama administration has also already overseen the release of four official defense and engagement reviews specifically designating climate change as a major consideration in planning global development and security strategies. This acknowledgment was prominently featured in the Congressionally mandated National Security Strategy of April 2010; the Defense Department's Quadrennial Defense Review, the administration's first-ever Quadrennial Diplomacy and Development Review; as well as the Presidential Policy Directive on Global Development.[11]

In a shocking misuse of taxpayer money, in February 2012, one week after the Palestinian Authority entered into a unity government with the Hamas Islamist terror organization, the U.S. announced the continuation of a $100 million, five-year program initiated in 2010 to construct "environmentally and socially sustainable" buildings for the Palestinians. The website for the U.S. consulate in Jerusalem posted the plans, which include a community center and school to be built to meet "stringent third-party-verified 'green' certification standards."[12] Already, the U.S. Agency for International Development, which is funding the projects, has constructed the Safeer Center, a West Bank child-care program, one of the first of the U.S.-funded Palestinian "green" buildings to open. "Its energy-efficient insulation (visible through a small cutout), rainwater collection system and temperature-regulating window shades provide a healthy facility for more than 3,000 children," boasted the U.S. consulate site. "These and others provide models for efficiency in the West Bank and Gaza Strip, where the mostly imported energy is expensive," the site added.

MORE UN HELMETS ON U.S. TROOPS

Getting back to seminal Unified Security Budget report, another one of its schemes is the creation of a standing international peacekeeping force, which is also a top priority of the Connect U.S. Fund, one of the report's sponsors. The Connect U.S. Fund is a Soros-funded organization promoting global governance. Its mission, according to the group's website, is to influence "policy through integrative collaborative grant making on human rights, non-proliferation, climate change and development, and effective foreign assistance."[13] The Connect Fund provides grants to pro-UN groups such as Human Rights First, which states it has used top military brass to secure U.S. politicians' commitments against torture. Another grantee, the Center for Victims of Torture, produced a 2008 draft executive order against torture endorsed by prominent national security figures.[14] Months later, a virtually identical executive order was issued by Obama.[15]

The Connect Fund is directly tied to the White House. Obama's handpicked assistant secretary of state for population, refugees, and migration, Eric P. Schwartz, served as the Connect Fund's executive director just prior to his White House appointment.[16] Even before his appointment, Schwartz coordinated meetings on behalf of Obama's White House transition team with the Washington Working Group on the International Criminal Court, a group that openly advocates placing more blue United Nations helmets on U.S. troops and coercing the U.S. to join the UN's International Criminal Court, which could prosecute American citizens and soldiers for "war crimes" and other offenses.[17]

PANETTA'S CHECKERED PAST AND OBAMA'S SECOND-TERM PLANS

Here it is instructive to detail how the Unified Security Budget's publisher, the Institute for Policy Studies, is tied to Defense Secretary Leon Panetta. In Aaron Klein's articles and in our most recent book, *Red Army*, we showed how a review of Panetta's voting record, while a member of Congress from 1977 to 1993, evidenced a strong affinity for the IPS agenda. Panetta was also reportedly on the IPS official 20th Anniversary Committee, celebrated in April 1983, at a time when the group was closely aligned with the Soviet Union. In his authoritative book, *Covert Cadre: Inside the Institute for Policy Studies*, author S. Steven Powell writes:

> April 5, 1983, IPS threw a large twentieth-anniversary celebration to raise funds. On the fundraising committee for the event were 14 then-current members of the U.S. House of Representatives, including Leon E. Panetta (D-CA), chairman of Budget Process Task Force of the House Committee on Budget (chairman of Subcommittee on Police and Personnel, Ninety-ninth Congress).[18]

Researcher Trevor Loudon, a specialist on communism, obtained and posted IPS literature documenting members of the 20th Anniversary Committee, which also included Sens. Chris Dodd (D-CT), and Gary Hart (D-CO), with an endorsement by Sen. Mark Hatfield (R-OR). Besides Panetta, Congressmen on the IPS committee included Les Aspin (D-WI), George E. Brown Jr. (D-CA), Philip Burton (D-CA), George Crockett (D-MI), Tom Harkin (D-IA), and Richard Ottinger (D-NY).

Along with serving on the IPS committee, Panetta supported the IPS "Coalition for a New Foreign and Military Policy Line" in 1983.[19]

Powell wrote that in the 1980s, Panetta commissioned the IPS to produce an "alternative" budget that dramatically cut defense spending, meaning Panetta has a history of promoting IPS defense reports.[20] According to Powell, writing in the November 1983 issue of the *American Opinion*:

> The congressional supporters for the Institute for Policy Studies included many of those who biennially commission I.P.S. to produce an 'Alternative' Budget that dramatically cuts defense spending while increasing the spending for social welfare to levels only dreamed of by Karl Marx.[21]

"In this pact of I.P.S. intimates [are] such luminaries as...Leon Panetta (D-CA), Chairman of the Budget Process Task Force," wrote Powell.

Just as Panetta promoted IPS military reports twenty to thirty years ago when he was a U.S. Congressman, current IPS military reports deeply influence legislation proposed by progressive politicians. For example, Rep. Barney Frank's (D-MA) Sustainable Defense Task Force reached conclusions that are strikingly similar to the IPS 2010 Unified Security Budget report. Frank's task force concluded the Pentagon could cut $960 billion between 2011 and 2020 (virtually identical to Obama's proposed $1 trillion reduction in Defense spending over ten years). The Navy would be drastically cut back to 8 aircraft carriers, instead of 12 planned, and 7 air wings. The overall Navy fleet would be slashed to 230 ships instead of the current 285, let alone the 313 envisioned by the service. Eight ballistic missile submarines will be cut from the planned force of 14, leaving just 6. Building of nuclear attack submarines will be cut in half, leaving a force of 40 by 2020. The 4 active guided missile submarines would be cut too. Destroyer building would be frozen and the new DDG-1000 Destroyer program cancelled.[22]

Meanwhile, groups funded by Schwartz's Connect Fund organized a January 2009 national conference calling for a "Responsible U.S. Global Engagement" agenda for Obama's new administration.[23] It is exactly that "responsible" engagement that will most likely spell out the future of warfare during Obama's second term, a "responsibility" doctrine that could remake no less than the Middle East, North Africa, and the very purpose of armed force itself, as we shall now see.

"RESPONSIBILITY TO PROTECT" (R2P) AND REMAKING NATIONS

A core doctrine of progressive international relations thinking is called "Responsibility to Protect." The joint CAP and IPS report specifically cites the need for the U.S. and the international community to "carry out its Responsibility to Protect (R2P) duty when civilian populations are in danger around the globe." Recent events in Libya, the report notes, "illustrate the need to protect civilians from governments who would subject them to mass atrocities." "Responsibility to Protect" was the military doctrine cited repeatedly by Obama as the main justification for U.S. and international airstrikes against Libya. Indeed, the Libya bombings have been widely regarded as a test of R2P.[24]

In *Red Army* and throughout Aaron Klein's reporting, concerns about the origins of "Responsibility to Protect" have been raised, with connections that tie right into the sponsors of the IPS Unified Security Budget report, most prominently George Soros's Open Society Institute.

Responsibility to Protect, or Responsibility to Act, as cited by Obama, is a set of principles, now backed by the United Nations, based on the idea that sovereignty is not a privilege but a responsibility that can be revoked if a country is accused of "war crimes," "genocide," "crimes against humanity," or "ethnic cleansing."[25] The term "war crimes" has, at times, been used indiscriminately by various UN-backed international bodies—including the International Criminal Court, or ICC—which has applied it to Israeli anti-terror operations in Gaza. There is also concern the ICC could be used to prosecute U.S. troops.[26]

Soros's Open Society is one of only three nongovernmental funders of the Global Centre for the Responsibility to Protect, the main body behind the doctrine. Government sponsors include Australia, Belgium, Canada, the Netherlands, Norway, Rwanda, and the United Kingdom.[27] In *Red Army*, we showed how the R2P center's patrons include former UN secretary-General Kofi Annan, former Irish president Mary Robinson, and South African activist Desmond Tutu.[28] Robinson and Tutu have made solidarity visits to the Hamas-controlled Gaza Strip as members of a group called The Elders, which includes former president Jimmy Carter.[29] Annan once famously stated:

> State sovereignty, in its most basic sense, is being redefined—not least by the forces of globalization and international co-operation. States are . . . instruments at the service of their peoples and not vice versa.[30]

The Carr Center for Human Rights Policy served on the advisory board of a 2001 commission that originally formulated R2P. The center was led at the time by Samantha Power, who is now National Security Council special adviser to Obama for human rights. Power is reported to have heavily influenced Obama in consultations leading to the decision to bomb Libya.[31] That 2001 commission was named the International Commission on Intervention and State Sovereignty. It invented the term "Responsibility to Protect" and defined its guidelines.[32] Also on the advisory board was Arab League secretary general Amre Moussa as well as Palestinian legislator Hanan Ashrawi, a virulent denier of the Holocaust who long served as the deputy of late Palestinian Liberation Organization chairman Yasser Arafat.[33]

Soros himself outlined the fundamentals of Responsibility to Protect in a 2004 *Foreign Policy* journal article titled "The People's Sovereignty: How a New Twist on an Old Idea Can Protect the World's Most Vulnerable Populations."[34] In the article, Soros wrote,

> True sovereignty belongs to the people, who in turn delegate it to their governments.
>
> [...]
>
> If governments abuse the authority entrusted to them and citizens have no opportunity to correct such abuses, outside interference is justified.
>
> [...]
>
> By specifying that sovereignty is based on the people, the international community can penetrate nation-states' borders to protect the rights of citizens.
>
> In particular, the principle of the people's sovereignty can help solve two modern challenges: the obstacles to delivering aid effectively to sovereign states, and the obstacles to global collective action dealing with states experiencing internal conflict.

The inventor of R2P doctrine, Ramesh Thakur, recently advocated for a "global rebalancing" and "international redistribution" to create a "New World Order." In a piece in the March 2010 issue of the *Ottawa Citizen* newspaper, Thakur wrote,

> Toward a new world order, Westerners must change lifestyles and support international redistribution.[35]

Here he was referring to a UN-brokered international climate treaty of which he argued, "Developing countries must reorient growth in cleaner and greener directions." In the opinion piece, Thakur also discussed recent military engagements and how the financial crisis has impacted the U.S. "The West's bullying approach to developing nations won't work anymore— global power is shifting to Asia . . . A much-needed global moral rebalancing is in train." Thakur continued:

> Westerners have lost their previous capacity to set standards and rules of behavior for the world. Unless they recognize this reality, there is little prospect of making significant progress in deadlocked international negotiations.

And, Thakur contended:

> [T]he demonstration of the limits to U.S. and NATO power in Iraq and Afghanistan has left many less fearful of "superior" western power.

Of course, should Obama be reelected, with the implementation of the progressives' agenda radically expanded, "Western power" would be diminished much, much further.

2

WHAT SOLYNDRA? NEW "GREEN" STIMULUS, FEDERAL "GREEN BANK"

PRESIDENT OBAMA'S "GREEN" initiatives are from the same mold as the rest of the progressives' political program: full of hidden agendas masked by crafty political rhetoric, loaded with corruption and favors for his donors and political cronies, founded on dubious science and "voodoo" economic principles, and aimed at weakening the U.S. economy and national defense.

In our most recent book, *Red Army*, we gave chapter and verse on how the progressives exploit the power of the environmental movement to weaken America. This, for example, is the usually concealed but sometimes explicit agenda of former Obama "Green Czar" Van Jones, the founder of a Communist revolutionary organization who adopted the Saul Alinsky stratagem of "boring from within" the system in order to destroy it. Jones was forced to resign after being exposed in 2009 by reporters including Aaron Klein. As we noted in *Red Army*, he has continued his work for groups advising the Obama White House, including the Center for American Progress and the Presidential Climate Action Project.[1]

Here we expose shocking second-term plans to "green" the Pentagon, even as America's true defense capabilities are radically diminished, as we documented in the previous chapter. Also uncovered herein is a giant international spread-the-wealth scheme, with Uncle Sam paying penalties to the developing world for our "climate crimes," based on the questionable "science" behind global warming. This second-term "green funding" includes a new massive "green" stimulus, even as crony pay-offs from Obama's 2009 "stimulus" bill are exposed amid wasteful spending schemes, with one of the authors of the green legislation providing hundreds of millions in federal funds to companies with which he is personally connected.

Also integral to the progressives' green agenda is the "shutting up" of conservative opposition to bogus "climate science," its corrupt cronyism and financially unsustainable green industries. This includes revived proposals for using the Federal Communications Commission to shut down conservative talk radio critics of the green (and greed) agenda.

In his January State of the Union address—his last before the 2012 election—President Obama laid out his vision for "an economy that's built to last—an economy built on American manufacturing, American energy, skills for American workers, and a renewal of American values."[2]

Just when the wisdom of investing in the solar energy boondoggle seemed most ludicrous, with numerous federally funded "green" companies embarrassingly filing for bankruptcy, Obama used SOTU to double-down on a "new energy future," seeking an "all-out, all-of-the-above strategy that develops every available source of American energy—a strategy that's cleaner, cheaper, and full of new jobs." Evidently reaching hard for an accomplishment to tout, after billions in wasted and corrupt "stimulus" spending, Obama boasted: "In three years, our partnership with the private sector has already positioned America to be the world's leading manufacturer of high-tech batteries."

The timing of the president's "battery boast" could not have been any worse. Just two days after his national speech, New York–based Enerl, the parent company of an electric car battery maker that received a $118 million "stimulus" grant from the Obama administration, filed for Chapter 11, becoming the third alternative energy corporation to seek bankruptcy protection after receiving stimulus funds from the Energy Department.[3]

Less than two months later, government-bailed-out General Motors announced it was slashing production of its battery-powered Volt model, putting 1,300 out of work, due to lack of customer demand for the green vehicle.[4]

Obama's State of the Union speech also came just after the colossal failure of the scandalous $535 million loan guarantee to the Solyndra solar company. "Some technologies don't pan out; some companies fail," Obama allowed. Still, he pledged, "I will not walk away from the promise of clean energy." Obama made clear that his future plans will even further increase the use of public money to finance so-called clean energy. "It was public research dollars, over the course of thirty years that helped develop the technologies to extract all this natural gas out of shale rock—reminding us that Government support is critical in helping businesses get new energy ideas off the ground."

What follows are Obama's specific second-term plans for billions more in federal funding to "green" companies, including a "green stimulus."

"GREEN" STIMULUS; FEDERAL GREEN BANK?

An organization that calls itself the Presidential Climate Action Project, or PCAP, has been working with the Obama administration since day one to help craft and implement White House environmental policy. Following Obama's victory in 2008, PCAP began working with John Podesta, co-chair of Obama's transition team, to help the incoming president formulate an initial one-hundred-day environmental agenda. Podesta, of course, is president and CEO of the highly influential progressive think tank Center for American Progress. In a November 2009 interview with Aaron Klein, PCAP's executive director, William S. Becker, boasted how his group's specific climate recommendations received a "very positive reception from the moment we delivered (the one-hundred-day proposal) last November to John Podesta."[5]

"We continue to work with some colleagues inside the (Obama) administration, as well as continuing to push for bold action from the outside," Becker said at the time, adding that the White House "adopted quite a few of our recommendations or variations of them."

Last January, PCAP released an extensive new list of recommendations for the White House in a seventy-five-page paper entitled, "Building the Obama Administration's Climate Legacy."[6]

Foremost among PCAP's recommendations is that the Department of Energy (DOE) should join three other Federal agencies—the Department of Housing and Urban Development (HUD), the Department of Transportation (DOT), and the Environmental Protection Agency (EPA)—in funding what is essentially a progressive slush fund called the Partnership for Sustainable Communities. The Partnership blandly proclaims it aims to "help communities nationwide improve access to affordable housing, increase transportation options, and lower transportation costs while protecting the environment."[7]

The Partnership has already granted over $409 million in financing to support what it calls "livability investments" in over two-hundred communities across the country. Additionally, the Partnership's Office of Sustainable Housing and Communities oversees two grant programs established by the Livable Communities Act. One grant program makes $2.2 billion available for communities to build and improve affordable housing, strengthen public transportation, promote transit-oriented development, and redevelop brownfield sites. A second grant program provides $500 million to support comprehensive regional planning that recognizes the interconnectedness of transportation, housing, community and economic development, and environmental sustainability.[8]

If Obama is reelected, progressive plans backed up by proposed legislation aim for an immediate and massive increase in federal funding for domestic "green" projects. A seminal November 2010 report by the de facto policy nerve center of the Obama White House, the Center for American Progress, titled "Cutting the Cost of Clean Energy 1.0," recommends a de facto federal "green bank" for the sole purpose of loaning or granting public funds to so-called clean energy companies.[9]

The report calls for a new "Energy Independence Trust," which could "borrow from the federal treasury to provide low-cost financing to private-sector investments in clean energy." Continues the CAP paper:

> Our proposed Energy Independence Trust would hold sufficient reserves to protect the Treasury from loan losses, and would be able to offer a variety of debt- and equity-based financial instruments, loan guarantees, and tax incentives to draw a wave of private capital into the clean energy sector.

The policy proposals outlined in this paper represent key elements of a strategy to begin immediately rebuilding the U.S. economy on a foundation of clean and efficient energy.

The program for rebuilding the U.S. economy using clean energy as an impractical and unworkable "foundation" is telling. Written a full fourteen months before Obama's most recent State of the Union, the paper proposes exactly what the president called for in his SOTU.

This should not surprise readers of our previous books in which we showed how proposals by progressive think tanks can incubate for years, even decades, as the policies are recrafted and perfected, with activists waiting for the right opportunity to foster a particular policy, such as health care or immigration reform, on the American public.

The direct links between the seven authors of CAP's Energy Trust report and the Obama administration leave little to the imagination about how the progressive think tank's recommendations become Obama's policies. One author, senior CAP Fellow Bracken Hendricks, served as a policy advisor to President Clinton's Global Initiative organization as well as to Obama's presidential campaign and 2009 White House transition team. Hendricks is also a founder and the first executive director of the Apollo Alliance, which reportedly helped craft key portions of Obama's 2009 stimulus. Last year, after a slew of negative publicity about the group, Apollo changed its name to the BlueGreen Alliance. Van Jones serves on Apollo's board. The group is funded by the George Soros–financed radical clearinghouse, the Tides Center. Energy Trust report authors Ken Berlin and Alex Kragie, meanwhile, also served on Obama's White House transition, after Kragie served as a regional field director on the Obama presidential campaign in 2008.

All CAP reports must be taken seriously, as they have the strong potential to shape Obama's presidential agenda. The U.S. House of Representatives has already attempted to translate CAP's "green bank" program into reality. The American-Made Energy Act of 2011, sponsored by Rep. Mike Ross (D-AR), seeks to establish an Energy Trust Fund for "alternative and renewable energy incentives and projects (e.g., wind, solar, biomass, and geothermal resources, waste to energy, hydropower, nuclear power, coal to liquid technology, compressed natural gas, and liquified natural gas)."[10]

This legislation comes right out of the CAP playbook, with Obama clearly in support.

That the CAP saw Obama's State of the Union as the public launching pad for its own energy agenda was declared by the progressive group itself. Writing on their website, CAP's vice president for energy policy, Kate Gordon, posted a piece called "Manufacturing America's Energy Future: Enacting President Obama's Blueprint Means Sustained Economic Growth." In the article, Gordon fawned over virtually every aspect of Obama's speech dealing with clean energy, while proclaiming the president's plan crucial to a clean energy future.[11]

Other legislation circulating in hopes of attracting support during a second Obama term calls for every sort of green scheme funding. A sampling includes sections of the Make It in America Act of 2011, to be discussed at length elsewhere in this book, as representing the mainstay of Obama's second-term economic policies. The Act calls for the manufacture of "renewable energy systems" costing billions spent on "clean technology." It authorizes federal funds to states for "green technologies that are 100% manufactured in the United States from articles, materials, or supplies that are 100% grown, produced, or manufactured in the United States."[12] Then there is the Solar Energy Regulatory Relief Act of 2011 (SERRA), introduced December 14, 2011, by Rep. Brian P. Bilbray (R-CA). SERRA calls for a federally funded program to provide competitive grants or challenge grants, or both, to local governments that have adopted or offer a commitment to adopt solar-friendly communities.[13]

SHUTTING UP TALK RADIO

Underlying Obama's environmental agenda is the highly questionable theory of global warming, which took a serious hit from the release in November 2009 of thousands of e-mails and other documents from the UK's University of East Anglia Climatic Research Unit (CRU). The e-mail bombshell revealed a conspiracy to suppress massive amounts of research that refuted, or at least disputed, the basic science underlying global warming theory. Some climate researchers had failed to share their contrary data with fellow scientists. Some conspired to falsify data crucial to the global warming consensus of international bodies, while others sought to keep researchers with dissenting views from publishing in leading scientific journals.[14]

Apparently, those helping to craft Obama's policies are so concerned the public might also question global warming theory that they want to silence the theory's critics in the public media. Case in point is the earlier referenced 2011 Presidential Climate Action Project report, which outrageously recommends that Obama reinstate the anti–free speech Fairness Doctrine in order to shut up some of global warming theory's most effective challengers. In one of its first recommendations, the PCAP report states:

> National discourse today is tainted—and in some cases poisoned— by unbalanced ideological use of the public airwaves . . . To improve and better inform public discourse, it is time for the Federal Communications Commission (FCC) to reinstate the Fairness Doctrine.

The Fairness Doctrine—rescinded under President Reagan between 1985 and 1987—was a legacy of the Telecommunications Act of 1934, which had also created the Federal Communications Commission. In an age before broadcast television, not to mention cable TV, satellite radio, the Internet, and the explosion of twenty-first-century media services, the doctrine required that holders of the relatively few radio broadcast licenses treat "controversial issues of public importance" in a "balanced" manner, giving equal time to both sides. Thus, no single station could, upon threat of losing its license, advocate principally for one point of view. Critics had long attacked the doctrine as an infringement on First Amendment rights, but with the explosion of new and diverse media sources in the mid-1980s, it was widely acknowledged to be obsolete.

But President Obama's advisory commission, it seems, cannot stomach the public raising questions about the "science" underlying global warming theory and the entire green agenda. Never mind the stunning revelation that much of the so-called settled science is, in fact, questionable, and that certain politically motivated scientists conspired, with evident success, to suppress that knowledge. For PCAP, the public, along with dissenting scientists, simply have no right to air such questions—not even Climate

Research Unit director Prof. Philip Jones, who publicly conceded the possibility that the world was warmer in medieval times than now—implying that global warming, if it is in fact occurring, may not be man-made at all. Jones said, for example, that for the fifteen years preceding 2009 there had been no "statistically significant" warming, although he qualified this was a blip rather than the long-term trend.[15]

Perhaps we should all just ignore the avalanche of news stories suggesting global warning "catastrophes" were really anything but. Central to the theory espoused by the global warming alarmists led by former senator Al Gore is that the oceans are rising due to the melting of ice caps and that soon the seas will be flooding thousands of miles of coastal lands around the globe. If CPAC has its way, we should never know about an April 2009 study that observed that ice is actually expanding in much of Antarctica.[16] The results of ice-core drilling and sea ice monitoring indicated there was no large-scale melting of ice over most of Antarctica (although experts stated they were concerned at ice losses on the continent's western coast). Antarctica contains 90 percent of the earth's ice and 80 percent of its fresh water.

Nor should we be permitted to know of scientific papers that found sea levels worldwide weren't rising. In one paper presented at the fourth International Conference on Climate Change (2009), Nils-Axel Morner, former emeritus head of the paleogeophysics and geodynamics department at the prestigious Stockholm University in Sweden, revealed that observational records from South Asia and the Pacific—including the Maldives, Bangladesh, India, Tuvalu, and Vanuatu—show the sea level not to be rising at all. Morner concluded there is no "alarming sea level rise" across the globe. His paper says a United Nations report warning of coastal cities being deluged by rising waters from melting polar ice caps "is utterly wrong." Profs. Manfred Wenzel and Jens Schröte, writing in the *Journal of Geophysical Research*, came to similar conclusions.[17]

The PCAP is not alone in calling for the silencing of global warming theory's critics. In a remarkable display of paranoia, just prior to his appointment as President Obama's so-called Regulatory Czar in 2009, Cass Sunstein wrote a lengthy academic paper suggesting the government should "infiltrate" social network websites, chat rooms and message boards. Such "cognitive infiltration," Sunstein argued, should be used to enforce a U.S.

government ban on "conspiracy theorizing."[18] Sunstein's official title—perhaps invented by a latter-day Orwell or Kafka—is Administrator of the White House Office of Information and Regulatory Affairs. Among the beliefs Sunstein classified in his paper as a "conspiracy theory" is advocacy that the theory of global warming is a deliberate fraud.

AUTHOR OF "STIMULUS" TIED TO COMPANIES FUNDED BY BILL

Easily overlooked in the morass of Obama's second-term drive for a radical increase in federal spending on "clean energy" is not simply the utter incompetence of some of the major recipients of "green stimulus" funds but also the rank corruption intrinsic to those hand-outs, as Washington cronyism is routinely ignored by the mainstream news media.

For starters there's BrightSource Energy, a solar energy company attempting to build the world's largest solar power plant amid concerns such a venture might be too risky an investment for the federal government. So BrightSource received a $1.37 billion federal loan guarantee, the largest the Department of Energy has ever given for a solar power project.[19] The loan guarantee is for the construction of a gigantic California desert solar plant known as the Ivanpah Solar Electric Generating System, featuring mirrors that reflect sunlight towards a massive central tower that is thereby heated to produce steam, spinning turbines that, in turn, produce electricity.[20]

BrightSource projects it will produce enough power to meet the needs of hundreds of thousands of Californians. During a national address last October, Obama mentioned the possible benefits of BrightSource Energy's "revolutionary new type of solar power plant." But some, including advocates for green power, have questioned whether the massive solar plant will actually work. The *Bay Citizen* quoted Michael Boyd, president of the nonprofit Californians for Renewable Energy, as saying there is "no evidence" BrightSource's project will succeed. Boyd also complained that most of the equipment used at the plant would be manufactured in China and Germany. "Stimulus money isn't going to jobs here in the U.S. It's going to jobs overseas," he said. Boyd's group in 2010 reportedly filed an administrative complaint seeking to block the U.S. loan guarantee, worrying that the solar project "could have the unintended consequences of killing innovation if these projects fail." But in a recent briefing, BrightSource CEO John Woolard exuded confidence his plant would significantly lower energy costs.[21]

Besides the question of risk, a giant elephant in the room has received nearly zero media attention. BrightSource's chairman at the time of the federal loan guarantee was John Bryson, who stepped down from the energy company before being sworn in on October 21, 2011, as the thirty-seventh secretary of the Department of Commerce.[22] In other words, the former employer of Obama's commerce secretary received the Energy Department's $1.4 billion loan guarantee. Of note is that Bryson also cofounded the Natural Resources Defense Council, an environmental activist group belonging to the controversial Apollo Alliance, which helped draft the "green" portions of Obama's 2009 stimulus, the very legislation that underwrote BrightSource's loan.

Bryson is not the exception. His inside deal should have been one of the biggest scandals of the Obama administration. Instead it is exclusive to this book, as the "watchdog" (actually lapdog) news media remain mysteriously uninterested in probing corruption within the monstrous expansion of government under Obama.

Here's another Obama crony we found playing a key role in developing the energy provisions of the stimulus bill while occupying the boards of several companies recently receiving Federal funds, including hundreds of millions in "stimulus" money. T. J. Glauthier served on Obama's 2008 White House Transition Team. He is widely credited with helping to craft the energy provisions of the American Recovery and Reinvestment Act of 2009, aka the "stimulus." In addition to serving on the boards of multiple major energy companies, Glauthier previously held two presidential appointments during the Clinton administration. He was the Energy Department's deputy secretary and chief operating officer, its second-highest-ranking official. Earlier, he served in the White House for five years as the associate director for Natural Resources, Energy and Science in the Office of Management and Budget. Glauthier is tied to several energy companies that benefited from the "stimulus" bill he helped to write.[23]

One such company investigated by these authors is GridPoint Inc, where

Glauthier was appointed to the board in March 2008.[24] GridPoint provides utilities software solutions for electrical grid management and electric power demand and supply balancing. The "stimulus" provides a whopping $4.5 billion for so-called smart grid projects, and GridPoint got paid from scores of smart grid deals funded by the "stimulus." The company partnered with the Electric Transportation Engineering Corporation (eTec), Nissan, the Idaho National Laboratory, and others in a project to deploy electric vehicles (EVs) and their charging infrastructure in five states.[25] The Energy Department had awarded eTec almost $100 million in "stimulus" funds to support the project. GridPoint's role in the eTec project was to supply smart charging and data logging capability to utilities located in strategic markets of eTec's program in Arizona, California, Oregon, Tennessee, and Washington.

GridPoint also benefited from "stimulus" funds when it recently provided home energy management, load management, and electric vehicle management software solutions for a KCP&L's Green Impact Zone SmartGrid Demonstration in Kansas City, Mo.[26]

Additionally, GridPoint helped the Sacramento Municipal Utility District, or SMUD, to manage power from its customers' rooftop solar panels.[27] SMUD had won $127.5 million in "stimulus" funds from the Department of Energy to carry out the project, which also includes deploying 600,000 smart meters in its service territory. Again, in early 2009, the Energy Department awarded Argonne National Laboratory nearly $2.7 million in "stimulus" funding for three solar energy–related research projects. Argonne reportedly shared another $5 million in "stimulus" funding for projects with GridPoint and other companies and the University of Illinois Sustainable Technology Center.[28]

Besides benefiting from "stimulus" grants, GridPoint, in 2010, won a separate $28 million contract with the U.S. Postal Service to install energy management systems in selected post office locations across the U.S.[29] At the same time, Gridpoint's founder, Peter L. Corsell, contributed the $50,000 maximum donation allowable to Obama's inauguration.[30]

Glauthier, meanwhile, came under some fire in the conservative blogosphere after Fox News reported the U.S. Navy has purchased 450,000 gallons of biofuel for about $16 a gallon, or about four times the price of its standard marine fuel, JP-5, which has been going for under $4 a gallon.

HotAir reported Glauthier is a "strategic advisor" to Solazyme, the California company that is selling a portion of the biofuel to the Navy.[31] *HotAir* noted Solazyme received a $21.8 million grant from the 2009 stimulus package. Also, writing at BigGovernment, Whitney Pitcher found that prior to serving as advisor to Solazyme and after his time as part of Obama's transition team, Glauthier served on the advisory board of SunRun, a solar financing company. In October of 2010, just a few short months after Glauthier joined SunRun's advisory board, SunRun secured a $6.73 million grant from this Treasury Department stimulus program.[32] The company was the ninth largest recipient of such programs through December 2010.

We've mentioned John Podesta and his CAP several times in this chapter. It bears noting that Podesta's sister-in-law served as the lobbyist for a wind power firm recently awarded a $135.8 million loan guarantee from the Department of Energy. The company is Brookfield Asset Management. It has a board of nine directors, including New York mayor Michael Bloomberg's longtime girlfriend.[33] The grant was finalized to build the 99-megawatt Granite Reliable wind project in New Hampshire's Coos County, making it the state's largest wind plant. Seventy-five percent of the new wind project is owned by BAIF Granite Holdings, which was created earlier this year by Brookfield Renewable Power, a subsidiary of Brookfield Asset Management of New York.[34]

Since 2009, Brookfield has been represented by the lobbying firm of Heather Podesta and Partners, LLC.[35] Podesta, a top financial bundler for Democrat politicians, is wife of lobbyist and art collector Tony Podesta, who is John's brother. Heather Podesta and her husband, in July 2011, topped the FEC's lobbyist bundler database, raising more money by far in the six prior months than any other lobbyists. Their fundraising was largely for Democrats.[36] According to White House visitor logs, Heather Podesta visited the White House eight times in Obama's first six months alone.[37] Brookfield, meanwhile, is a Toronto-based asset management company that manages a global portfolio of assets valued at over $120 billion. The firm's assets boast not only renewable power generation but also real state, including some of Manhattan's most famous skyline buildings. Brookfield also happens to own Zuccotti Park, the park "occupied" by Wall Street protesters in the fall of 2011.[38]

BIG ENERGY'S SELF-SERVING ENERGY BLUEPRINTS

A coalition of some of America's largest corporations, and a handful of "environmental" groups, issued the *Blueprint for Legislative Action* in January 2009 to "provide decision makers in the Administration and Congress with a framework for legislation." The *Blueprint*, according to USCAP, was to serve as a guide for "the development of legislation in the 111th Congress that can become law."[39]

In summary, the *Blueprint* blandly called for: an "increase [in] the overall energy efficiency of our Economy"; to "utilize responsibly our domestic supplies of coal, oil and natural gas"; to "develop and export the transportation technologies and fuels of the future"; and to "ensure the nation has an adequate supply of electricity produced from low-carbon resources, including wind, solar, next generation nuclear technology, and coal with carbon capture and sequestration."[40]

Two years earlier, in January 2007, USCAP called for "prompt enactment of national legislation in the United States to slow, stop and reverse the growth of greenhouse gas (GHG) emissions over the shortest time reasonably achievable."[41] GHG may have been the cover story, but history has shown us that some USCAP members—AIG, BP, Caterpiller Inc., Conoco-Phillips, Exelon, Duke Energy, Ford Motor Company, GM, and GE—had or still have a very different, less-earth-friendly agenda.

In fall 2008, in the waning days of the Bush presidency, insurance giant AIG received the largest corporate bailout in history—$182 billion in government funds. The leftist *Nation* magazine later observed that this should have been seen as "the Rosetta Stone for understanding the financial crisis and its costly aftermath." Why? While the financial dealings were "monstrously complicated," William Greider wrote, the "larger catastrophe" was because AIG's "collapse and subsequent rescue involved nearly all the critical elements, including delusion and deception."[42] Hold that thought.

Next on the list is Exelon, well connected to both Barack Obama and his first chief of staff, and current Chicago mayor, Rahm Emanuel. In late 1998, when Emanuel left the Clinton White House, he joined the boutique investment banking firm Wasserstein Perella & Company. The following year, Emanuel "landed an advisory role for Wasserstein in the $8.2 billion merger of two utility companies, Unicom, the parent company of Commonwealth Edison, [once headed by Tom Ayers, father of Weatherman Bill Ayers,] and Peco Energy, to create Exelon, now one of the nation's largest power companies." John W. Rowe, then Unicom CEO, assumed the same position at Exelon. Rowe is one of Obama's longest and most generous bundler backers.[43]

During the 2008 presidential campaign, candidate Sen. Hillary Clinton, said, "Barack has one of his biggest supporters in terms of funding, the Exelon Corporation, which has spent millions of dollars trying to make Yucca Mountain the waste depository." PolitiFact.com confirmed the veracity of her statement.[44] According to the company's website, Exelon Nuclear "represents approximately 20% of the U.S. nuclear industry's power capacity with 10 power plants and 17 reactors—located in Illinois, Pennsylvania, and New Jersey —and produces enough electricity to power 17 million average American homes annually. Approximately 93% of Exelon's total electricity generation is nuclear power."[45] That's a lot of power and "investment" to protect.

Besides three nuclear power plants, two in South Carolina and one in North Carolina, Duke Energy operates fourteen coal-fired energy plants, as well as several traditional hydro plants, oil- and gas-fired plants, and pumped-storage hydro plants.[46] Duke has already stepped up in this election cycle to subsidize the Democratic National Convention to the tune of a $10 million line of credit. Duke's CEO, Jim Rogers, has given more than $30,000 towards Obama's reelection and has contributed more than $210,000 to Democrats since 2008. Duke "pocketed $230 million in taxpayer money from Obama's stimulus" for so-called "green energy" projects and has "lobbied for and stands to profit from the sort of cap-and-trade policies President Obama supports, as well as other Obama green-energy subsidies."[47]

General Electric's influence in the "green" marketplace of ideas—or in the Obama White House—cannot be understated. In January 2011, President Obama chose GE chairman and CEO Jeffrey R. Immelt to replace former Federal Reserve chairman Paul Volcker as head of the Economic Advisory Panel. The "move," a *Huffington Post* writer observed, was the "latest salvo in the White House's continued aggressive and very public outreach to corporate America."[48]

BP, Caterpillar Inc., Conoco-Phillips, Ford Motor Company, and GM have all dropped out. The most recent withdrawal was Ford, which left in January 2012 following pressure from the National Center for Public Policy Research.[49]

The Free Enterprise Education Institute (FEEI) issued a press release challenging USCAP members—described as a "lobbying group supporting global warming regulation and cap-and-trade schemes"—to report their involvement with USCAP to the Securities and Exchange Commission. Of the twenty-one members, only five had "disclosed in their annual SEC filings that limits on greenhouse gas emissions pose[d] a business risk."[50]

NCPPR's national chairman, Amy Ridenour explained further: "The U.S. Climate Action Partnership was invented by environmentalists to try to get big businesses to come in [and] give them money to lobby for things like cap and trade and other limitations on greenhouse gases . . . And what the liberals do is they promise the corporations that they can maybe mitigate some of the damage to their own businesses.[51]

MORE BLUEPRINTS FOR ENERGY SECURITY

At the same time USCAP was formulating its blueprint, in June 2007, the Business Roundtable's CEOs came up with a *Blueprint for the U.S. Energy Future*.[52] (Members of the Business Roundtable include former and current USCAP members Caterpiller, Conoco-Phillips, Duke Energy, GE, General Motors, Ford Motor Company, Johnson and Johnson, Xerox, and more.[53])

Recommendations included: expanded use of bio-fuels "such as biobutanol and cellulosic ethanol as warranted by technology advances in the vehicles and fuels sectors"; developing and deploying energy efficient vehicle technologies to the maximum extent feasible"; "reducing energy intensity outside the transportation sector by at least 25 percent above the anticipated business-as-usual rate of improvement, which would mean an overall reduction in energy intensity of 40 percent by 2025 (energy intensity is energy consumed per unit of economic output)"; "expanded access to oil and natural gas supplies in the Rocky Mountains, along the Atlantic and Pacific Coasts and the Eastern Gulf of Mexico regions, and in Alaska"; "maintaining a viable and growing nuclear power sector"; and "increased use of coal-to-liquids and coal gasification processes to produce transportation fuels, and syngas for electricity production use in manufacturing feedstock."

A few months later, a reality check must have awakened some members, as the Roundtable walked back its "wish list" somewhat. The Roundtable explained that, although it supported actions to address global warming, not all members were in agreement. For example, it stated, there was a "range of views and preferences about the policy tools that will best achieve that objective." While some companies supported "mandatory approaches," others did not. Therefore, the Business Roundtable revised its position somewhat, now stating that it "supports an open and constructive dialogue about the principles that should shape climate policy and the pros and cons of various options."[54]

In May 2009, the Union of Concerned Scientists released its 239-page *National Blueprint for a Clean Energy Economy,* which included many of the same requests in great detail, all predicated upon the perceived threat of global warming.[55]

The Union of Concerned Scientists, according to *Discover the Networks,* other than expressing environmental concerns, consistently "denounces American military campaigns" and "opposes U.S. development of [a] missile defense system." UCS "circulated a petition that drew the signatures of some 1,600 scientific experts demanding that the United States ratify the Kyoto Protocol." In a declaration entitled "Restoring Scientific Integrity in Policy Making," USC charged that the Bush administration "[had] continued to distort and suppress science in pursuit of its political goals — despite a plea from top U.S. scientists to restore scientific integrity to the policy-making process." However, as DTN exposes, while the petition's signers "portrayed themselves as objective scientists with no political agenda," in reality "over half of them were financial contributors to the Democratic Party, Democratic candidates, or a variety of leftist causes."[56]

OBAMA'S ALL-OF-THE-ABOVE ENERGY STRATEGY

A Friday the 13th of April executive order signed by President Obama—"Supporting Safe and Responsible Development of Unconventional Domestic Natural Gas Resources"—states:

> "While natural gas production is carried out by private firms, and States are the primary regulators of onshore oil and gas activities, the Federal Government has an important role to play by regulating oil and gas activities on public and Indian trust lands, encouraging greater use of natural gas in transportation, supporting research and development aimed at improving the safety of natural gas development and transportation activities, and setting sensible, cost-effective public health and environmental standards to implement Federal law and augment State safeguards."

In short, in 2011, natural gas produced 25 percent of our energy. The federal government "must control this source of energy in order to deliver on the promise of making gasoline prices rise to $10 per gallon, bankrupt the coal industry, and cause energy prices to skyrocket," Dr. Ileana Johnson Paugh, a freelance writer at the *Canada Free Press*, commented on April 14.[57]

This is not at all surprising. At the end of March 2011, Obama's newly-released energy blueprint pushed natural gas to forefront.[58] By July, conservative websites reported that Texas hedge-fund operator and natural gas-magnate T. Boone Pickens, and George Soros, stood to gain from legislation that "would create very generous tax credits to manufacturers who retrofit existing work vehicles to run on natural gas rather than on that terrifying global menace known as oil."[59]

Also, Soros had been observed making "some intriguing investments into alternative fuel companies of late, specifically those at the forefront of natural gas." Soros has a track record of "accurately predict[ing] both economic bubbles and quickly growing industries. As a result, Soros's funds have turned out a 30% return on investments since their inception."[60] Likewise not surprising.

The truth of the matter is that no one can be sure what the president intends.

Robert Bradley Jr. explained why a few days earlier at *Forbes* magazine online:

> President Obama just can't seem to make up his mind on Keystone XL. Earlier this year, he denied federal approval for the project, which would have unleashed construction of a 2,600-mile pipeline to transport crude oil from Canadian shales to refineries in the American south.
>
> Yet just a few days ago, at a campaign stop in Cushing, Oklahoma, the Energy-Impresario-in-Chief said that he actually did support the pipeline—well, part of it at least. He announced a plan to fast-track construction of Keystone's southern leg, a 484-mile track running from Cushing to the Gulf Coast, representing about 29 percent of the overall route.[61]

Bradley continued: "A White House that high-handedly rejects a major energy project one day, then boldly demands fast-track approval for that same project the next day, hasn't exactly established a coherent energy policy."[62]

As Bradley pointed out, this is what Obama calls "an 'all of the above' energy strategy." His administration "will support any project that promises to ramp up overall supply, bring down prices, and reduce national dependence on foreign energy sources — including the oil and gas sector Democrats have been so hostile [to] in the past."[63]

The only problem is, Bradley concluded, Obama's "'all of the above' approach is heavily biased toward 'green tech' and does not even include coal, which accounts for more domestic electricity generation than any other energy source."[64]

Another indication that Obama's energy plans are not carved in stone is the one-year progress report on his *Blueprint for a Secure Energy Future*. The heretofore all-important GHG (greenhouse gas) goal was no longer mentioned.[65]

On March 12, 2012, Brad Johnson took the president to task at *Think Progress*, the Center for American Progress's online propaganda site.

"Few challenges facing America, and the world, are more urgent than combating climate change," President-elect Barack Obama said on November 19, 2008. "My presidency will mark a new chapter in America's leadership on climate change that will strengthen our security and create millions of new jobs in the process," he promised.[66]

"Obama reiterated the pledge he made on the campaign trail and in his transition-team energy and environment agenda," Johnson wrote. Obama said: "We will establish strong annual targets that set us on a course to reduce emissions to their 1990 levels by 2020 and reduce them an additional 80 percent by 2050."[67]

"The blueprint does make several mentions of programs that reduce greenhouse pollution in individual sectors, but the Environmental Protection Agency's work to regulate carbon pollution from power plants is not one of them," Johnson continued. The "abandonment of the goal of cutting carbon pollution in line with international obligations and scientific reality is a sad reflection of the power of the fossil fuel industry over American politics."[68]

Speaking to Obama's possible political motivation, Johnson offered a caveat: "It may also reflect the mistaken political calculation that Americans won't support a leader who is willing to publicly fight the urgent challenge of climate change."[69]

One thing we do know for certain is that investors like T. Boone Pickens and George Soros will not lose one dime—nor will Big Energy.

3

OPEN BORDERS, AMNESTY FOR ILLEGALS

URING HIS 2008 presidential campaign, Barack Obama pledged amnesty for over 13 million illegal immigrants. Having failed to fulfill that pledge in his first term, but running for reelection, the savvy politician responded to a challenge over his failure in a February 2012 interview with Hispanic market Univision Radio: "My presidency is not over. I've got another five years coming up. We're going to get this done," Obama pledged yet again.[1]

President Obama first described his plan for amnesty during a December 4, 2007, campaign debate with Hillary Clinton:

> As president of the United States, I will make sure that the federal government does what it's supposed to do, which is to do a better job of closing our borders and preventing hundreds of thousands of people to pour in, have much tougher enforcement standards when it comes to employers, and create a pathway of citizenship for the 12 million people who are already here.[2]

Later in that debate, Obama elaborated:

> After illegal aliens pay their fine and get on his "pathway," they can then stay here and they can have the ability to enforce a minimum

wage that they're paid, make sure the worker safety laws are available, make sure that they can join a union.[3]

Since becoming president, Obama has made abundantly clear that amnesty for illegal immigrants (or undocumented workers, as progressives love to call them) is a main policy goal. For more than two years, he has waged a high-profile political war over this issue with the State of Arizona and its governor, Jan Brewer. But Obama also understands that a solid majority of Americans remains opposed to mass amnesty for illegals. Despite repeated pledges to oversee such "comprehensive" immigration reform, it would be difficult for Obama to get any amnesty bill passed in Congress, even if Democrats should retake the House during a second Obama term.

Instead, as we show here, Obama has already quietly begun to bypass the will of Congress and the American people—using his power as the nation's chief executive through an incremental series of orders.

This antidemocratic game plan is bad enough. But in attempting to divine Obama's specific agenda for immigration amnesty, we have also uncovered shocking new elements of progressive plans for a second Obama term that would impede U.S. border security, flood the country with an untold number of new immigrants, and change the very nature of the American electorate. The political skill and duplicity of Obama and his progressive comrades should never be underestimated.

EXECUTIVE AMNESTY

New orders weakening the deportation criteria for illegals were issued on June 17, 2011. The head of Immigration and Customs Enforcement (ICE), John Morton, instructed ICE staff to exercise "prosecutorial discretion" in weighing any future deportations. Among the factors newly to be considered—an illegal's "contributions to the community, including family relationships; the person's age, with particular consideration given to minors and the elderly; whether the person or the person's spouse is pregnant or nursing."[4] Leniency was also mandated for "individuals present in the United States since childhood; and individuals with serious health conditions," among scores of other disqualifications.

The subtext of Morton's memo is clear: Stop enforcing nearly all measures against illegals. The only deportation "priorities" under the new ICE guidelines are "individuals who pose a clear risk to national security; serious felons, repeat offenders, or individuals with a lengthy criminal record of any kind; known gang members or other individuals who pose a clear danger to public safety; and individuals with an egregious record of immigration violations, including those with a record of illegal re-entry and those who have engaged in immigration fraud." Shortly, we will reveal second-term Obama plans to expand these exemptions even further.

A month after Morton's order, Homeland Security Secretary Janet Napolitano announced a two-pronged initiative to limit deportations to those persons deemed by her department most dangerous to the country, rather than on the general population of millions of illegals.[5] Napolitano said the Obama administration would limit deportation proceedings on a case-by-case basis for illegal immigrants who meet certain criteria, such as attending school, having family in the military, or having primary responsibility for other family members' care.[6] In other words, without any Congressional approval—much less public knowledge—the Obama administration has already taken major steps toward comprehensive amnesty for illegals.

In reviewing deportation orders for just the first three months of FY 2012, a nonpartisan research center—the Transactional Records Access Clearinghouse (TRAC)—found historic drops in deportations and historic increases in illegals allowed to stay. Illegals were deported in only half of the cases on record, marking the lowest rate for the past two decades. "Clearly, the Obama Administration's stealth amnesty plan to suspend the deportations of most illegal aliens is in play here," complained Judicial Watch, referencing the TRAC statistics.[7]

Obama's administration has again signaled its strategy of "executive amnesty" by appointing, in January 2012, a longtime open-borders advocate to direct the White House Domestic Policy Council, the executive body mainly tasked with immigration issues. Cecilia Muñoz had been a senior vice president for the National Council of La Raza, a group lobbying for open borders, mass immigration, and amnesty for illegal aliens. Muñoz also chaired the board of the Coalition for Comprehensive Immigration Reform.[8]

Just how many illegal immigrants are there in the United States today?

The estimated number varies widely and is the subject of considerable debate. A little over half a decade ago, Sen. John McCain (R-AZ) shocked the public when he estimated—based on illegal immigrant apprehension statistics of the U.S. Border Patrol—*that nearly four million people had crossed the U.S. border illegally in 2002 alone.* In September 2004, *Time* magazine put the illegal population somewhere around 11 million. An independent study of the underground economy by Wall Street firm Bear Stearns, released in January 2005, estimated 18 to 20 million illegals in the United States.[9]

There is, of course, nothing new about the concept of amnesty for illegal immigrants. Indeed, since the radically liberalized Immigration and Nationality Act of 1965, there have been a total of seven amnesties.[10] The first was the Immigration and Reform Control Act of 1986 in which President Ronald Reagan approved amnesty for 2.7 million people, providing forgiveness for those who entered illegally, and setting them on the path to citizenship. Of the 1.3 million amnesty applications that ensued, more than 90 percent were for a specialized program for agricultural workers. The number of illegal aliens seeking amnesty exceeded expectations, however, and there was reportedly widespread document fraud, with as many as a third of the applicants having been granted amnesty improperly.[11] Reagan's IRCA was a failure: it neither stemmed the tide of illegal immigrants through the strengthening of border security, nor increased immigration enforcement against employers, as was intended.[12]

During the Clinton administration, there were six more amnesties granted. In 1994, there was a temporary, rolling amnesty for 578,000 illegal immigrants, with an Extension Amnesty in 1997. Also in 1997, there was the Nicaraguan Adjustment and Central American Relief Act, which granted amnesty for nearly one million Central American illegal immigrants. The Haitian Refugee Immigration Fairness Act Amnesty in 1998 granted amnesty for 125,000 Haitian illegal immigrants.[13] In 2000, there were two more amnesties. One, called the Late Amnesty, granted amnesty to an estimated 400,000 illegal immigrants who claimed they should have been amnestied under IRCA in 1986. The second, called the LIFE Act Amnesty, reinstated the 1994 rolling amnesty and included 900,000 more.[14]

Obama and progressives fully understand that documenting millions of illegal immigrants and putting them on the path to citizenship can fundamentally transform our country in so many obvious ways, most prominently ensuring Democrat rule into the long term. Before we divulge specific second-term schemes to make this happen, it is instrumental to take a look at U.S. border enforcement, where plans are afoot to drastically transform the country's ability to stem the flow of illegals into our country.

OPEN THE BORDERS

In searching for future border policies, our extensive research eventually led to one major piece of legislation, the 645-page "Comprehensive Immigration Reform for America's Security and Prosperity Act of 2009." Within the bill, we find the specific handiwork of the usual suspects, the major progressive groups that have already been so instrumental in crafting Obama's major first-term initiatives, most notably ObamaCare and the so-called stimulus bill.

For those scratching their heads in wonderment as to why we would return to a 2009 bill to divine Obama's border plans for a second term, rest assured there is good reason. It is important to recall how we thoroughly documented in our previous book, *Red Army*, the way in which progressive legislation and research papers that traced back to 2002 and, in some cases even to the 1990s, eventually made their way into what became Obama's health care bill. In other words, the foundations for ObamaCare had been hiding in plain view for over a decade. We also showed how progressive politicians strategically introduced such legislation over time, working with the liberal think tanks to craft and perfect the bills.

Following our review of much border and immigration reform legislation as well as progressive research and policy papers on the topics, it became clear that significant blueprints for future border policies were strategically placed within the 2009 bill, a piece of legislation that we doubt many reporters or critical analysts have bothered to read in full, if at all.

The bill was introduced on December 15, 2009, by Reps. Solomon Ortiz (D-TX) and Luis Gutierrez (D-IL), with ninety-one original co-*sponsors, including many members of the Congressional Progressive Caucus.*[15] *(The CPC was founded by the Democratic Socialists of America, the largest socialist* organization in the United States, and the principal U.S. affiliate of the *Socialist* International, the world's largest socialist umbrella group.)

The bill immediately minimizes the capabilities of U.S. border agents to conduct searches or to carry out actions intended to root out the smuggling of illegal aliens. Because it mandates the creation of a Border Communities Liaison Office in every border sector (there are nine border sectors along the U.S. border with Mexico),[16] civilians living in those border communities—some of whom may be actively involved in illicit actions—would be warned by such "liaisons" ahead of time about the operational plans of border agents intended to curtail smuggling. Each new "liaison office" would be required to consult with border communities on the "directives," "laws," "strategies," and "operational issues" of border patrol authorities.

The Armed Forces, including the National Guard, would be prohibited under this bill from ever acting on the U.S. border unless the president first declared a national emergency. The only exception would be for specific counterterrorism duties, and even then the military would not be allowed to conduct armed operations within twenty-five miles of the border.

The vast majority—96.6 percent—of apprehensions of illegal aliens by the Border Patrol in 2010 occurred along the southwest border.[17] It does not take a genius to realize that the construction of a barrier along the entire 1,951-mile border between the United States and Mexico could curtail a large number of smuggling attempts. Already, the Homeland Security Department under President George W. Bush built 190 miles of pedestrian border fence and 154.3 miles of vehicle border fence—about one-fifth of the total length needed—mainly in New Mexico, Arizona, and California.

Throughout the years there have been calls for a barrier along the entire U.S.-Mexico border. For example, Rep. Duncan Hunter (R-CA), then chairman of the House Armed Services Committee, proposed a plan on November 3, 2005, calling for the construction of a reinforced fence along the entire border. In 2006, President Bush supported a major upgrade in border security with calls for a network of fences, cameras, radar, and communications gear to help speed the response of U.S. Border Patrol officers.

Under Obama, however, the fence project was halted, with Homeland Security spending nearly $90 million on environmental analysis and mitigation measures it claims are aimed at blunting any adverse impact the fence could possibly have on the environment.[18] The proposed 645-page immigration reform bill contains detailed provisions on how barriers cannot be constructed on areas if the fence will impede "wildlife migration corridors, key habitats, and the ecologically functional connectivity between and among key habitats sufficient to ensure that species (whether or not designated as rare, protected, or of concern) remain viable." Furthermore, the bill is concerned with whether such unspecified species are "able to adapt to the impacts of climate change." In other words, a security border fence could not be constructed where it would somehow impede a turtle's ability to adapt to so-called global warming. (If you're reading this book out of order, please see the previous chapter for more such uses of "global warming" to push a second-term progressive agenda.)

"Racist" to Enforce Border Security?

When it comes to border security, the progressives' greatest fear does not concern illegals infiltrating or terrorists making their way into our population zones. Apparently, their biggest concern is whether border agents exercise "racism" or violate the "civil liberties" of illegal aliens. A close reading of the bill makes clear the "racism" canard is actually a carefully constructed stratagem to impede border agents' ability to confront illegal immigration. The scheme mandates the collection of ethnic data on border searches to determine "the existence or absence of racial profiling." So if a border agent along the Mexican border searches, let's say, um, a lot of Mexicans (in other words, he/she does his/her job!) . . . that agent could be cited for racial profiling. There's more. Progressives are planning for every authorized border agent to be trained "on constitutional, privacy, civil rights, and civil liberties issues related to such searches." Let us imagine the training manual for agents at the Mexico border: *"Agents are advised not to apprehend more than 17 percent of suspects from any given ethnic group lest agents be subject to prosecution under Article 8, Subsection 6 of the Progressive Penal Code . . ."*

Backdoor Amnesty

What about the apprehension of illegals already within the United States?

The bill invents a new class of illegals—those from "community-based" and "faith-based" organizations. The bill would make it illegal to apprehend "undocumented" persons in the "premises or in the immediate vicinity of a childcare provider; a school; a legal-service provider; a Federal court or State court proceeding; an administrative proceeding; a funeral home; a cemetery; a college, university, or community services agency; a social service agency; a hospital or emergency care center; a health care clinic; a place of worship; a day care center; a head start center; a school bus stop; a recreation center; a mental health facility; and a community center."

Had enough? The bill also prohibits the apprehension of pregnant or disabled illegals.

There would also be new restrictions placed on apprehending illegals who are members of a newly defined "vulnerable population." Included is this neologism: "Individuals who have been determined by a medically trained professional to have medical or mental health needs." Afraid of deportation? A doctor's note claiming "medical needs" (a hangnail?) or a social worker documenting "anxiety" might suffice. Also in the "vulnerable population" are "individuals who provide financial, physical, and other direct support to their minor children, parents, or other dependents"—in other words, virtually every single illegal alien inside the United States.

Perhaps the biggest proponents of these new sensitivities would be the illegals themselves. Once they understood the litany of new perks they'd receive in detention in the U.S. under Obama, they'd be lining up to be arrested (although their arrests could be prevented under the law's anti-racial profiling provisions)!

The bill contains many more pages of scandalous, newfound "rights" provided to all illegals held in detention centers. Each detainee, for example, would have a right to "prompt and adequate medical care, designed to ensure continuity of care, at no cost to the detainee." Included would be "care to address medical needs that existed prior to detention; and primary care, emergency care, chronic care, prenatal care, dental care, eye care, mental health care, and other medically necessary specialized care." This is better coverage than some of the most expensive private health plans. And it is only the beginning of the taxpayer-funded madness that could comprise Obama's second-term agenda on illegal immigration. Also included in the completely free, mandated coverage for detained illegals would be "medication, prenatal care, prenatal vitamins, hormonal therapies, and birth control." Every detainee's needs would be met since, upon detention, each inmate is to get a "comprehensive medical, dental, and mental health intake screening."

BRING IN MORE IMMIGRANTS

Other second-term progressive immigration plans—some of which are included in the amnesty bill detailed above—*actually call for more immigrants to enter the United States*, albeit legally. John Podesta's Center for American Progress, the "idea center" of the Obama White House, highlighted those plans in a January 2012 report—"Immigration for Innovation: How to Attract the World's Best Talent While Ensuring America Remains the Land of Opportunity for All."[19] Podesta's recommendations include eliminating the cap on the number of the H-1B visas provided to foreigners. H-1B is the most widely used high-skilled immigration classification for temporary workers. Currently, the system is regulated by a Congressionally established annual cap set at about 85,000 H-1B visas per year. The report also complains we aren't giving out enough "green cards" (currently about 140,000 employment-based permanent visas, or "green cards," are available each year) and demands that the cap on those highly restricted visas be removed, as well.

To be fair, this particular progressive goal—an increase in legal immigration of highly skilled foreigners—is shared by many fiscal conservatives. Many of those in business already live in ethnically diverse American cities, and have not experienced the sense of cultural inundation of average Americans forced to adjust to large waves of illegal aliens flooding into their more ethnically homogenous communities. Fiscal conservatives also see the economic contributions of highly skilled immigrants as compensating for the services they receive in the U.S., in a way that the poorer, and much more numerous, illegals do not.

The 2009 amnesty bill itself makes precisely the same CAP arguments for lifting the cap on visas in a section entitled "Visa Reform." But its solution is to take the regulation of legal immigration away from Congress, and vest it in an agency within the executive branch. The so-called Commission on Immigration and Labor Markets would establish "employment-based immigration policies that promote America's economic growth and competitiveness while minimizing job displacement, wage depression and unauthorized employment in the United States." The executive branch would henceforth determine the numbers of new immigrants, as well as to whom visas would be issued. Viewed another way, it would oversee the flow of an untold number of new immigrants into the U.S., in addition to the unknown number currently inside of, and still entering, the country.

ENSURING DEMOCRAT RULE

As noted earlier, mass amnesty for 10 to 20 million illegals would profoundly alter the American electorate. Many champions of amnesty have noted this openly, although the news media routinely neglect to report it. A good example is Eliseo Medina, the SEIU's international secretary-treasurer, who was appointed in November 2008 to serve on Obama's transition team committee for immigration.[20] Medina made some very revealing, if largely unreported, remarks at the 2009 session of the annual progressive conference organized by Campaign for America's Future. Medina said of Latino voters:

> [W]hen they voted in November [2008], they voted overwhelmingly for progressive candidates. Barack Obama got two out of every three voters that showed up.[21]

Medina continued:

> So I think there's two things, very quickly, that matter for the progressive community.
> Number one. If we are to expand this electorate to win, the progressive community needs to solidly be on the side of immigrants, then we'll solidify and expand the progressive coalition for the future . . . When you are in the middle of a fight for your life you will remember who was there with you. And immigrants count on progressives to be able to do that.

Number two. We reform the immigration laws, it puts 12 million people on the path to citizenship and eventually voters. Can you imagine if we have, even the same ratio, two out of three? If we have eight million new voters that care about our [winning?] and be voting, we will be creating a governing coalition for the long term, not just for an election cycle.[22]

Medina was boasting to a friendly audience that granting citizenship to millions of illegals would expand the *progressive* electorate and help ensure a *Democrat* governing coalition for the long term.

This is not mere rhetoric. We discovered specific, second-term plans for government agencies to immediately register as voters the new Americans who would receive amnesty. One such plan was outlined in a thirty-two-page report from the progressive think tank Demos—"From Citizenship to Voting: Improving Registration for New Americans."[23] In future chapters, we will show how Demos, like the CAP, has been highly influential in crafting White House policy. This particular Demos report was authored by Tova Andrea Wang, a senior fellow at both Demos, and at a group called the Century Foundation, which works closely with the Center for American Progress.

The Demos report calls for the United States Citizenship and Immigrant Services (USCIS) to fully implement a new policy to ensure "new Americans" are provided with a voter registration application at all administrative naturalization ceremonies. Ultimately, USCIS should be designated as a full voter registration agency under the National Voter Registration Act so that every newly naturalized American is automatically given the opportunity to register to vote. The report also wants state and local elections officials to be proactive in registering new citizens to vote by reaching out to their communities through every possible means.

4

A JOBS PLAN FOR AMERICA

PRESIDENT OBAMA ACTUALLY laid out much of his plan for a second administration in the final State of the Union address of his first. On the subject of jobs, the forty-fourth president's broad outline was vague, but he telegraphed unspecified intentions by repeatedly invoking the theme of "fairness":

> No challenge is more urgent. No debate is more important. We can either settle for a country where a shrinking number of people do really well, while a growing number of Americans barely get by. Or we can restore an economy where everyone gets a fair shot, everyone does their fair share, and everyone plays by the same set of rules.[1]

As we shall see, this progressive president's "job fairness" agenda would never be the traditional American one of *fairness of opportunity* for all. Rather he seeks to implement the progressive socialists' "fairness" of politically driven outcomes. Fortunately thus far—and in spite of record unemployment—the ruinous jobs agenda of the far left that we expose here has not won much support from the American people, nor in Congress, and has virtually no chance of being enacted—unless Obama is reelected to a second term.

In the fall of 2011, Obama was already nearly six months into reelection campaign mode. He was desperately trying to salvage his disastrous first term by pushing for nearly half a trillion dollars in new "jobs creation" spending. His memorable speech to a joint session of Congress, on September 8, found him demanding of those he'd assembled to just "pass this jobs bill"—a $447 billion package of tax cuts and a pork-barrel overflowing with new spending.[2]

Certainly most of Congress was not buying into yet another ruinous spending package. And the president surely had no expectation at that stage of their approval. (Rather, he is shrewdly campaigning on their recalcitrance.) But about one-sixth of the U.S. House today are members of the Congressional Progressive Caucus (with seventy-five members in the House, plus one in the U.S. Senate), who have complete allegiance to the so-called "fair jobs" agenda. The CPC's own literature describes its fair jobs schemes as rooted in core principles embodied in its Progressive Promise—Fairness for All.[3] The specific ways these core principles are translated into a tsunami of progressive policies and legislation, we detail here and throughout this book.

It is important to note that the Congressional Progressive Caucus was launched, in 1992, with the help of the Democratic Socialists of America. DSA is a full member of the Socialist International, a worldwide organization of 162 social democratic, socialist, and labor political parties and organizations.[4] On its website, DSA laments that the "vision of socialism" has taken root everywhere in the world—except in the United States.[5] For progressive socialists worldwide, a major goal is government-created jobs. As the DSA stated on its website in 2011, "We . . . have long been calling for jobs, good jobs, and lots of them,"[6] but at the same time DSA was critical of the progressive president. "Obama has proposed creating jobs, but his program is too small, and most of it goes to tax incentives, not to direct job creation."[7] But the DSA and its progressive allies were working overtime to get their wish.

JOBS, BUT BAD JOBS

The same day as Obama's jobs speech to the joint session of Congress, a far-left think tank called Demos issued its response. Based on the idea of wealth redistribution, Demos claims to be nonpartisan, and lobbies federal and state policymakers to address "economic insecurity and inequality" in American society. It advocates for a "more steeply progressive income-tax structure, on the premise that 'the rich must pay their fair share if communities are to thrive.'"[8]

The authors of *Help Wanted: American Needs a Better Jobs Plan* are David Callahan and Tamara Draut, Demos' co-founder and vice president, respectively. In response to the president's speech, on behalf of Demos, they were only mildly impressed with Obama's jobs plan, asserting it did not go far enough. In particular, the almost half-trillion dollars just proposed by the president was not nearly enough. Moreover, Obama's speech failed to push for something Callahan and Draut characterized as an "urgent effort"—to ensure "better jobs."[9]

The Demos officials referenced a paper—barely a week old—written for the group by Prof. Paul Osterman, of MIT's Sloan School of Management. Osterman believes "far too many jobs fall below the standard that most Americans would consider decent work."[10] Osterman's co-author on a 2011 book is Beth Shulman, and together they assert that *good jobs* are those that "pay enough to support a family and provide decent, safe conditions." They say that "many middle-class jobs have disappeared or deteriorated into low-wage ones that cause families to fall below the poverty line."[11] Here they are referring to the *underemployed*, meaning those employed below their abilities and ability to earn more. According to the Bureau of Labor statistics, almost a half million people, as of October 2011, were underemployed.[12]

A month after the president's speech to the Congressional joint session, two other Demos analysts published a report called *Worth Working For: Strategies for Turning Bad Jobs into Quality Employment*. Just finding a job, "while critical," is not enough, wrote Ben Peck and Amy Traub. Hard work should be rewarded with "more jobs capable of supporting a family with a decent standard of living." "Millions of workers," Peck and Traub asserted, were unable to achieve or remain in the middle class due to the recession, leading to an "earnings shortfall." The majority of jobs lost were middle-income positions, they claimed, "yet the majority of jobs gained during the recovery have been in low-wage occupations."[13]

Peck and Traub's assertions about the state of the job market may or may not be accurate. These, as well as their questionable claim that there has actually been any economic "recovery," are matters for experts to debate. One notable point is that Peck and Traub identified the cause of the purported underemployment malaise as . . . corporate greed.

Further, among the utopian solutions they advocate would be a family leave law such as the proposed Family Leave Insurance Act. The new bill, first introduced in the House of Representatives in 2005, builds upon the Family and Medical Leave Act of 1993. This measure afforded eligible workers *unpaid family leave*, while preserving a worker's job or a comparable job upon return.[14]

But the new plan goes a giant step further—from job preservation to a new form of entitlement. It would provide *twelve weeks of paid benefits* to employees who need time off—to care for a new child, a sick family member, or their own illness. This would allegedly be financed through employees paying premiums into a trust fund, who would then be eligible through a tiered system after having paid into the trust for six months. Yet besides the cost of such a scheme, nowhere in their paper do the authors address the impact of the easily imaginable scenario of dozens of employees taking up to three months of paid leave simultaneously.

Peck and Traub also want to amend the Fair Labor Standards Act to give workers the right to refuse overtime. It is hard to see how that squares with predictions by the Department of Labor that the largest job growth in the next decade will be in "low-paying occupations, such as home health aides, food service workers, and retail salespeople." Workers in lower-paying jobs are often desirous of overtime and less likely to be looking for ways to get out of it. Conversely, employers need to be able to rely upon their workers to get the job done. Moreover, add this to the aforementioned three months of paid family leave, and it is easy to see how the two plans could virtually shut down a business's operations. The silver lining Peck and Traub find here is that these low-paying jobs cannot be outsourced and will need to be filled by resident workers—if employers can stay in operation.

For Demos contributors Osterman and Shulman, a kind of shock therapy will be needed in order to inaugurate such changes:

> The status quo overall will not change unless companies are subjected to an external "shock" that forces them to rethink the way

they do business. [Such a shock] can come from laws enacted at the federal, state or local levels; from workers themselves organizing a union; or from the larger community demanding better quality jobs in exchange for some public benefit.[15]

SOLVE ECONOMIC INEQUALITY WITH UNION JOBS!

For Peck and Traub, nearly all of their prescriptions point to a familiar progressive constituency—unions. They remind us that "even manufacturing jobs were not 'good jobs' until employers, government and unions adopted strategies to improve them generations ago." They observe that people working low-wage jobs do not have as much buying power as workers who are better paid, that many of them are struggling, overburdened, and have to juggle "rigid and unpredictable work schedules" which may keep them from participation with family obligations or other tasks. So they prescribe one remedy: a higher minimum wage that would "raise the floor for all employees." In addition, non-wage benefits such as "sick leave, paid family leave, and more control over their work schedules" would be included.

Demos executives Callahan and Draut concur, adding that government "can and should play a vigorous role in encouraging employers to create good jobs—perhaps by providing tax incentives that require employers to pay a living wage."[16]

The reference to a "living wage" comes straight from the pen of Karl Marx, author of the 1848 *Communist Manifesto*. In his book on the living wage, Donald R. Stabile, professor of economics at St. Mary's College of Maryland, wrote, "Marx believed that only under communism could he find support for his ultimate goal of a living wage, 'From each according to his ability, to each according to his needs.'"[17]

Here is the real-world scenario of what a nationally mandated living wage could mean for America should Barack Obama win a second term. In the winter 2003 issue of *City Journal*, Manhattan Institute scholar Steve Malanga wrote that for more than a decade,

"[a] savvy left-wing political movement, supported by radical economic groups, liberal foundations, and urban activists" had lobbied for a "government-guaranteed 'living wage' for low-income workers, considerably higher than the current minimum wage."[18]

The living wage movement had succeeded in no fewer than eighty cities as of 2003. But as Malanga showed, this brought with it plenty of bad news:

> The living wage poses a big threat to [the cities'] economic health, because the costs and restrictions it imposes on the private sector will destroy jobs—especially low-wage jobs—and send businesses fleeing to other locales. Worse still, the living-wage movement's agenda doesn't end with forcing private employers to increase wages. It includes opposing privatization schemes, strong-arming companies into unionizing, and other economic policies equally harmful to urban health.

Malanga cites Baltimore as exhibit number one. Baltimore embraced the living wage in the mid-1990s but failed to become a "workers' paradise." Instead, the city saw its economy "crash and burn" while 58,000 jobs disappeared at the same time other cities across Maryland added 120,000 jobs and "other cities across the country prospered." Malanga stated that the living-wage bill was "just one expression of a fiercely anti-business climate that helped precipitate Baltimore's economic collapse."

While you might expect the Baltimore experience to serve as an example of what *not* to do, nothing could be farther from reality. Malanga wrote,

> Baltimore "became the poster child for future activism," where a "host of left-wing groups, including Ralph Nader's Citizens Action and the Association for Community Reform Now, or ACORN, joined forces in 1995 in a national 'Campaign for an America That Works,' which made the living wage central to its demands."

The impact, Malanga wrote, was national in scope as radicals took the "living wage" movement to "city after city."

Central to this campaign was the anti-capitalist ACORN—the Association of Community Organizations for Reform Now. ACORN was created around 1970 by former Students for a Democratic Society radical Wade Rathke. A 1960s colleague of Weatherman terrorists Bill Ayers and Bernardine Dohrn, Rathke is also the founder of an SEIU Local in New Orleans. The ACORN *People's Platform* of 1979 (updated in 1990) states:

> [O]nly the people shall rule. Corporations shall have no role: producing jobs, providing products, paying taxes. No more, no less. They shall obey our wishes, respond to our needs, serve our communities.[19]

As for the role of government, ACORN states, it is a "public servant for our good, fast follower to our sure steps. No more, no less."

In fact, Malanga wrote, following on its 2002 success in getting New Orleans—ACORN's national headquarters—to enact living wage legislation, ACORN created a step-by-step manual, which "echoes" the coalition-building organizational techniques of influential radical theorist Saul Alinsky. The ACORN manual is a blueprint to everything one could want to know on how it was done and how it could be replicated elsewhere. Money is not a problem. Malanga discovered that ACORN had lots of it available to push the living-wage campaign. He cites two sources: the Tides Foundation, which had "given hundreds of thousands of dollars to local and national living-wage groups . . . [while] the Ford Foundation has been another big contributor."

The Tides Foundation is a major legal money-laundering funding funnel for a myriad of progressive groups and causes. Rathke was a Tides founding board member along with Drummond Pike, has served as board chairman, and continues to serve as a senior adviser.[20]

Malanga draws a clear picture for us of how ACORN—which has now rebranded itself with a number of state organizations since being exposed a few years back for corruption[21]—and similar groups, will advance the "living wage" via a stealth campaign:[22]

> Living-wage campaigns have repeatedly outflanked the business community by practicing what ACORN calls "legislative outmaneuver." Local groups work behind the scenes for months before going public. They draft partisan economists to release timely studies on the

prospective benefits of the living wage before opponents can come up with any countering data, and they try to keep any actual legislation off the table until the very last minute, so that there's no fixed target for opponents to get a bead on.

THE ROLE OF "PARTISAN ECONOMISTS"

Demos is our exhibit number one for such "partisan economists."

Demos officials Callahan and Draut contend that, because the U.S. economy is stuck in a downturn, that is reason enough to make it "easier" for workers to join unions and put more disposable income into their pockets.[23] To prop up this straw man, the authors cite a separate contemporary report by Demos staffer Amy Traub, who asserts that "organized labor has traditionally played a crucial role in ensuring that working people—who make up most consumers—receive a larger share of the economy's gains." Taking this to its logical conclusion, Peck and Traub write that legislation should be drawn up that would "more effectively" protect the "right of workers to bargain collectively for improved wages and benefits."[24]

Let us examine the flaws in this argument, bearing in mind the progressive strategem of not allowing enough time for public consideration of progressive think tank blather before their legislation can be rammed through.

First of all, we fact checked Traub's false and misleading statement that working people "make up most consumers." *Everyone* residing in the United States is a consumer, and fewer than half are active members of the workforce at any given time. Second, nothing legally bars workers from joining unions. If a union exists and people want to join it, who will stop them? And why does the Federal government need to have a role in removing a nonexistent barrier? Since 1935, with the passage of the National Labor Relations Act, or Wagner Act, it has been a matter of federal law that workers in the private sector have the right to create labor unions and enter into collective bargaining, without discrimination. And since June 1963 (*Labor Board v. General Motors Corp.* 373 U.S. 734), although employees have the right to join and assist unions, they also have a right to refrain from supporting them. They cannot be required to join a union that represents their bargaining unit, to remain in said union, or to pay full dues in the union (or they can pay but with the express exclusion of that portion used by the union for political purposes). By law, employees are not required to join a union or to pay full dues as a condition of their employment.[25]

It is outrageous that progressive socialists in America have deemed union workers to be more equal than nonunion workers. Demos and its fellow travelers are actively promoting a massive political realignment in which union workers are entitled to a "larger share of the economy's gains" than nonunion workers. This is the progressive "fair share"!

And now we can proceed to how Barack Obama would use a second term to push for a "living wage."

In February 2010, the Associated Press reported that a company paying a "living wage" to its workers "could gain an advantage in bidding on government contracts under a new policy the White House is considering."[26] Called "high road" contracting, the White House move would be designed to lead to a "larger debate over whether the government should use public purse strings to strengthen the middle class and promote higher labor standards." As we have seen, in reality this would benefit mainly unions and union workers, and so, unsurprisingly, the unions were all for the plan, claiming that "too many jobs financed by government contracts come with low wages and limited benefits and support companies that violate employment laws." Nor would the advantages contained in the Obama living-wage plan be exclusive to wages (as was shown above in the Demos literature). It would also promote benefits such as health insurance, retirement funds, and paid leave.

Right on cue, "partisan economists" at a leading progressive think tank, the Economic Policy Institute, estimated "nearly 20 percent of the 2 million federal contract workers in the U.S. earn less than the poverty threshold wage of $9.91 per hour." The über-progressive think tank, the Center for American Progress, chimed in that there was "evidence that better-paid workers are more efficient and productive."

Another deceptive claim is that unions "raise compensation for workers they don't represent." The Demos officials based this claim on a March 2011 study by two professors—Bruce Western of Harvard and Jake Rosenfeld of the University of Washington–Seattle.[27] In essence, Western and Rosenfeld view union membership as an equality redistribution mechanism for all wage earners. They note the steep decline in private-sector union membership between 1973 and 2007 and then postulate that if union membership would expand, wages for all workers—union and nonunion—would necessarily go up. But, in the real world, boosting union membership benefits unions, who, in turn, spend billions of dollars of union membership dues supporting Democratic candidates, who, in turn, support the union bosses' interests. Yet another form of incestuous, progressive cronyism.

REGULATE, REGULATE, REGULATE

A universal theme for all aforementioned progressive think tanks is more regulation.

And if there is one thing at which the Obama administration has succeeded spectacularly, it is the explosive proliferation in the number of federal regulations in less than four years, particularly job-destroying ones. (An Internet search on "Obama + regulations" reveals two results competing for the highest returns: *Obama regulations costing jobs* and *Obama regulations killing jobs*. Not a good sign.) Eight months into Obama's administration, a Minneapolis–St. Paul labor lawyer warned her colleagues:

> The Obama administration is slated to awaken this slumbering dragon.... Attorneys who represent employers, employees, and unions would be wise to remain apprised of these impending changes.[28]

Over at the online publication of the communist Workers World Party— *People's World*—its co-editor could scarcely contain his jubilation when he reported, in January 2012, that the Obama administration had "moved under the radar over the last month to issue some of the most pro-worker rules the country has seen in 35 years. The new rules cover union elections, hours of work and wages, among other things."[29]

Exactly how was Obama already moving "under the radar" on behalf of Big Labor? And what kind of stealth actions might lie ahead in a second Obama administration?

Barely a week after the 2008 election, the Associated Press was writing:

"Unions look to Obama to help advance their agenda."[30] "The labor unions that helped Barack Obama win the White House are looking for some payback," reporter Jim Abrams wrote.

One key organization in this effort is the president's Economic Recovery Advisory Board. Created in early February 2009, the board included two of the top union officials in America: Anna Burger and Richard L. Trumka.

Anna Burger was then secretary-treasurer of the corrupt community action group ACORN, and its affiliate, the Service Employees International Union, and was chairman, until August 2010, of the SEIU-affiliated Change to Win federation. Burger was also a board member of the union-affiliated Economic Policy Institute.

Richard L. Trumka at the time was secretary-treasurer of the AFL-CIO, soon to be elected president in September 2009. Trumka now serves on the president's Council on Jobs and Competitiveness and is an EPI board member.

Another union heavy-weight and former EPI board member is Andrew L. Stern, SEIU's president until April 2010. SEIU is the second largest labor union in the U.S. and Stern was one of the most frequent visitors to the Obama White House. We reported in our previous book—*Red Army*—that Stern told a *Los Angeles Times* reporter that SEIU has had a close relationship with Obama since 2004, when Obama ran for the U.S. Senate from Illinois. In February 2008, during the Democrat presidential primary contest between Obama and a Hillary Clinton who was still widely considered to be "unbeatable," Stern announced that the SEIU was endorsing Obama in the name of its 1.9 million members. Stern's union would ultimately deposit some $60 million in the Obama campaign piggy bank. But the real debt owed by unions to their progressive president in the White House is incalculable.

And if unions are the workers' best friend, then greedy corporate America is their worst enemy.

"[F]ar more American workers would like to be part of a union than is now the case," claimed Demos officials, citing unspecified polls. The reason for this, they assert, is that Big Business lobbyists have worked for decades to "water down the nation's labor regulations so that corporations can, with near impunity, obstruct their employees' efforts to choose a union."[31]

The Demos solution for this troubling situation is for Congress to pass the controversial Employee Free Choice Act (EFCA), also known as Card Check. If passed (though they concede the bill's prospects are doubtful), EFCA would "streamline the process of forming unions in the workplace and prohibit some current forms of union-busting by employers."

There have been many pros and cons bandied about regarding EFCA. One negative consequence, for employers as well as employees, was explained in February 2009, by a group called the Center for Union Facts:[32]

> Consider current labor election procedures. If union organizers hit a threshold of employee signatures, a federal agency conducts a secret ballot election, usually within 60 days. In that time period, employees have the opportunity to hear from both sides regarding the pros and cons of unionization.
>
> As in a presidential campaign, the campaign window allows people to make the best decision by giving access to all the information about the "candidates." But [the] "your signature equals your vote" process means a small workplace unit can be unionized overnight. Employers could be blindsided with little chance for informing their employees about the downsides of a union-run workplace.

Not to mention the fact that the workers could show up the next workday to discover they are working in a union shop against their will.

Beyond "Card Check," the Demos group wants an increase in the federally mandated minimum wage to $10 per hour.[33] The problem is that pushing up the minimum wage has the corollary effect of eliminating many jobs. As a senior fellow at conservative Colorado think tank, the Independence Institute wrote:

> In practice they often price low-skilled workers out of the labor market. Employers typically are not willing to pay a worker more than the value of the additional product that he produces. This means that an unskilled youth who produces $4.00 worth of goods in an hour will have a very difficult time finding a job if he must, by law, be paid $5.15 an hour.[34]

Again, Demos touts Obama's proposal to extend unemployment benefits as being "among the most urgent elements of his plan." But there were problems. Congress has already extended unemployment benefits a number of times, and the "average duration of unemployment" has reached a postwar record of ten months. In the debt ceiling deal reached by Congress in August 2011, unemployment benefits that were due to expire by the end of the year were not extended.

Meanwhile, the unemployment rate passed a new milestone in February 2012. Despite coming in at 8.3 percent—a three-year low—the rate had exceeded 8.0 percent for the longest stretch since the Great Depression.[35] According to the Bureau of Labor Statistics, the actual number of non-farm unemployed stood at 12.8 million. The long-term unemployed—those who had been jobless for 27 weeks and more—remained at 5.4 million, and accounted for 42.6 percent of all those unemployed.[36]

Speaking of unemployment benefits, Obama's closest political confidant—senior White House adviser Valerie Jarrett—shockingly told a Durham, North Carolina, university audience in February 2012:

> Even though we had a terrible economic crisis three years ago, throughout our country many people were suffering before the last three years, particularly in the black community. And so we need to make sure that we continue to support that important safety net. It not only is good for the family, but it's good for the economy. People who receive that unemployment check go out and spend it and help stimulate the economy, so that's healthy as well.[37]

Her clear implication was that unemployment—and not simply unemployment benefits—is "good for the economy." But Jarrett was simply pushing an official progressive political message in advance of the 2012 presidential election: that Congress's failure to extend unemployment benefits would be exploited to the maximum advantage.

Some of the leading Keynesian economists have consistently promoted the idea that unemployment is good for the economy. For example, Alan S. Blinder served on the Clinton administration's Council of Economic Advisors and was appointed by Clinton to the board of the Federal Reserve, while Mark Zandi is chief economist of Moody's Analytics and served as economic advisor in 2008 to Senator John McCain. Both claim that the $787 billion "stimulus" of 2009 has worked.[38] In July 2010, they claimed that unemployment benefits are "among the most potent forms of economic stimulus available." Why? Because, they rationalize, most unemployed workers "spend their benefits immediately." With a total price tag for benefits approaching $300 billion, they claimed economic activity like this made "such spending far more effective than most tax cuts."[39]

A study from the Economic Policy Institute claimed that failure to extend the payroll tax and emergency unemployment insurance would reduce U.S. GDP by $241 billion in calendar year 2012, a decrease of 1.5 percent, relative to projected levels. EPI's study claimed it would also "decrease economic activity by $70 billion (–0.4 percent) and decrease employment by roughly 528,000 jobs."[40] Thus, at the end of January 2012, President Obama and Congress extended unemployment benefits for an additional two months, though they did not add any benefits beyond the current ninety-nine-week mark.[41]

How the Obama administration intends to deal with the needs of a massive labor force that is no longer seeking employment has not been addressed. In March 2012, for example, while the "good for the economy" unemployment rate declined from 8.3 percent to 8.2 percent, the dip in the unemployment rate was accompanied by an all-time high of 87,897,000 people no longer seeking employment.[42]

THE "FALLING UNEMPLOYMENT" SCAM

This leads us to the gigantic—and completely false—spin Democrats gave to official employment numbers released at the beginning of 2012.

New jobs and unemployment data from the Bureau of Labor Statistics were released on February 3. On the one hand, they showed an improved 8.3 percent unemployment rate—still much higher than Obama had inherited, or promised, but the lowest rate since February 2009. At the same time, the BLS numbers also revealed *that 1.2 million people had disappeared from the workforce in a single month.*[43] So the unemployment rate had "improved" by 1.2 million Americans exiting from the workforce altogether!

This sleight of hand was well explained at ZeroHedge.com, an American financial blog:

> Do the following calculation with us: using BLS data, the US civilian non-institutional population was 242,269[,000] in January, an increase of 1.7 million month over month: apply the long-term average labor force participation rate of 65.8% to this number. . . . and you get 159.4 million: that is what the real labor force should be. The BLS reported 154.4 million: a tiny 5 million difference. Then add these people who the BLS is purposefully ignoring yet who most certainly are in dire need of labor and/or a job to the 12.758 million reported unemployed by the BLS and you get 17.776 million in real unemployed workers. What does this mean? . . . [The] real unemployment rate actually rose in January to 11.5%.
>
> [. . .]
>
> It also means that the spread between the reported and implied unemployment rate just soared to a fresh thirty-year high of 3.2 percent. And that is how with a calculator and just one minute of math, one strips away countless hours of BLS propaganda.[44]

Jim Pethokoukis, writing in the *American Enterprise*, put it another way:

> We need only to go back to January 2011, when the "unemployment rate was 9.1 percent with a participation rate of 64.2 percent." At the current participation rate, the unemployment rate would be 8.9 percent, instead of 8.3 percent, he wrote, adding, "As an analysis from Hamilton Place Strategies concludes, *most of the shift of the past year is due not to the improvement in the labor market, but the continued drop in participation in the labor force.*"[45] [Emphasis added.]

This "rosy ruse" of an 8.3 percent unemployment rate was deconstructed further by John Crudele in the *New York Post*. "Seasonal adjustments," he said, are intended to "smooth out holiday bumps" in employment numbers. A milder-than-expected winter meant fewer layoffs and fewer people laid off than expected, which further skewed the numbers.[46]

THE WORK SHARE FOR LESS OPTION

Yet another Demos plan from their September 2011 offensive—"work-sharing programs"—would "compensate employers who reduce hours for workers, but don't fire them."[47] President Obama had, in fact, already included a measure in his proposed American Jobs Act that would support all fifty states in creating work-sharing programs.[48] Or, as the Center for Economic and Policy Research progressive think tank put it, at the same time Demos was pushing the idea:

> [The] quickest, and likely cheapest, way to increase employment would be to aggressively promote a policy of work sharing, for which President Obama already proposed some funding in his 2012 budget.[49]

(It should be noted that CEPR is a prominent supporter of, and apologist for, Venezuela's communist president, Hugo Chavez, and is supported in part by George Soros's Open Society Institute.[50])

A further rationale for work-share dollars came from Demos:

> Work-sharing payments allow employers to retain workers and avoid the disruption of lay-offs even as they lower their labor costs during a downturn. They also deliver even more stimulus bang for the buck than traditional unemployment benefits.

Demos also reported that some work-share assistance had already been provided to states as part of the initial federal "stimulus" in 2009.

CEPR's co-director, Dean Baker, elaborated on the purported "stimulus" benefit to work-share:

> In an economy that is operating well below its potential—and projected to remain so for much of the next decade—work sharing may be the most viable way of bringing the economy back closer to full employment.

Baker also claimed his work-sharing proposal would "give employers an incentive to maintain workers on their payroll at reduced hours as an alternative to laying them off"; would be "attached to the existing system of unemployment compensation, with short-time compensation as an alternative to unemployment compensation"; and would not require any "new" government bureaucracy.[51]

Unfortunately for Baker—given the recent nosedive in Europe's economy—his plan holds up for emulation the failed role models of Spain, Germany, and Italy. Each of these European Union countries tried work sharing to help avoid massive unemployment. But the numbers speak for themselves. For Spain, the unadjusted unemployment rate from July 2010 to December 2011 was around 23 percent. Using adjusted unemployment figures for the same time period, Germany showed around a 7.5 percent rate, and Italy 9 percent—all according to the U.S. Bureau of Labor Statistics.[52]

In a more recent article for the UK *Guardian*, Baker finds a major flaw in the Obama economic blueprint.

He cites a December, 2008, memo by Larry Summers, who headed Obama's National Economic Council, showing the economy to be in "much worse shape than was implied by the projections the Obama administration used in crafting its stimulus." In short, the numbers were "hugely overly optimistic." The administration expected that "job loss would peak at around 5 million in the 4th quarter of 2009." But they expected to regain all jobs lost by the end of 2011. Instead, by May 2009, almost 7 million jobs had been lost, and the hemorrhaging, in Baker's estimation, did not end until February 2010. Baker claimed the "stimulus" had failed to keep the job loss from falling even further, resulting on 6 million jobs lost below the pre-recession level.[53] The "unemployment rate had already hit 9.4%," he wrote, "when the stimulus first started to be felt in May of 2009. It eventually peaked at 10.0% in October of 2009."

We can see the results of implementing flawed "stimulus" plans in the name of job creation—especially in a period of high unemployment, excessive spending, and an out-of-control national debt. Yet another Obama plan would provide a $4,000 tax credit to businesses that hire workers who have been unemployed for at least six months. The Demos officials Callahan and Draut had one reservation, but it is not that the president would be doubling down on already ruinous policies. "This incentive could be useful," they wrote, "but care must be taken to ensure that employers are not pocketing funds for hires they would have made anyway."

Apparently untroubling to them would be the price tag of such a program, not to mention the wasteful expansion of government bureaucracy required to monitor it.

On the other hand, Callahan and Draut were unenthusiastic about an Obama proposal for "new government spending that ties unemployment insurance to job training." This idea is modeled after a Georgia program, which hands unemployment benefits over to employers—in the form of a stipend—who have hired the unemployed as trainees. But the Georgia results were dismal. Only 16.4 percent of workers who participated between 2003 and 2010 actually got hired by the "company where they were placed, and only 24 percent got jobs at all," according to the Georgia Department of Labor. And again, as with the above-mentioned tax credit plan, monitoring a "U.S. Works" program would require expanding the bureaucracy, an unfunded expense America can ill afford.[54]

PAYROLL TAX HOLIDAY

One Obama recommendation—deemed the "costliest and most ambitious element" of Obama's plan—did meet with the Demos officials' full approval: the extension of the payroll tax holiday. A payroll tax reduction of 2 percent for all workers in 2011, they wrote, "now delivers benefits to 121 million workers averaging about $934."[55]

But the Center for Budget and Policy Priorities wanted Obama to go farther. CBPP agreed that the expiration of the tax holiday, at the end of December 2011, would be a "self-inflicted wound to the economy" and "shrink the paychecks of nearly all Americans." Therefore, the CBPP wrote, Obama should not only propose to extend the tax cut for another year but also permanently expand it by cutting it in half for "all workers and employers up to the first $5 million of payroll. (The holiday rate would be 3.1 percent for employees and 3.1 percent for employers, as opposed to the normal 6.2 percent for each or the existing holiday rate of 4.2 percent just for workers.)" In addition, employers who added to their workforce or increased wages would be exempt from having to pay any payroll tax at all.[56]

(The CBPP, it should be noted, is a George Soros–funded, public policy think tank. Jared Bernstein, a CBPP senior fellow, formerly worked at the Economic Policy Institute. In December 2008, Bernstein became chief economist and economic policy adviser to Vice President Biden.[57])

In one of the more honest statements in their report, Demos' Callahan and Draut touted the payroll tax holiday for its "potential political viability." They added that Demos senior fellow and Cornell economist Robert Frank "advocated suspending this tax altogether for workers, which would increase most workers' paychecks by 4.2 percent immediately." But Frank wanted "the 6.2 percent employer side of this levy [to] be left in place for existing workers while there should be a full holiday for the tax on all new hires until the economy recovers from the current downturn." Another political windfall cited by Callahan and Draut: University of Delaware economist Larry Seidman "estimated that suspending the employee's share of the payroll tax would cause the national unemployment rate to decline by a full percentage point by the end of 2012 relative to what it would have been otherwise."[58] For Obama's reelection campaign, just in time!

The Demos officials note another, more far-reaching proposal, from 2010, by the bipartisan task force the president and Congress had created to develop a broad deficit-reduction plan (the Domenici-Rivlin Commission of the Bipartisan Policy Center). It "would [have suspended] the entire payroll tax for both workers and employers for one year—a move the commission estimated would create between 2.5 million and 7 million jobs." They also "proposed reimbursing the Social Security Trust Fund for lost revenues to ensure its long term solvency."[59]

A more radical perspective on payroll-tax-reduction-as-stimulus came from the Institute for Policy Studies. IPS is by far the most left-leaning progressive think tank in America today. The IPS has a long record of anti-capitalism, not to mention support for, and involvement with, Communist, Marxist, and anti-American causes around the world.

Putting more money in the hands of those who already have jobs so they can buy more Chinese imports does very little to put Americans to work in good jobs that pay good wages.[60]

So wrote John Cavanagh and David Korten for the IPS in November 2011.[61] They were optimistic about the current political environment: "Democrats are more likely to see a need for appropriate regulation, a progressive tax system, and government stimulus spending."[62] And they were anxious to get beyond the traditional American formula of economic expansion coupled to a strong work ethic: "Beyond just creating jobs, we need to help people shift from jobs that are harmful or simply unproductive to jobs that address currently unmet needs."[63]

In other words, Americans need the benevolent guiding hand of Big Brother to understand the fruitlessness of continuing in "harmful or simply unproductive" jobs that only meet their basic needs. In fact, Cavanagh and Korten epitomize the progressive ideal of the nanny state that wants to shape, direct, and control every aspect of Americans' lives:

> Examples include the transition from jobs in military industries to jobs in environmental remediation and elder care, and from jobs guarding prisons to jobs rehabilitating ex-offenders. We need to shift the resources we're squandering marketing junk food to children to teaching them, from mining coal to installing and maintaining solar panels, and from building an ever-increasing number of automobiles to expanding public transportation. More broadly, we need to shift from mining to recycling, from growing urban sprawl to retrofitting cities for sustainable living, and from financial speculation to the local financing of productive enterprises.[64]

The White House estimate of its proposed payroll tax holiday was also attacked by Demos. Obama's payroll tax cut would benefit 160 million workers and raise household incomes by $1,500 the following year for an average family. But Demos objected that the measure would cause $240 billion in lost federal tax revenue. Additionally, they complained that a payroll tax cut is "not as effective as direct government spending in stimulating economic activity." Moreover, they did not believe that tax cuts for all workers would be as effective as tax cuts "more sharply focused on low-income Americans." Still, they argued, a payroll tax cut is "highly effective at stimulating growth because it increases the size of ordinary people's paychecks and most of this money gets immediately spent."[65]

Here Demos is promoting the reinstatement of a tax credit called Making Work Pay. The MWP tax credit was included in the $787 billion 2009 "stimulus" bill. If the MWP credit were reinstated, estimates from the Economic Policy Institute predict it would "boost employment by 409,000 jobs in fiscal 2012 and 532,000 jobs in fiscal 2013."[66] During the years 2009 and 2010, MWP "provided a refundable tax credit of up to $400 for working individuals and up to $800 for married taxpayers filing joint returns," according to the IRS.[67] However, the tax credit was replaced in 2011 with a payroll tax cut, which "cut taxes for higher-income workers, raised taxes for some low-wage workers, and nearly doubled the amount of lost tax revenue," according to a former official with the Congressional Budget Office.[68]

Reinstatement of the MWP tax credit is now included in a major piece of progressive legislation called the Act for the 99%. The name is a short form of the Restore the American Dream for the 99% Act. The Act for the 99% is a major initiative of the Congressional Progressive Caucus, introduced on December 13, 2011. The reference to "99%" comes from a political slogan of the Occupy Wall Street movement—*We Are the 99%*—after their first New York City protest on September 17, 2011.[69] OWS protesters claimed the slogan called attention to the fact that "marchers [were] not part of the one percent of Americans who hold a vast portion of the nation's wealth."[70]

Progressive Caucus co-chairs, Reps. Keith Ellison (D-MN) and Raúl Grijalva (D-CA), claimed that the proposal was a "package of near-term job-creation measures and budgetary policy reforms that would meaningfully boost employment and improve the long-term fiscal outlook."[71] But in reality, the CPC created the Act for the 99% by cobbling together a bundle of dead-end legislation. Each bill had failed to make its way out of at least one committee or subcommittee. The danger is that this legislation, like so many others, would become a central initiative of a second Obama term.

In their Capitol Hill press conference, Ellison and Grijalva claimed the bill would not only create 5 million jobs in two years but it would also save more than $2 trillion over ten years.[72] But the math does not add up, even according to progressive experts. Rutgers Professor Philip L. Harvey, writing for Demos, wondered in 2011 what it would take to bring "unemployment back down to 5 percent and consumer demand back up to pre-recession levels?" If the 2009 stimulus bill's $787 billion price tag had only bought 3–4 million jobs, how much would it take to "double that amount over again to create the 6–8 million additional jobs needed"?[73] The implication of Harvey's question is: *an additional expenditure of nearly $1.6 trillion.*

Viewed another way, in June 2011, over 14 million people were reported as unemployed. The U.S. economy had lost an officially reported 7 million jobs, "wiping out every job gained since 2000." Real job losses were said to be closer to 10.5 million, with an estimated 3 million people who have quit looking for work.[74]

Plus, new numbers for the "Obama Jobs Gap"—far worse than those from less than a year earlier—were revealed in early April 2012, by the U.S. Bureau of Labor Statistics: 15 million missing jobs. Just to catch up, the jobs gap would require 14.8 million net jobs "to restore the ratio of unemployed people to [the] total population"—and just to return to 2007 levels, before the Great Recession.[75]

So the only other way—besides a new $1.6 trillion "double stimulus"—that the Progressive Caucus's plan could create 5 million jobs is if they are government jobs, paid for using taxpayer and borrowed money. Where is the saving? How can the progressives' plan possibly close the jobs gap?

JOBS CHALLENGE

The Center for American Progress took a less-detailed approach to jobs creation. A quick reminder that CAP has been one of the key organizations—along with other progressive groups—in crafting legislation for the Obama administration. CAP's January 2012 offering—*20 Ideas for Job Creation*—is based on its December 2009 report, *Meeting the Jobs Challenge.*[76] In the more recent publication, CAP pushes several items having nothing to do with "jobs created or saved;" for example: CAP proposes the "extension of emergency unemployment benefits to [more than 700,000] long-term unemployed workers" and the "expansion of the payroll tax cut for employees and [extension of] it to employers through 2012." Somehow CAP rationalizes these measures as saving more than 1 million jobs. Then

CAP rationalizes protecting 247,000 National Park Service jobs from "budget cuts, corporate interests, and antigovernment rhetoric" is jobs creation. CAP's plan also calls for rejection of a "federal proposal to mandate employer use of the E-Verify eligibility verification system"—as of now a voluntary program to verify the citizenship or legal residence eligibility of potential private sector employees—in order to protect 770,000 American jobs.

The pure fiction of "jobs created or saved" was spelled out by Caroline Baum, a columnist for Bloomberg News (October 2009).[77] According to the Obama administration's own reporting (at recovery.gov), between February 17, 2009—when the president signed the $787 billion "stimulus" bill—and October 27, the date of Baum's report, a grand total of 30,383 jobs had been "created or saved."[78] Baum cited the chief economist at the National Federation of Independent Business, Bill Dunkelberg, who called government job creation an oxymoron. "It is only by depriving the private sector of funds that government can hire or subsidize hiring," Baum pointed out. And when, on October 22, Obama's former chief economic adviser, Christina Romer, testified before Congress's Joint Economic Committee, the impact of the stimulus bill was, as Baum put it, *kaput*:

> What was most puzzling about Romer's Oct. 22 testimony was her comment on the waning effect of fiscal stimulus.
>
> "Most analysts predict that the fiscal stimulus will have its greatest impact on growth in the second and third quarters of 2009," Romer said. "By mid-2010, fiscal stimulus will likely be contributing little to growth."

What Baum and Romer did not mention was that the economy lost 216,000 jobs in the month of August 2009 (though a loss of 60,000 fewer than the month prior). National Economic Council director Larry Summers admitted in September 2009 that unemployment was exceptionally high and would, "by all forecasts, remain unacceptably high for a number of years." The national unemployment rate was at 9.7 percent, a twenty-six year high. It was estimated that 6.9 million jobs had been lost in the recession, "which economists call the worst since the Great Depression."[79]

While the Center for American Progress's plan suggests many possibilities, it provides little by way of concrete numbers, and nothing that comes even close to the creation of the millions of jobs that are needed.

"GREEN" JOBS

Shortly after the Obama inauguration, in early February 2009, Progressive Caucus Democrats in Congress teamed up with Big Labor and Big Green to push for a "Green American Dream."[80] Sen. Debbie Stabenow (D-MI) and Rep. Jay Inslee (D-WA) held a press conference with Laborers' International Union general president Terence O'Sullivan, Sierra Club political director Cathy Duvall, and other "clean energy" business leaders to "urge Congressional leaders to take bold action to create a new Green American Dream for working people by making sure the newly created green jobs are good jobs that can sustain families and fuel economic recovery."[81] (Inslee has since resigned from Congress to run for governor of Washington State. He was one of nearly two dozen House Democrats in 2012 not seeking reelection.[82])

As a result of Progressive–Big Labor–Big Green pressure, the $787 billion "stimulus" bill of 2009 was the first piece of legislation to include "green job creation" projects. Three of these programs were set to expire at the end of 2011. They were supposed to have created over 100,000 jobs: 55,000 in conjunction with projects for wind; 45,000 jobs for solar; and 11,200 jobs for geothermal.[83] Using "stimulus" funds, for example, sixty-two grant awards of between $42,000 and $100,000 were made by the Department of Labor's Employment and Training Administration to "fund both green job training and evaluation projects" and to "teach workers the skills required in emerging industries including energy efficiency and renewable energy."[84] But in November 2011, a U.S. Department of Labor audit asked where the money gone. The audit revealed that the program had an "underwhelming success rate." About $500 million in "stimulus" funds were allocated nationwide to train nearly 125,000 people for "green careers." The audit found only about 53,000 people had been trained, of which only a little over 8,000 actually found jobs.[85] Half a billion dollars spent to train 8,000 employees!

The BlueGreen Alliance, or BGA, put forth its own nationwide blueprint,

Jobs21! Good Jobs for the 21st Century, to solve the jobs crisis in August 2011.[86] BGA is one of the main progressive political alliances between Big Labor and Big Green—and a partner in Al Gore's Alliance for Climate Protection. BGA was created in 2006 by the Sierra Club and the United Steel Workers union and now includes a long list of unions like the AFL-CIO and SEIU.[87] It also now incorporates the radical Apollo Alliance Project, which claimed credit in February 2009 for "influencing" the content of many provisions in the $787 billion "stimulus" bill.[88] Sometime in 2011 BGA absorbed the Apollo Alliance, which itself had been spun off from its founding organizations, Campaign for America's Future and COWS (Center for Wisconsin Strategy), in late 2007.

BGA's plan identifies federal tax incentives and loan guarantees, purportedly to "provide the clean energy sector with the tools it needs to produce energy, to make the parts for wind turbines, solar panels and other equipment, and to connect to new supply chains and markets while spurring private investment and job creation." But at the top of BGA's list is the creation of a "Green Bank," to provide both seed money and a consistent funding source for renewable energy companies. BGA claims this would "encourage private investment to support loans for an array of advanced clean energy technologies."

The Center for American Progress had also proposed a public Green Bank in May 2009. CAP's John Podesta and Karen Kornbluh saw the creation of a Green Bank as critical to the progressive Big Green agenda.[89] Such a bank, they wrote, "could lead to the steady and reliable creation of clean-energy jobs and would be a crucial element of the transition to a clean-energy economy." The Green Bank would magically open credit markets and "motivate businesses to invest again" and would enable clean-energy technologies (wind, solar, geothermal, advanced biomass, and energy efficiency) to be "deployed on a large scale and become commercially viable at current electricity costs." It would allow the U.S. to "lead the world in the transformation to a global economy powered by low-carbon energy," Podesta and Kornbluh claimed.

As a jobs creator, this plan is more pie in the sky. Moreover, in our chapter on "green energy," we show in detail how the Obama administration's green loan guarantees have, to date, been a supersized bust for taxpayers, while those receiving billions of dollars in federal backing have literally made off like bandits.

The BlueGreen Alliance, in addition to a Green Bank, also wants a Green Manufacturing revolving loan fund. BGA claims this would create 680,000 manufacturing jobs and 1,972,000 additional jobs over five years.[90] BGA also wants a new regulation—the National Renewable Electricity Standard—which would mandate production of 25 percent of the country's electricity from renewable energy sources by 2025. BGA projects the creation of 850,000 jobs in existing manufacturing firms and even designates eight of the largest American states with the "greatest potential": California, Illinois, Indiana, Michigan, New York, Ohio, Pennsylvania, and Wisconsin.

The chairman of the U.S. Senate Energy and Natural Resources Committee, Sen. Jeff Bingaman (D-NM), introduced the Clean Energy Standard Act on March 2, 2012. Bingaman's bill would inaugurate a Clean Energy Standard, or CES, beginning in 2015.[91] Utilities "would need to sell a percentage of their electricity from clean energy sources, and each year would need to sell a slightly greater amount of clean energy."[92] Bingaman and Sen. Sam Brownback (R-KS) had introduced the same bill two years earlier. But Michael Williams, the legislative representative for the BGA, had complained in September 2010 that the previous bill "does not meet the targets laid out in our report [Building a Clean Energy Assembly Line], but understanding the difficulty of passing nearly anything this year, Bingaman-Brownback may just thread the needle as evidenced by the bill's diverse and large number of cosponsors."[93]

In reality, this is a backdoor plan to introduce cap and trade legislation. The tipoff is: "All generators of clean energy would be given credits based upon their carbon emissions."[94] The BGA's Williams added that there were "other pieces of legislation that can move with the CES. Home Star and Building Star are residential and commercial energy efficiency measures with strong bipartisan support." The BGA proposal for residential energy efficiency includes a Weatherization Assistance Program (WAP), Home Star, and Rural Star. Home Star alone was predicted to generate 168,000 jobs based on a proposed $6 billion two-year rebate program.[95] The Center for American Progress was yet more rapturous. It claimed passage of Home Star, Building Star, and Rural Star legislation would create 250,000 new jobs a year.[96]

BGA calls for yet another federal mandate: the National Energy Efficiency Resource Standard. NEERS would "encourage more efficient generation, transmission, and use of electricity and natural gas," *et voila*, would create 220,000 jobs over ten years. CAP's plan imagines that just generating 20 percent of power using wind would create more than 500,000 jobs. But CAP does not provide a time frame.[97]

Many more blueprints for "green jobs" have appeared since 2009. Most of them differ only in their imagination of the number of jobs they will create. In an Obama second term, you can be sure you would see and hear about various schemes tucked into another bill that could never pass Congress on their own. That is how we got all the lovely hidden aspects of ObamaCare.

5

IT'S BACK! FDR'S WORKS PROGRESS ADMINISTRATION AND OTHER OBAMA JOB NIGHTMARES

THE NATION IS facing a jobs crisis unlike any in our history. This crisis goes far beyond any temporary fluctuations in official unemployment statistics.

It begins with millions of American youth who are not even included in the standard employment indices. Some 6.7 million are "neither enrolled in school nor participating in the labor market." They are not "investing in their human capital or earning income," according to a January 2012 report of the White House Council for Community Solutions and the Corporation for National and Community Service.[1] The bad news was only partially revealed in the report's conclusion: in the 16–24 age group, at least 6.7 million (17 percent) are currently "opportunity youth." Actually, the White House–generated crisis scenario is short of the mark. Bureau of Labor Statistics data for February 2012 showed teenage unemployment (partially a lower age bracket) at 24 percent, higher than the White House estimate by more than one-third.[2]

Many of the "opportunity youth," according to the administration's report, have dropped out of high school or college and been unable to find work. Others have become involved in the criminal justice system. Some have mental or other health conditions. Others have care-giving responsibilities to their families. The White House report estimated a "chronic opportunity youth" population of approximately 3.4 million, as well as an "under-attached opportunity youth population" of about 3.3 million.

In its own January 2012 report, the leading "progressive" think tank, the Center for American Progress, predicted that full-time national service programs could produce jobs for 60,000 youth.[3] But given an "opportunity youth" population of 6.7 million, 60,000 jobs—even if taxpayers could afford to create them out of thin air—would hardly make a dent.

One "progressive" economist, Heidi Shierlolz at the Economic Policy Institute, stated in September 2010 that in order to get "the national unemployment rate back to 5 percent, where it was before the 2008 downturn, the economy would be required to generate about 17 million jobs—or about 285,000 a month for five straight years."[4] A partnership of three progressive think tanks—the Economic Policy Institute, Demos, and the Century Foundation—working together under the rubric of Our Fiscal Security, produced a budget blueprint in November 2011 for "economic recovery and fiscal responsibility":

> Jobs and economic growth are essential to our capacity to reduce deficits.
> [...]
> There should be no across-the-board spending reductions until the economy fully recovers. We believe there should be no consideration of overall spending reductions until unemployment has fallen to 6% and remained at or below that level for six months.[5]

But if six months of continuous 6 percent unemployment—let alone the pre-downturn rate of 5 percent—is the goal, then that goal would never be reached and the spending would never end.

EXPERTS BEG TO DIFFER

Barack Obama claimed in his 2012 State of the Union address that jobs creation would be the driving force behind his second term. "Join me," Obama said, "in a national commitment to train two million Americans with skills that will lead directly to a job."[6] In response, a warning was issued by David B. Muhlhausen, of the Heritage Foundation:

> Before Congress signs off on any new initiatives, we must recognize that President Obama wants to add several new programs on top of the 47 job-training programs already operated by the federal government. Further complicating the matter, the U.S. Government Accountability Office has concluded that there is little evidence that these programs are effective.[7]

Muhlhausen, who has been expounding on the Job Corps scheme for at least five years, directs our attention to the abject failure of the federal government's "flagship program for hard-to-employ youth." Participants in the Job Corps, he wrote, earned fewer high school diplomas than non-participants; were no more likely to attend or complete college; earned only $22 more per week than a control group; and only earned $0.22 more in hourly wages than the control group.[8]

But the failure of federal jobs training is an old story. More than twenty-five years ago (in 1986) James Bovard—dubbed by the *Wall Street Journal* as the "roving inspector general of the modern State"[9]—penned an article about it for the Cato Institute.[10] Bovard's opening salvo looked back a further twenty-five years to the 1960s, to John F. Kennedy's "New Frontier" and Lyndon Johnson's "War on Poverty" programs. The results of these programs were brutal:

> Federal job-training programs have harmed the careers of millions of Americans, failed to impart valuable job skills to the poor, and squandered billions of dollars annually. For 25 years, government programs have warped work ethics, helped disillusion generations of disadvantaged youth, and deluged America with fraudulent statistics. After spending over a hundred billion dollars on manpower programs we have learned little or nothing: today's programs merely repeat the mistakes of the early 1960s. Federal programs have reduced the incomes of millions of trainees and have helped create a growing underclass of permanently unemployed Americans.

"Even worse, government-funded jobs training diminishes the available job pool for the private sector and damages the economy," Bovard wrote.

"Instead of adding new programs to an already bloated job training system," Muhlhausen concluded, the president and Congress "should stop wasting taxpayer dollars by terminating these programs."[11]

WASTED "JOBS TRAINING," WASTED "JOBS CREATING"

A failed Keynesian concept even more harmful than government "jobs training" was described by the Cato Institute's Thomas DiLorenzo at about the same time. In a February 1984 paper, *The Myth of Government Job Creation*,[12] he wrote:

> The "cost" of government jobs programs, regardless of how they are financed, is therefore best viewed as the reduction of private sector production and the employment that production creates. Those who believe that government jobs programs can create jobs fail to realize or acknowledge that they also destroy jobs elsewhere in the economy. Government jobs programs alter the composition of jobs in the economy—more government employment, less private employment—but do not increase the number of jobs. Some may prefer a larger government sector relative to the private sector—and this is what government job programs give us—but it is misleading to pursue this objective under the guise of creating jobs.

"More government employment and less private employment"—a progressive's dream! And so, in the fourth component of its December 2009 *American Jobs Plan*, the progressives called for the government's direct creation of jobs "by putting unemployed people to work in jobs that will benefit their communities."[13] "If the private sector can't put people back to work, then the public sector must," the Economic Policy Institute declared.

Clearly, if unrestrained by Congress during a second term in office—or using the power of the presidency to circumvent Congress and issue executive orders—Obama would inevitably push these jobs programs or a variety of others like them.

Onward, Jobs Programs, Onward

As for terminating any existing programs, Democrats inside and outside Congress are adamantly opposed. In fact, the progressive Democrats' game plan is to introduce, re-introduce, and cut and paste jobs legislation until— like the 2009 stimulus package and the gargantuan 2010 ObamaCare bill ("Let's pass it and then we'll find out what's in it")—they manage to force through more and more taxpayer-funded government-controlled jobs and entitlement programs.

A good example of government-as-job-provider boosterism comes from Dr. Philip L. Harvey, professor of law and economics at Rutgers University, who champions the "direct creation" of jobs in his 2011 Demos report, *Back to Work: A Public Jobs Proposal for Economic Recovery*:

> The advantage of the direct job-creation strategy lies in its unique ability to serve the goals of anti-recessionary fiscal policy at the same time that it is serving the social welfare needs of jobless workers. There is no other anti-recession strategy that can do either of these things as well as a direct job-creation program, let alone combine them in a single programmatic initiative.[14]

Clearly a Keynesian economist, Harvey claims that the direct creation of jobs by federal spending includes a "multiplier effect" of more jobs created per dollar because the government can target where jobs are needed at who needs them most. The government, he claims, can make jobs available immediately. And all this will be paid for without raising the federal deficit. Evidently Harvey envisions a revival of FDR's New Deal. Participants would fulfill community needs such as "construction work (e.g., the rehabilitation of abandoned or substandard housing), conservation measures (e.g., caulking windows and doors in private dwellings), the construction of new affordable housing units, the improvement of existing public parks, the construction of new parks, and the beautification and maintenance of indoor and outdoor public spaces." Then it could be expanded to improve "the quality of public services in areas such as health care, child care, education, recreation, elder care, and cultural enrichment."

And who would operate and oversee such massive programs for the necessary 8.2 million jobs Harvey projects would be required to reduce the unemployment rate to 4.5 percent? Government, government, government: federal, state, and local. Participants would be paid at "approximately the same wage that persons with similar qualifications and experience reasonably can expect to receive in the regular labor market." But individuals would not be *guaranteed* the same wages they'd enjoyed in their last jobs. Rather, they would be paid the "prevailing wage for the positions they were offered based on their qualifications and experience."

In his estimation, Harvey includes employer-provided health insurance and child-care services for the workforce. He presumes participants would have access to affordable health insurance and all workers would be guaranteed paid sick leave. Additionally, Harvey states the "easiest way to guarantee access to affordable housing would be to turn the Section VIII housing voucher program (or its equivalent) into a legal entitlement"—at an estimated annual cost of about $50 billion. Ultimately laying bare his socialist roots, Harvey calls his wage policy nonessential, but "the equal pay for equal work principle argues in its favor." New Dealers, he concludes, generally favored reducing the number of hours worked rather than reducing the hourly wage.

CUT, PASTE, REGROUP, PUSH ON

Not to worry. Progressives in Congress have all this covered.

When the U.S. Senate voted on it, October 7, 2011, Barack Obama's sweeping jobs bill—the American Jobs Act of 2011—failed to pass.[15] Ten days later, October 17,[16] Sen. Robert Menendez (D-NJ) reintroduced the first piece of legislation from the package, the $447 billion Teachers and First Responders Back to Work Act.[17] But three days later, the Senate also voted this down.[18]

Later that week, October 20, Democrats returned with another piece of the president's defeated jobs bill and introduced the $60 billion Rebuild America Jobs Act. It would have provided "an infusion of funding to rebuild roads, bridges, airports and rail, and create a national infrastructure bank that would leverage private and public capital to finance projects."[19] On

November 3, the Obama administration "strongly supported" passage of the bill, claiming it would "put hundreds of thousands of construction workers back on the job and modernize America's crumbling infrastructure."[20] The bill would have poured an immediate $50 billion into U.S. highways, transit, rail, and aviation—but was defeated 51–49 in the Senate the same day.

The August 2011 progressive blueprint of the BlueGreen Alliance (BGA)—*Jobs21! Good Jobs for the 21st Century*—uses similar language. It calls for investment in America's highways, rail, transit systems, and biking and walking infrastructure to make America "more energy independent and globally competitive." BGA claims 13,700 jobs would be created or sustained (more jobs "created or saved") with a mere $1 billion investment. It also calls for a whopping six-year, $550 billion reauthorization bill to create a total of 7.7 million jobs.[21] (It's unclear how that multiplier works.) BGA also calls for a $1 billion investment to create or sustain 20,000 jobs for high-speed passenger and freight rail—and to reduce oil dependence and pollution.

BGA's claims are based on a group of progressive reports, principally *The Job Impact of Transportation Reauthorization: Research and Ideas for Shared Prosperity,* by Ethan Pollack of the Economic Policy Institute (June 2010), as well as another June 2010 report by Pollack, a May 2010 report by the Economic Policy Institute and the BlueGreen Alliance, and an October 2010 report by EPI's Pollack and Becky Thiess.

BULLET TRAINS TO BANKRUPTCY

In the original "stimulus" bill, Obama included $8 billion for high-speed rail and called for $1 billion per year for five years in his proposed budget to get his projects "off the ground."[22] Grant awards were designated to lay the "groundwork for 13 new, large-scale high-speed rail corridors across the country . . . part of a total of 31 states receiving investments, including smaller projects and planning work that will help lay the groundwork for future high-speed intercity rail service," as the White House claimed in April 2009.[23]

Grant awards were not announced until nine months later (January 28, 2010). Almost two years after that, in November 2011, the U.S. Department of Transportation announced that 2012 was "shaping up to be the year of significant high-speed activity." Contracts had been let by states for design work, planning work, construction materials, and supplies.[24]

A closer look at one of these high-speed rail projects is instructive.

Stanford University economist Thomas Sowell wrote at the end of January 2012 about California's prospective "Bridge to Nowhere."[25] Sowell pointed to Japan's famous high-speed rail system between Tokyo and Osaka, in "one of the most densely populated countries in the world." The "bullet train" carries 130 million riders a year. He compares this to the proposed first leg of California's system, the route between Fresno and Bakersfield. Tokyo has a population three times that of San Francisco and Los Angeles combined. Fresno and Bakersfield are much smaller communities in the agricultural San Joaquin Valley. The 2010 population for all of San Joaquin County was 685,306.[26] "You can bet the rent money that high-speed rail traffic between Fresno and Bakersfield will never come within shouting distance of covering the operating costs," Sowell wrote. "Some people have analogized putting such a rail line between these two towns to the infamous 'bridge to nowhere' in Alaska."

Why *is* the project in the sparsely populated Valley? Politics. It's about politics. If the high-speed train started where California's governor, Jerry Brown, and Obama wanted it to go—between the mega coastal cities—environmentalists, and politicians connected with environmentalists, would lie down on the tracks to stop the trains, Sowell wrote. Instead, California gets federal taxpayer dollars, and Brown and Obama look like heroes.

Another section of the Rebuild America Jobs legislation claimed it would

> take special steps to enhance infrastructure-related job training opportunities for individuals from underrepresented groups and ensure that small businesses can compete for infrastructure contracts.

BGA gives its recommendation to programs like those found in the Green Jobs Act to expand federal, state, and local support for "green industry career programs in high schools and community colleges."[27]

The Green Jobs Act of 2007 (GJA) was introduced by then representative Hilda Solis (D-CA)—who is now the secretary of labor—and Rep. John Tierney (D-MA). GJA authorized up to $125 million in funding to establish national and state job training programs, which would be administered by the U.S. Department of Labor. GJA became part of the Energy Independence and Security Act (the "2007 Energy Bill") signed by President Bush in late 2007.[28] Congress appropriated $500 million for the Green Jobs Act through the stimulus bill in February 2009.

The final item in the Rebuild America Jobs bill threw $10 billion into the creation of an "innovative American Infrastructure Financing Authority" to "leverage private and public capital and to invest in a broad range of infrastructure projects of national and regional significance, without earmarks or political influence." (The topic of creating an infrastructure bank is covered in the following chapter.)

But from where would this $10 billion come? Entirely through a surtax on Americans making over $1 million per year. But as Scott Wong at *Politico* noted, the bill "is almost certainly doomed given that Republicans are unified against any tax hikes."[29] Wong was correct. For the third time within a month, progressive Democrats failed to get a jobs bill passed in the Senate.[30]

One particularly trenchant comment came from a retired clergyman in the Philadelphia area, James A. Glasscock. Obama's proposals were merely updated versions of Franklin Roosevelt's Depression-era Works Progress Administration, he wrote. The projects were "not a long range plan for economic stability and job creation" but would rely entirely on borrowed money. "It is not free money."[31] "Ironically, the legislative plan that President Obama proposes in 2011 in his Rebuild America Jobs Act borrows heavily from the blueprints adopted by Fascism and National Socialism, and FDR's New Deal," Glasscock continued. "The end results of the Depression years of the 1930s remain with us in 2011, because our national politicians have not learned any lessons of the past."

21ST CENTURY WORKS PROGRESS ADMINISTRATION

One such politician is Sen. Frank R. Lautenberg (D-NJ), who introduced the 21st Century Works Progress Administration Act on September 7, 2011. The old/new legislation would "immediately put Americans to work rebuilding our nation and strengthening our communities," Lautenberg claimed when he introduced it.[32]

Across the country, we continue to benefit from projects com-
pleted under President Roosevelt's WPA, which employed more than
three million Americans during a time of great need. A 21st Century
WPA would tackle our nation's job crisis head-on and accelerate our
economic recovery.[33]

From union quarters, not surprisingly, came a similar meme. Speaking in late January 2012 at a Labor Summit sponsored by the Democratic
Governors Association, R. Thomas "Tom" Buffenbarger, president of the
International Association of Machinists and Aerospace Workers, "urged a
renewed focus" on a 21st Century Works Progress Administration.[34]

Buffenbarger's promotion of a new WPA carries substantial weight,
because he is also a member of the executive council of the AFL-CIO and
a member of the Economic Policy Institute's board of directors, serves as
chairman of the Labor Advisory Committee to the U.S. Trade Representative, and is a past member of the U.S. Treasury Department's Advisory
Committee to the International Monetary Fund. Buffenbarger also once
served on the National Advisory Board of the far-left Apollo Alliance
and was one of the original 130 founders of the Campaign for America's
Future.[35]

So Buffenbarger has arguably been cheerleader-in-chief for a 21st Century WPA. A lengthy article of his published on the Democratic Socialists
of America's labor blog (September 2011) called for the establishment of a
21st Century WPA by the next Labor Day.[36]

Soon Buffenbarger and Senator Lautenberg were to get big-caliber
support in the press. *New York Times* columnist Paul Krugman (a Nobel
Prize–winning economist and erstwhile solid Obama partisan, who'd veered
sharply off the reservation by April 2011[37]) called specifically for a 21st
Century WPA:[38] On January 3, 2012, Krugman wrote,

So what can be done to accelerate this all-too-slow process of
healing? A rational political system would long since have created a
21st-century version of the Works Progress Administration—we'd
be putting the unemployed to work doing what needs to be done,
repairing and improving our fraying infrastructure.

Despite such big-time boosterism, the WPA projects of the 1930s and early 1940s are, in reality, a cautionary tale for today. The original Works Progress Administration was established in 1935 by President Franklin Roosevelt, via executive order, as a "relief" agency. Congress provided the initial $4.9 billion in funding, a gargantuan sum for nearly eighty years ago. The WPA "offered work to the unemployed on an unprecedented scale by spending money on a wide variety of programs, including highways and building construction, slum clearance, reforestation, and rural rehabilitation."[39]

"A noble conception gave rise to the idea that the dangers to morale resulting from the dole"—more gently referenced today as unemployment or welfare benefits—"were to be avoided through work relief, despite its relatively high cost," authors Lewis Meriam and Laurence F. Schmeckebier wrote in 1939.[40] The government took charge of construction projects that would normally have been done by private contractors or municipal governments, had funding been available to them, and local governments benefited from more favorable funding terms than those for "ordinary municipal loans," they pointed out. Additionally, WPA money was "added to the national debt and not to the local debt and created in the minds of the local taxpayers the idea that they were getting something for nothing."

In fact, taxpayers and those privately employed appear to have benefitted less than those who worked for the WPA. Meriam and Schmeckebier wrote:

> The Works Progress Administration became, as it was intended to be, a safe haven in which the unemployed could weather the storm at wages approximating the prevailing local wage, with enough work to insure a living. The assumption of course was that it would all be temporary. . . . [Some political and economic forces sought to make the WPA] permanent. It tended in some instances to make the [WPA] worker better off in respect to hours, wages, and perquisites, particularly the surplus commodities he was given, than were persons who were still working for wages. Surplus commodities were purchased in many cases in order to sustain the price which privately employed persons had to pay for commodities given the unemployed and the

[WPA] workers. Thus the tendency was to establish contemporane-
ously two different economic systems. [41]

The 21st Century reincarnation of Roosevelt's WPA would operate
under the auspices of a Works Progress Administration created within
the Department of Labor and headed by the secretary of labor.[42] Lautenberg's bill proposes projects similar to those of the earlier era, including
residential and commercial building weatherization; residential and commercial water use efficiency improvement; highway, bridge, and rail repair
and maintenance; manufacturing projects; school, library, and firehouse
construction; soil erosion and pesticide runoff prevention; National Park
and trail maintenance; and "other projects that are proposed by the eligible departments and determined appropriate by the Administration."[43]

While the new WPA legislation is vague on the matter of how many jobs
would be created, Lautenberg's pie-in-the-sky press release claims that funds
would be awarded to "economically-beneficial job creation project proposals";
"provide businesses unable to locate a worker with suitable skills with a WPA
fellow, who would receive on-the-job training from the business and be paid
by the WPA"; and "provide funding to communities to improve public safety
by hiring unemployed Americans as firefighters and police officers." When
asked how long it would take for people to get hired for these projects (October
18, 2011), Lautenberg replied, "'A couple of months, maybe. People can get
on the job before projects break ground,' since most would require architects,
planning and a variety of other managerial, professional and administrative
workers to get started."[44] As the 21st Century WPA boondoggle has not
come into being, the estimated time frame is inevitably pushed forward into
a hoped-for second Obama administration, to 2013 and beyond.

The 21st Century WPA public works legislation does provide information for how the new programs will be funded, claiming it would be "fully
paid for through a surtax on income exceeding $1 million ($2 million for
joint filers)." For sheer chutzpah, Lautenberg's bill was dubbed "the most
expensive bill of the week" by the National Taxpayers Union Foundation,[45]
projected to cost $250 billion over the next two years. Lautenberg, for his
part, claimed the new WPA program would "reduce the deficit by approximately $133 billion over 10 years."

21st Century Civilian Conservation Corps Act

A December 1, 2011, article by Lawrence Mishel of the progressive Economic Policy Institute admonished the Obama administration to "stop digging us into an even deeper hole!"[46]

Mishel was not, however, referencing the president's spending proclivities run amok. Instead Mishel's beef was with the Democrats' proposed expansion of the payroll tax holiday. "Direct spending on infrastructure or even on government hiring people to perform useful public jobs (as was done by the Works Progress Administration and Civilian Conservation Corps) is more effective in raising demand and generating jobs" than any tax relief, he asserted.

Months earlier (January 26, 2011), a companion bill to the 21st Century WPA Act—the 21st Century Civilian Conservation Corps Act—had been introduced, but was immediately referred to the Committee on Education and the Workforce.[47] Its sponsor was Rep. Marcy Kaptur (D-OH). Kaptur had introduced the same legislation in November 2010, but it likewise failed to get out of committee.

In its "People's Budget for 2012," the annual spending blueprint cooked up by the seventy-five-member Congressional Progressive Caucus, the reestablishment of a Civilian Conservation Corps is also invoked. It's part of a proposed overall expenditure of $1.45 trillion (that's "trillion," with a *t*) for "job creation, education, clean energy and broadband infrastructure, housing, and R&D." (Note: all charts and projections in the Progressive Caucus report were created by the Economic Policy Institute.)[48]

The ancestor of this progressive fantasy—the original Civilian Conservation Corps—operated from 1933 to 1942. It was the first, and credited by some as the most popular, of Roosevelt's New Deal programs, also known as Roosevelt's Tree Army. The CCC was "credited with renewing the nation's decimated forests by planting an estimated three billion trees."[49]

In those days, eligibility for enrollment in Roosevelt's "peacetime army" was restricted to U.S. citizens. The CCC mandated "sound physical fitness" for those employed because of the hard physical labor involved. Additionally, men had to be "unemployed, unmarried, and between the ages of eighteen and twenty-six, although the rules were eventually relaxed for war veterans." Enlistment was for six months, "although many reenlisted after their allotted time was up." In Representative Kaptur's bill, the only requirements are that jobs would be for unemployed or underemployed U.S. citizens. Hiring preference purportedly would be for unemployed members of the U.S. armed forces or those unemployed who have exhausted their unemployment benefits. Jobs would be in construction, maintenance, and public works programs, which would obviously require significant physical ability.

Beyond a laborer's job, CCC employees could be furnished housing, meals, clothing, medical care and hospitalization, and a cash allowance while they are so employed, as well as transportation to and from places of employment. The Kaptur bill called for an appropriation of $64 billion—that's $16 billion for each fiscal year 2012 through 2015. The 21st Civilian Conservation Corps Act also earned the "most expensive bill of the week" distinction in December 2010 from the National Taxpayers Union Foundation.[50]

21ST CENTURY CONSERVATION CORPS— "A POWER GRAB"

By the time President Obama bypassed Congress and issued a little-noticed memorandum—*A 21st Century Strategy for America's Great Outdoors*—in April 2010, key members of his administration tasked with environmental policy had set in motion a chain of events culminating in what is now the 21st Century Conservation Service Corps (21CSC).[51] Funding for the "Great Outdoors" initiative comes from the Land and Water Conservation Fund, which, in turn, gets its money through fees paid to the Bureau of Ocean Energy Management, Regulation and Enforcement by companies drilling offshore for oil and gas. LWCF's budget cap is $900 million.[52]

A nongovernmental publication about America's parks, the *National Parks Traveler*, wondered in February 2011 how timely was the Great Outdoors initiative in "light of current fiscal and political winds."[53] Veteran journalist Kurt Repanshek reasonably asked: "And while the America's Great Outdoors, or AGO, initiative proposes a Conservation Services Corps to draw youth outdoors, don't groups such as the Student Conservation Association, the Boy and Girl scouts, and Big Brothers and Big Sisters already do that?"

But as Kristen Brengel, director of legislative and governmental affairs for the National Parks Conservation Association, observed, the AGO initiative "seeks to tie together the various land-management agencies on shared concerns."[54] This is one way to describe the agenda in President Obama's 2012 State of the Union speech, in which he said,

> The executive branch also needs to change. Too often, it's inefficient, outdated and remote. That's why I've asked this Congress to grant me the authority to consolidate the federal bureaucracy so that our Government is leaner, quicker, and more responsive to the needs of the American people.[55]

Another way to view this consolidation of America's land-management agencies is that it puts their control squarely under the weighted thumb of the president.

The Obama administration's 2013 budget significantly increases taxes for U.S.-based multinational oil companies as well as domestic producers through "proposed onshore drilling permit processing fees, offshore inspection fees, and fees for not meeting lease development deadlines."[56] The budget was released February 13, 2012, on the heels of Obama's SOTU, in which he spoke of more domestic oil and gas production. But how much of the proposed $10.72 billion increase in taxes over ten years from the oil industry would end up in the Land and Water Conservation Fund—funds which could be used for Obama's conservation projects—is unknown.

The week after Obama's America's Great Outdoors executive fiat, Center for American Progress president and CEO John Podesta took center stage. CAP's new Public Lands Project convened a forum on "Building a Conservation Legacy from the Ground Up," where Podesta delivered the welcoming remarks. Of two panelists, secretary of the interior Ken Salazar was one.[57] Podesta identified the "core strategy" for the AGO initiative: to "target resources to the needs identified by local communities" and to "make it easier for Americans to get jobs working on conservation efforts by lowering obstacles to working with federal agencies."

Around the same time, in the February/March 2011 time frame, Obama announced the launch of the 21st Century Service Corps as part of his administration's Youth in the Great Outdoors Initiative.[58] The 21CSC programs—aimed at youth between fifteen and twenty-five—are conducted on a year-round or seasonal basis, and range from eight to ten weeks during the summer to full-time employment.[59]

Consolidation was well under way. The 21CSC umbrella includes a dizzying array of taxpayer-funded agencies: the Public Land Corps, managed by nonprofit organizations that partner with the Federal land management agencies; the United States Youth Conservation Corps; Americorps; the Youth Internship Program; the Career Discovery Internship Program; and Conservation and Land Management Internships. Civilian partners include the Sierra Club and the BlueGreen Alliance.[60]

There's nothing like creating a huge government agency like 21CSC, in reverse. Nearly ten months after announcing 21CSC's launch, in November 2011, Obama got around to establishing a 21CSC Advisory Committee,[61] replete with a budget of $325,324 for all direct and indirect expenses and 1.5 staff years.[62] This "discretionary federal advisory committee"[63] was assembled to advise America's Great Outdoors Council, through the secretary of the interior, on how to create a 21CSC to work through "public-private and non-profit partnerships to engage citizens in hands-on service and job training experiences on public lands, waterways, cultural heritage sites, and community green spaces."[64] In other words, spread taxpayers' wealth around among community organizations in sync with the Obama administration's goals. And note that the total authorized annual budget for the Land and Water Conservation Fund is $900 million.

As yet unanswered is, from where will the funds for the 21CSC programs come? Also unknown is how much of a crossover there will be with the proposed 21st Century Civilian Conservation Corps and those operated by the 21st Century WPA.

And, will there be any crossover between these and the several corps outlined in the Emergency Jobs to Restore the American Dream Act (discussed below), now included in the Restore the American Dream Act for the 99 percent?

CORPS, CORPS, AND YET MORE CORPS

Yet another grand progressive spending scheme—the Restore the American Dream for the 99% Act—was introduced December 3, 2011. A product of the Congressional Progressive Caucus, it would enact, if passed, yet another jobs bill, the Emergency Jobs to Restore the American Dream Act of Rep. Jan Schakowsky (D-IL).[65] Schakowsky is "an outspoken progressive, one of the leftmost members" of the Democratic Caucus. Like Barack Obama, she has been supported throughout her political career by the Democratic Socialists of America, the socialist New Party, the AFL-CIO, AFSCME, and the SEIU.[66]

Schakowsky originally introduced her Emergency Jobs Act in September 2011. It was sent to the Committee on Higher Education and Workforce Training on November 18.[67] About the same time on September 7, 2011, the same day Senator Lautenberg introduced his 21st Century WPA Act, Rep. Keith Ellison (D-MN) introduced another version of Schakowsky's bill, called the Emergency Jobs Now Act. It was also referred to the committees, where it remains as of this writing.[68]

Schakowsky's Emergency Jobs Act would create seven new "corps" spending $100 billion to create 650,000 new jobs: *School Improvement Corps* (400,000 construction and 250,000 maintenance jobs to fix American schools); *Park Improvement Corps* (100,000 jobs for youth between the ages of 16 and 25, to improve our nation's parks); *Student Job Corps* (250,000 part-time, work study jobs for eligible college students); *Neighborhood Heroes Corps* (300,000 teachers, 40,000 police officers, 12,000 firefighters); *Health Corps* (40,000 health care providers, including physicians, nurse practitioners, physician assistants, and health care workers); *Community Corps* (750,000 jobs including energy audits and conservation upgrades, urban land reclamation and addressing blight, public property maintenance and beautification, housing rehabilitation, and new construction); and *Child Care Corps* (100,000 jobs in early childhood care and education).[69]

In early March 2009, the Center for American Progress along with eighty labor, environmental, civic, and policy groups proposed a Clean Energy Corps. But it appears that this corps is similar to Schakowsky's Community Corps.[70]

Yet another progressive cabal, the Clean Energy Corps Working Group—which included representatives of the Apollo Alliance, Center for American Progress Action Fund, Center for Economic and Policy Research, COWS (Center on Wisconsin Strategy), and Green For All—recommended combining "job creation, service, and training to combat global warming." These groups also wanted the new corps to be led by President Barack Obama and administered through a new executive-level Energy Security Council comparable to the existing National Security Council. Corps workers would supposedly apply energy-efficient measures to over 15 million existing buildings. The retrofit would be financed by borrowed money, a federal revolving loan fund, with the loan wondrously paid back from savings in energy bills.

The School Improvement Corps program in Schakowsky's bill is also known as Fix America's Schools Today (FAST!). FAST! was developed by another alphabet soup of progressive groups: the Economic Policy Institute, the Center on Budget and Policy Priorities, and the 21st Century School Fund.[71] Several of the new corps would result from direct-hiring programs targeting "youths in high unemployment areas; idle construction workers who could be deployed on school refurbishing projects; and laid-off police, firefighters, teachers and health care workers."[72]

But as one commentator saw it:

> The bill is a scream of frustration at the president's failure to make life better for angry voters who will soon decide whether lawmakers like Schakowsky get to keep their jobs. . . . America became an economic superpower because of wealth-creating industry, not because the Federal Government decided to become an employment agency.[73]

And who will pay for all of Schakowsky's corps?[74] Michelle Chen put it this way in the August 2011 edition of the socialist journal *In These Times*:[75]

> The financing of FAST!, as outlined in Schakowsky's jobs proposal (and possibly in a parallel plan to be floated by the Obama administration) is an open question. But the EPI suggests a funding formula based on the needs of individual school districts and estimates of how many jobs would be generated and how much energy would be saved.

Schakowsky claimed it will all be paid for through separate legislation creating higher tax brackets for millionaires and billionaires, eliminating subsidies for Big Oil, and loopholes for corporations that ship American jobs overseas.

But, the commentator continued:

> The bill uses the "fully paid for" approach to funding. To Republicans, this means spending cuts. To Democrats, it means a tax increase. Schakowsky proposes that we take $227 billion from the unjustly enriched to resurrect the ghost of FDR.[76]

AND A VETERANS JOBS CORPS

In his 2012 State of the Union address, Obama also called for a Veterans Job Corps "that will help our communities hire veterans as cops and firefighters, so that America is as strong as those who defend her."[77] Obama proposed putting U.S. veterans returning home from the wars in Iraq and Afghanistan to work rebuilding roads, national park trails, and other public works projects, in an effort to cut the unemployment rate among veterans, according to Brian Koenig in the *New American*.[78] However, even without the president's scheme, the jobless rate for veterans serving post-9/11 fell significantly in January 2012 to 9.1 percent, while the jobless rate for veterans separated from active duty since the 2001 terrorist attacks is down from 13.3 percent in December and from 15.2 percent a year ago, in figures reported by *Army Times*.[79]

In case there is any doubt that a second Obama administration would try to implement a 21st Century version of FDR's 1930s New Deal programs, Secretary of the Interior Ken Salazar put it explicitly in those terms: the $1 billion program that would put an estimated 20,000 veterans to work "restoring habitat and eradicating invasive species, among other activities," Salazar said, is reminiscent of FDR's "Tree Army."[80]

> When one looks back at the legacy of the Civilian Conservation Corps, we take great comfort that those who take on these kinds of activities will leave a lasting legacy for the United States.

Where Does This Leave the Unions?

We are ultimately left with this question and many more. Will Lautenberger's 21st Century WPA be unionized? How about Kaptur's 21st Century Civilian Conservation Corps and all of Schakowsky's corps? Will they be unionized, too? And how about those returning and unemployed veterans? Will they find themselves part of a unionized Veterans Job Corps?

And finally, how could these massive government-owned-and-operated entitlement schemes be paid for by taxing only the rich?

6

BLUEPRINT FOR A NEW ECONOMY, NATIONAL INFRASTRUCTURE BANK

N O ONE OWNS the deplorable and dangerous state of today's American economy other than Barack Obama.

The new president promised, in his inaugural address, "action, bold and swift, and we will act—not only to create new jobs, but to lay a new foundation for growth."[1] Just ten days earlier, on January 10, 2009, the U.S. unemployment rate had hit a 16-year high—7.3 percent (a number we envy today). Obama soon claimed his record three-quarters-of-a-trillion-dollar "stimulus plan" would *create or save* 3–4 million jobs, nearly 90 percent of which would be in the private sector. He also assured Americans that the "stimulus" would keep unemployment from rising above 8 percent.[2]

Jobs saved or created? In presidential rhetoric, but not in reality. The $787 billion "stimulus" had only "created" an anemic 150,000 jobs by June. Still, Obama's silk-tongued staff promised an additional 600,000 would be *saved or created* by late summer.

"Of course, the inability to measure Mr. Obama's jobs formula is part of its attraction," William McGurn wrote in the *Wall Street Journal*.[3]

Never mind that no one—not the Labor Department, not the Treasury, not the Bureau of Labor Statistics—actually measures "jobs saved." As the *New York Times* delicately reports, Mr. Obama's jobs claims are "based on macroeconomic estimates, not an actual counting of jobs." Nice work if you can get away with it.[4]

Former Bush economic adviser N. Gregory Mankiw added: "[T]here is no way to measure how many jobs are saved. Even if things get much, much worse, the president can say that there would have been 4 million fewer jobs without the [$787 billion] stimulus."[5]

The reality—as opposed to the rhetoric—was shockingly worse. A mere four months after Congress approved the "stimulus," by June 2009, the economy had lost nearly 1.6 million jobs and unemployment officially hit 9.4 percent.[6] Speaking at an August 2009 rally in Virginia for State Senator Creigh Deeds, the Democratic candidate for governor, a petulant Obama told critics to just "get out of the way" so his administration could clean up the economic "mess" Republicans had left for him.[7]

I don't want the folks who created the mess to do a lot of talking. I want them to get out of the way so we can clean up the mess. I don't mind cleaning up after them, but don't do a lot of talking.[8]

Fast-forward three years. In his 2012 State of the Union address, Obama was still talking about acting, talking about creating new jobs, and talking about another new foundation for growth:

I want to speak about how we move forward, and lay out a blueprint for an economy that's built to last—an economy built on American manufacturing, American energy, skills for American workers, and a renewal of American values. This blueprint begins with American manufacturing."[9]

What is this blueprint? What is Obama's basis for "American manufacturing?" Why, old wine in new bottles—more and more of the same legislation, regurgitated from years gone by.

NOT JUST ANOTHER STIMULUS: A NATIONAL INFRASTRUCTURE BANK

Let's state right up front: as proposed, a national infrastructure bank, or NIB, wholly owned by the U.S. government, would be a veritable klondike for corruption, presenting unlimited opportunities for politically motivated mischief, not to mention fraud, waste, and abuse beyond the wildest dreams of the most corrupt crony capitalist—regardless of what President Obama and the progressives pretend.

Federal spending on infrastructure projects has a "long and painful history of pork-barrel politics and bureaucratic bungling, with money often going to wasteful and environmentally damaging projects," wrote Chris Edwards, director of tax policy studies at the Cato Institute, in October 2011.[10] The federal government should not be in the infrastructure business, Edwards added. While there are "plenty of examples of the downside of federal infrastructure," the histories of the two oldest infrastructure agencies—the Army Corps of Engineers and the Bureau of Reclamation—show that "state governments and the private sector are best equipped to provide it."

Also, as Edwards and Peter Van Doren explained in December 2008, "the main problem with government infrastructure spending is the lack of efficiency."

> More roads and transit capacity may or may not make sense depending on whether the benefits exceed the costs. One sure way to find out is to have private provision and user charges. If users are not willing to pay the costs of extra or newer capacity, then calls for taxpayer involvement probably imply subsidy of some at the expense of others rather than efficiency.

Additionally, the U.S. would be bucking a global trend to shift infrastructure responsibility to the private sector in favor of centralizing more bureaucratic control. Edwards and Van Doren continued:

> While America debates higher government spending on infrastructure, governments on every continent have sold off state-owned assets

to private investors in recent decades. Airports, railroads, energy utilities, and many other assets have been privatized. Heathrow airport in London is privately owned and operated. Air-traffic control services are fully private in Canada. In Italy and France, limited access highways are private concessions funded with toll revenue. In many areas, the U.S. is a laggard in the world on private infrastructure provision.[11]

So just when Europeans and Canadians—not to mention some of America's states—have been privatizing the infrastructure business, President Obama and progressive Democrats continue to push a national infrastructure bank.

The avalanche of waste—not to mention funds simply unaccounted for—already thrown away in the original "stimulus" bill pushed through by Obama and the Reid/Pelosi Democrats will take years to uncover. From the Chevy Volt and Solyndra to a $100 million train station renovation in Delaware named after Vice President Joe Biden—these are just the tip of the failed first "stimulus" iceberg. But the creation in a second Obama term of a national infrastructure bank—with taxpayer-funded capitalization at $60 billion just for starters—besides being a hideously inefficient way to address a legitimate problem, would concentrate ever more power in Washington while creating a giant cesspool for government cronyism and corruption.

Already, while on the 2008 campaign trail, Obama was pushing a National Infrastructure Bank. In a February 13, 2008, economic policy speech at the General Motors assembly plant in Janesville, Wisconsin, Obama said,

> For our economy, our safety, and our workers, we have to rebuild America. I'm proposing a National Infrastructure Reinvestment Bank that will invest $60 billion over ten years. This investment will multiply into almost half a trillion dollars of additional infrastructure spending and generate nearly two million new jobs—many of them in the construction industry that's been hard hit by this housing crisis. The repairs will be determined not by politics, but by what will maximize our safety and homeland security; what will keep our environment clean and our economy strong. [12]

By the end of the first year of his presidency, with the enormous "stimulus" already passed, the leading progressive think tanks were already clamoring for more. A briefing paper of the Economic Policy Institute—*Street Smart—Reforming the Transportation Budget Process*—noted how many different versions of an infrastructure bank were being proposed, and their similarities. All the proposed NIBs, EPI found, would finance "transportation infrastructure, housing, energy, telecommunications, drinking water, wastewater, and other infrastructures."[13]

All attempts, thus far, by progressive Democrats to pass National Infrastructure Bank legislation have failed. Their attempts to address the "infrastructure crisis" by creating a national infrastructure bank date back to at least the 1980s. Harvard economist Herman B. Leonard, in his 1986 study, *Checks Unbalanced*, described it this way:

> Never the most exciting of subjects, infrastructure nonetheless claimed top billing in the public finance spotlight as deterioration in basic public service systems—highways, bridges, waterways, ports, mass transit, water, sewers—became increasingly obvious.[14]

At the time, there was "dim prospect for improvement," in Leonard's judgment, as this came into collision with "tremendous fiscal pressure on federal, state, and local governments as grass roots movements to limit taxes and spending gained hearings at state and federal levels. The result was declining levels of public investment and rising levels of public attention, official oratory, and media comment."[15] A contemporary estimate of the national cost of infrastructure improvements came from economists Pat Choate and Susan Walter. Between $2.5 and $3 trillion would be required (as of the 1980s) "to prevent the further deterioration of public services." And, as Leonard pointed out, (in the early 1980s) this was roughly equal to one year's gross national product. Leonard proposed "annual public investment levels . . . between 5 and 10 percent of the GNP."[16]

But more accurate national estimates, Leonard admitted, were those prepared by the Congressional Budget Office—which "reflected a more conservative definition of what constituted 'need' than did earlier figures."[17] Moreover, Leonard described well the overreach of national bank "solutions":

Proposals for infrastructure banks generally agreed on financing but differed on everything else, like the degree of federal control that should be exercised in selecting projects and setting engineering standards. Little interest was shown in specifying the operational details of the banks' functions. The proposals were a reflex response to insufficient infrastructure spending, and they were intended to increase it sharply.[18]

This "reflex response" of a big, fix-it-all government infrastructure bank has now persisted over nearly four decades.

THE NEW PUSH FOR A NIB

One of the leading progressive think tanks—the New America Foundation—set forth its vision of a federally capitalized and controlled national infrastructure bank in a June 2008 policy brief—*Financing America's Infrastructure: Putting Global Capital to Work*.[19] While NAF's funding comes from a plethora of progressive funders and foundations, NAF claims its views are in the "radical center," and its focus is on promoting "a New Deal for the 21st Century."[20]

According to the NAF paper's authors, Heidi Crebo-Rediker and Douglas Rediker, the source of many of their ideas is legislation proposed by U.S. Rep. Rosa DeLauro's (D-CT) in 2007 to create a National Infrastructure Finance Enterprise.[21] DeLauro is one of the (at present) seventy-five members of the Congressional Progressive Caucus; it was she who introduced the National Infrastructure Development Act of 2007 (H.R.3896). Supporters for a similar DeLauro bill, introduced in 2009, included the U.S. Chamber of Commerce, the SEIU, the AFL-CIO, and the Campaign for America's Future.[22]

Rediker/Crebo-Rediker's proposal would set up a "government-owned and -capitalized infrastructure financing entity," that "would pool, package, and sell existing and future public infrastructure securities in the capital markets," as well as "seek to develop an in-house capability to originate infrastructure loans and would be able to fund itself through the international capital markets." But the capitalization they envision would be at a far higher level than is proposed in the DeLauro bill. In fact, they added, the scope should extend beyond that of the National Infrastructure Bank then being proposed by then Senator Christopher J. Dodd (D-CT) and Sen. Chuck Hagel (R-NE).[23] Dodd and Hagel had introduced the Senate version of the 2007 National Infrastructure Act of 2007.[24] Then presidential candidates Barack Obama and Hillary Clinton were co-sponsors.[25] The House version was introduced by Rep. Keith Ellison (D-MN) who is co-chair of the Congressional Progressive Caucus.[26]

The failed Dodd-Hagel bill would have provided for an independent government entity with a five-member board appointed by the president and confirmed by the Senate. The bank would have been financed with $60 billion in bonds used to leverage private capital. State and local sponsors would submit candidate projects—roads, bridges, mass transit systems, wastewater treatment facilities, and public housing—for the bank's sponsorship.[27] Clearly, this projected bond-offering fell far short of the 1980s estimate of $2.5 to $3 trillion required "to prevent the further deterioration of public services." Nor did it approach a $1.6 trillion national infrastructure deficit estimated in March 2008 by the American Society of Civil Engineers.[28]

THE "RADICAL CENTER" PARTNERS WITH WALL STREET

So where would the trillions of needed dollars come from, based on a $60 billion stake of federal taxpayer dollars? The answer was to be: from private capital, "backed by the full faith and credit of the U.S. Government." And this is where the "radical center" of the progressives would be backed by more "moderate" Democrats and Republicans, including Wall Street.

The source of Dodd and Hagel's bill was Wall Street finance wizard Felix Rohatyn, a trustee of the Center for Strategic and International Studies (CSIS), and co-chair, with former senator Warren Rudman, of the CSIS Commission on Public Infrastructure.[29] Dodd (who retired from the Senate in January 2011) was then serving as chairman of the Senate Committee on Banking, Housing and Urban Affairs; he and Hagel were also members of the CSIS infrastructure commission. In 2009, shortly after Obama's inauguration, Dodd wrote that he, Hagel, Rohatyn, and Rudman had developed his "bipartisan idea . . . over the course of several years."[30] CSIS, for its part, claimed the Dodd-Hagel legislation followed two CSIS reports released in 2005 and 2006 "that highlighted the urgent need for a national plan and investments to improve infrastructure needs across the nation."[31]

Here is how CSIS described its proposed National Infrastructure Bank would work:[32] It would be modeled after the Federal Deposit Insurance Corporation, which is led by a five-member board of directors appointed by the president and confirmed by the Senate. The NIB's board would create a bureaucracy, headed by an inspector general to oversee the NIB's daily operations and report to Congress.

Only infrastructure projects with a potential public "investment" (i.e., spending) of at least $75 million would receive NIB consideration. A project sponsor, or consortium of sponsors, would apply to the NIB, which would then use a "sliding scale" to evaluate them, based on criteria including: the type of infrastructure system or systems, project location, project cost, current and projected usage, non-federal revenue, regional or national significance, promotion of economic growth and community development, reduction in traffic congestion, environmental benefits, land use policies that promote smart growth, and mobility improvements."

CSIS also explained how the government's "investment" would be leveraged in the private capital markets once a project were selected.

The NIB would develop a financing package backed "with full faith and credit from the government." A financing package could include "direct subsidies, direct loan guarantees, long-term tax-credit general purpose bonds, and long-term tax-credit infrastructure project specific bonds." The *initial* ceiling to issue bonds would be set at $60 billion. (But the NIB would not "displace existing formula grants and earmarks for infrastructure" as it "targets specifically large capacity-building projects that are not adequately served by current financing mechanisms.")

Following a smaller-than-projected job growth report the previous week, President Obama told a July 11, 2011, news conference that the infrastructure bank he was proposing would be "relatively small." But, he asked,

> [C]ould we imagine a project where we're rebuilding roads, bridges and ports and schools and broadband lines and smart-grids and taking all those construction workers and putting them back to work right now?

I can imagine a very aggressive program like that I think the American people would rally around and that I think would be good for the economy not just next year or the year after, but for the next 20 or 30 years.[33]

Obama's "aggressive program" probably stemmed from a plan laid out by Sen. John Kerry (D-MA) in testimony of September 10, 2010, before the Senate Banking, Housing, and Urban Affairs Committee, where Kerry pushed hard for an infrastructure bank.[34] A few days earlier, on September 6, Kerry had announced he was committed to National Infrastructure Bank legislation, proposing an entity similar to the European Investment Bank that "financed $350 billion in projects from just 2005 to 2009 across the European continent, helping modernize seaports, expand airports, build rail lines and reconfigure city centers."[35]

Kerry's vision would have Uncle Sam emulate the world's "largest international non-sovereign lender and borrower." The European Investment Bank's sphere of influence is worldwide, linked to 150 countries, from Southeast Europe; the Mediterranean partner countries; the African, Caribbean, and Pacific countries; Asia and Latin America; Central Asia; Russia; and other neighbors to the East.[36] A not-for-profit institution, the EIB "raises the resources it needs to finance its lending activities by borrowing on the capital markets, mainly through public bond issues." It can do so because of its AAA credit rating, which "enables it to obtain the best terms on the market."[37]

(But the United States no longer holds an AAA credit rating, which now makes it more expensive for us to raise capital. On August 5, 2011, the Standard and Poor's downgraded Washington's credit for the first time in history (to AA+), in what was described as a "sharply worded critique of the American political system." S&P found that the Obama administration's proposed $2.1 trillion in budget savings, following its virtually unrestrained spending spree, "fell short of what was necessary to tame the nation's debt over time and predicted that leaders would not be likely to achieve more savings in the future." S&P determined Obama's mounting national debt had "made the U.S. government's ability to manage its finances 'less stable, less effective and less predictable.'"[38])

Since his original proposal for a national infrastructure bank had not sold, by mid-March, 2011, Kerry simply re-branded it.[39] (Kerry had tried to call his earlier infrastructure bank bill "bipartisan," although it had the backing of but a single Republican, Sen. John Thune of South Dakota.) Kerry introduced his new legislation, dubbed the BUILD Act, at a March 15 press conference, with a supporting cast including Sen. Kay Bailey Hutchison (R-TX) (ranking member of the Commerce, Science, and Transportation Committee), and Thomas J. Donohue (president and CEO, U.S. Chamber of Commerce). Also present was AFL-CIO president Richard Trumka.[40] Besides the better bipartisan atmospherics, Kerry was now saying he wanted to establish an American Infrastructure Financing Authority (AIFA). Replete with rhetorical boosterism about his "bold solution," the American Infrastructure Financing Authority to be set up by Kerry's BUILD Act was nothing more than a national infrastructure bank by another name.[41] According to *The Hill*, citing Obama's transportation secretary, Ray LaHood, Kerry's newly branded national infrastructure bank would "receive $30 billion over six years as part of a proposed comprehensive six-year, $556 billion plan."[42]

This half-a-trillion-dollar scheme, according to Kerry, would also be "independent of the political process." AIFA would "fund the most important and most economically viable projects across the country, our states, and our communities." It would also be "fiscally responsible," after receiving its initial funding from the government. Later, Kerry's team claimed, AIFA would become self-sustaining. It would be able to rely on the private sector, as AIFA could never provide more than 50 percent of a project's costs, "and in many cases would provide much less, just enough to bring in private investment."[43]

Kerry claimed his plan for AIFA would closely follow the Export-Import Bank model. The Export-Import Bank of the United States finances and insures purchases of U.S. goods by foreign customers who are either unable or unwilling to accept credit risk. The purpose is to create and sustain U.S. jobs by financing sales of U.S. exports to international buyers.[44] But Timothy P. Carney, author of *Obamanomics* and *The Big Ripoff*, labeled Kerry's AIFA a "corporate welfare slush fund" and a "prime example of unaccountability." As to parallels with the Ex-Im Bank:

The agency is independent of any cabinet department, and it hands out loans and loan guarantees basically at its own discretion. Congress typically gives [the Export-Import Bank] lengthy reauthorizations, thus minimizing congressional oversight. In recent years, Ex-Im was moved off-budget, meaning it funds itself with the repayments from old loans and the fees from new ones. So it's kind of like Fannie Mae was, before its exposure became real and the taxpayers had to come in and bail it out.[45]

THE NEW BANK: GOVERNMENT–WALL STREET CRONYISM

A meeting between U.S. Treasury officials, bankers, pension funds, and hedge fund managers was convened on June 28, 2011, by NYU professor Michael Likosky "to discuss how such a bank [i.e., NIB] might work."[46] As a program on National Public Radio put it, the group discussed how greedy Wall Street capitalists "can help the government launch a national infrastructure bank."[47] Likosky—who calls the plan "Obama's bank"—is a leading academic cheerleader for the Kerry plan, an "expert on public-private partnerships," and the author of *Obama's Bank: Financing a Durable New Deal.*[48]

An opposite take on the virtues of the scheme (September 2010) comes from Glen Ford of *The Black Agenda Report*:

The so-called infrastructure bank masquerades as the beginning of an industrial policy to reverse the export of jobs from the United States. Obama is spinning the scheme as his variation on Franklin Roosevelt's New Deal, when the federal government directly created millions of jobs and invested public monies in a vast, new infrastructure, much of which we are still using, today.

But in reality, the president's proposed bank bears no resemblance to the New Deal of the 1930s. Rather, it is yet another ploy to create a new windfall for the private bankers on Wall Street—a public-private scam. The scheme would transfer billions in public funds to a new banking entity, to attract the mega-bankers, whose investments would be guaranteed by the U.S. government. The Obama bank would then lend these monies to selected projects, overseen by a board heavily weighted with representatives of those same Wall Street firms and their corporate allies.

[...]

Essentially, the same Wall Street players that have relentlessly and methodically de-industrialized the United States for the past 30 years would direct the economic makeover of the country, all the while earning interest on the borrowed funds. That's not a New Deal, that's a license for yet more no-risk self-dealing by Wall Street, guaranteed by the full faith and credit of the United States. It is a travesty and a swindle.[49]

In order to sell this grand new crony capitalism scheme, Obama and the progressives touted it as the solution to an emergency (the jobs emergency) just as they had "never let a good crisis go to waste"—in Rahm Emanuel's memorable turn of phrase—in ramming through the "stimulus" package, and then ObamaCare. Obama's flim flam was already in full swing at the September 2010 Laborfest in Milwaukee, when he pitched his bank scheme as a jobs plan to union workers and their families. Obama "called for a push to build or repair 150,000 miles of roads, 4,000 miles of railway and 150 miles of runway—and an update to the air traffic control systems," ABC News' Jake Tapper reported.[50] Obama told several thousand union members:

"We used to have the best infrastructure in the world and we can have it again. We want to change the way Washington spends your tax dollars; we want to reform the way we fund and maintain our infra-structure to focus less on wasteful earmarks and outdated formulas, and we want competition and innovation that gives us the best bang for the buck," he said, adding "this is a plan that will be fully paid for, it will not add to the deficit over time—we're going to work with Congress to see to that."[51]

Progressives in Congress were soon on board this monumental "change [in] the way Washington spends your tax dollars." Congressional Progressive

Caucus co-chairs, Reps. Raúl Grijalva (D-AZ) and Keith Ellison (D-MI), pushed Obama to "champion sweeping investments in the nation's crumbling infrastructure as a way to create jobs and jolt the sluggish economy." In September 2011, they wrote to Obama with a plea for "bold action" that required "federal emergency jobs legislation." In particular, Grijalva and Ellison urged Obama to promote an estimated $2.2 trillion "investment" in a national infrastructure bank, which they described as a "public-private partnership designed to fund the nation's aging roads, bridges, railways and other vital structures." The proposal was included in the Make It in America agenda progressive Democrats had pushed all year.[52]

In fact, a whole host of infrastructure bank bills was introduced in Congress that year (2011). In addition to the aforementioned acts, Obama's defeated American Jobs Act had called for the creation of an American Infrastructure Financing Authority.[53] The Rebuild America Jobs Act, introduced October 31 by Sen. Amy Klobuchar (D-MN), included plans for an AIFA.[54] The Act for the 99% (discussed in our chapter on the New WPA) would create the National Infrastructure Development Bank Act of 2011, intended to provide "$25 billion in seed money in the next five years."[55] Sen. Sherrod Brown (D-OH) introduced the National Infrastructure Bank Act of 2011 on September 13, and Rep. Marcia L. Fudge (D-OH) introduced a bill by the same name on October 25.

In his September 8, 2011, jobs speech, Obama gave Kerry and Hutchinson credit for their contribution in respect of the infrastructure bank contained in his proposed American Jobs Act.[56] In his pitch for the act, Obama called for $80 billion in spending on "new building projects, from school modernization to roads and bridges."[57] Notably missing from Obama's speech was any reference to "green energy" or the environment, one of the main pillars of the Progressive agenda. But, as Sen. Barbara Mikulski (D-MD) put it, though the president's speech had neglected "the bipartisan topic of energy efficiency," the infrastructure bank in Obama's plan could well be used to finance green projects. Mikulski claimed it would be "a major step forward in improving the environment."[58]

For the record, the details of the newly branded American Infrastructure Financing Authority creation are fairly straightforward: It would be incorporated at the first meeting of a seven-member board of directors appointed by the president. No more than four members would come from one political party. The chairman and three voting members would serve four-year terms; the other three members would serve two-year terms. The president would also appoint a non-voting chief executive officer to run the AIFA for a term of six years.[59] Capitalized with an initial $10 billion, AIFA would provide direct loans and loan guarantees to "facilitate infrastructure projects," as well as to "leverage private and public capital and to invest in a broad range of infrastructure projects of national and regional significance, without earmarks or political influence."[60]

There would also be ample opportunities for "back-room deals" and abuse. For example, a meeting quorum would be five voting board members, and, by a majority vote, could be closed to the public "if, during the meeting to be closed, there is likely to be disclosed proprietary or sensitive information regarding an infrastructure project under consideration for assistance." So it would be fairly easy to avoid transparency and/or a situation could easily arise where the "bi-partisan" quorum could be, say, four Democrats and one Republican. And while minutes of each meeting would be prepared, in some circumstances said minutes would not be made available for up to one full year from the date of the meeting, "with any necessary redactions to protect any proprietary or sensitive information." So any discussions and decisions made at such meetings would remain secret long after votes were cast and funds were allocated.

In short, we would have an un-transparent, Big Government–Big Finance *star chamber* allocating tens of billions of dollars (of taxpayers' money the U.S. does not have and cannot afford). Such a national infrastructure bank, by any name, would "effectively centralize another key area of our economy, namely infrastructure, into a government-run enterprise that mostly benefits the private capital of the global elite," Patrick Wood wrote in the August Corporation's *Forecast and Review* (September 2010).[61]

Can you say *crony-capitalism*? No wonder Obama and the progressives are working overtime to get some kind of New Deal scheme for a national infrastructure bank enacted.

FINANCIAL CRIMES UNIT—BUSINESS FRAUD, BUT NOT GOVERNMENT FRAUD

Another "progressive" agenda item of the Obama team is the establishment of a Financial Crimes Unit under the Justice Department. This would serve a number of purposes in the expansion of executive power, by:

- centralizing and greatly intensifying prosecution of the financial industry at the federal level;
- allowing the president's surrogates to select who would be targeted for investigation (as well as who not); and,
- keeping the public and government focused on business fraud rather than on government corruption.

Thus did Obama, in his 2012 State of the Union address, admonish Congress to enact legislation to "makes the penalties for fraud count," while announcing his establishment of a Financial Crimes Unit of "highly trained investigators to crack down on large-scale fraud and protect people's investments."[62] Obama tasked attorney general Eric Holder to "create a special unit of federal prosecutors and leading state attorneys general to expand our investigations into the abusive lending and packaging of risky mortgages that led to the housing crisis. This new unit," he said, "will hold accountable those who broke the law, speed assistance to homeowners, and help turn the page on an era of recklessness that hurt so many Americans."

Not mentioned by the president was that the U.S. Treasury Department has operated a Financial Crimes Enforcement Network, known as FinCEN, for a number of years to track and prosecute terrorism and drug dealer financing and both domestic and international money laundering. It involves at least thirty law enforcement agencies, including the FBI, CIA, and Border Patrol. It is also linked with more than fifty countries to act as a Financial Intelligence Unit.[63] In addition, many states and cities have their own Financial Crimes units.

Commenting on Obama's new executive agency, David John of the Heritage Foundation wrote:

Almost all of the crimes it will consider ranging from insider trading to fraud to stealing are now crimes and have been for many years. And it is not like the Justice Department has been sitting on its hands since 2008.

The newly announced task force may be worth a few minutes of new TV time, but it is really just doing what hard working professionals have been doing for some time. . . . The implication that it will do even more is an insult to the prosecutors who have been doing the same thing.[64]

The Heritage Foundation's Joe Luppino-Esposito asked, "When is enough, enough?" He challenged the president's claim that he needed "even more fraud laws and penalties on the books for financial institutions"[65] Luppino-Esposito also quoted former U.S. attorney general Edwin Meese III, then chairman of the Center for Legal & Judicial Studies of the Heritage Foundation, in his December 13, 2011, Congressional testimony before a subcommittee of the House Judiciary Committee. Meese asked:

Will we, as a society, not be taken seriously about fighting fraud unless we double, triple, and quadruple the number of iterations of this crime?[66]

"For Obama," Luppino-Esposito wrote, "the answer is a resounding, albeit ridiculous, 'Yes.'"

MORE EXECUTIVE ENFORCEMENT OVER FINANCE

Yet another front in the war over centralization of executive power—again targeting the U.S. finance industry—centers on an agency newly created (July 2011) by the so-called Dodd-Frank Wall Street reform bill, called the Consumer Financial Protection Bureau. The CFPB is essentially an executive-level enforcement operation, with broad authority not only over banking, but also over the gigantic student loan and real estate mortgage industries.

A political storm erupted over the CFPB in mid-December 2011, as Congress was heading into winter recess. Senate Republicans had been blocking confirmation of President Obama's nominee to head the CFPB, because they "wanted the White House to agree to a Senate GOP proposal to alter the bureau's leadership infrastructure in new legislation." Republicans wanted "a board in charge rather than an individual."[67]

In the words of Sen. Richard Shelby (R-AL):

> Unless Congress enacts reform, it is only a matter of time before this concentration of power is abused or misused to the detriment of American businesses and consumers.
>
> On May 5, 43 of my senate colleagues joined me in writing a letter to President Obama informing him that we will not confirm any nominee to head the bureau absent structural changes that will make it accountable to those it seeks to protect.[68]

Unfortunately, the political storm that erupted was not over what concerned the GOP Senators, that is, the centralized command structure of Dodd-Frank's new enforcement arm. Instead, the brouhaha was over a highly controversial—and probably unconstitutional—tactic employed by Obama to circumvent the GOP senators' refusal to confirm.[69] Still, the battle for control of the CFPB has probably only been postponed, pending the election of a new Congress in November 2012:

> By statute, the CFPB director is supposed to serve a five-year term. But a recess appointment only remains effective for the duration of the existing Congress, giving [the president's "recess" appointee] roughly a year as director before the 112th Congress draws to a close at the end of 2012. The president could re-nominate [him] to the position after that shortened term expired, but he would likely face even fiercer opposition from Senate Republicans a second time around.[70]

CENTRALIZING CONTROL OVER U.S. TRADE

Marching ever onward in his expansion of government—and, whenever possible, executive—power, on February 28, 2012, Obama established, by executive order, an Interagency Trade Enforcement Center.[71] As one "citizen commentator" observed of this president's methods:

> [Obama] again circumvented Congress with his latest Executive Order . . . The Constitution gives the president no such power to regulate commerce. This power is exclusive to the Congress.
> This falls in line with the president's "We Can't Wait" campaign, which, contrary to appearances, is not as much a dig on Congress as it is a realization he only has until January to institute as much of his destructive policies as he can before he loses his job, as have millions of Americans during his administration.[72]

Whether Obama is about to lose his job remains to be seen. But he had given advance warning of his intention to create the Trade Enforcement Unit in his landmark 2012 State of the Union address. Obama claimed the purpose of the TEU would be "investigating unfair trade practices in countries like China."

> There will be more inspections to prevent counterfeit or unsafe goods from crossing our borders. And this Congress should make sure that no foreign company has an advantage over American manufacturing when it comes to accessing finance or new markets like Russia. Our workers are the most productive on Earth, and if the playing field is level, I promise you—America will always win.[73]

As usual, Obama's rhetoric concealed more than it revealed. His real agenda appears to be:

- centralizing trade controls within the executive branch, and from a plethora of existing agencies;

- being able to swiftly implement protectionist policies, when needed, to reward the progressive base amongst organized labor; and
- relentlessly promoting American "green energy" technology, into which billions upon billions more of federal dollars would be poured.

After SOTU 2012, *PolicyMic* editor Jordan Wolf wondered what a new TEU would do:

> [Obama] talked about setting up a trade enforcement division, and it wasn't clear what this would do. The WTO already monitors this sort of thing and it seems that there is very little the U.S. can really do about this, otherwise why would we not be doing it?[74]

Glimpses of insight into the true purpose of the trade regulatory agency ·can be gleaned from the progressive think tank, the Third Way, which proudly touts its influence in setting the progressive agenda:

> Third Way's policy and political work has been incorporated into President Obama's State of the Union addresses, introduced in more than fifty bills in Congress, included as part of major bipartisan budget deals and the President's Deficit Commission recommendations, cited by the Vice President's Task Force on the Middle Class, and used by dozens of candidates, from first-time House candidates to the Senate Majority Leader.[75]

A February 2010 Third Way policy paper—"Getting Our Share of Clean Energy Trade," by Ed Gerwin, Anne Kim, and Josh Freed—laid out a blueprint for the Obama trade enforcement point by point, much of which found its way into three pieces of legislation introduced in 2011. A principal concern of the authors is overcoming impediments to American "clean energy" exports:

> These impediments hamstring U.S. clean energy exporters, who face foreign competitors backed by robust, highly strategic and agile government export promotion efforts.[76]

On March 31, 2011, Sen. Sherrod Brown (D-OH) introduced the Trade Enforcement Priorities Act, with two co-sponsors, Sens. Robert P. Casey Jr. (D-PA) and Debbie Stabenow (D-MI).[77] A complementary House bill was then introduced on April 13 by Rep. Mark S. Critz (D-PA), with one co-sponsor, Rep. Linda T. Sanchez (D-CA).[78] And a third bill, the Trade Prosecutor Act of 2011, was proffered November 8—again by Senator Stabenow—along with co-sponsor, Sen. Lindsey Graham (R-SC), rendering the bill "bi-partisan."[79]

The Stabenow-Graham measure would heed President Obama's SOTU exhortation to Congress, by establishing a completely new government bureaucracy—a Trade Enforcement Division within the Office of the United States Trade Representative. Its ostensible purpose would be to "ensure that United States trading partners comply with trade agreements to which the United States is a party." Under Stabenow-Graham, three new senior positions would be created: a Deputy United States trade representative for trade enforcement, a chief agricultural negotiator, and a chief manufacturing negotiator.

The Third Way authors assert that the U.S. does not have enough trade rules in place. While U.S. trade officials have "crisscrossed the globe to sign trade deals designed to assure that American goods and services have access to foreign markets," new rules are needed to help to open trade for U.S. clean energy exports. Too few USTR staffers are currently devoted to trade enforcement and monitoring activities. Trade enforcement, they write, "often takes a back seat." Even though trade has grown rapidly, and there are new trade agreements to monitor, the size of the USTR bureaucracy has not—nor has its funding.

Noting that there are already seventeen federal agencies involved in trade enforcement, including "multiple units within USTR and the Departments of Agriculture, Commerce, and State," the problem is that they fail to "effectively coordinate their activities or pool their resources well." Needed is a national strategy for getting "our share" of clean energy trade:

> For America to win a larger share of future job growth in clean energy, U.S. companies must produce innovative, efficient, competitive and high quality clean energy products and technologies.

In addition to government support, according to Third Way's authors, the U.S. government should "incentivize American clean energy firms by putting a price on carbon, developing smart domestic energy policies and making robust investments in clean energy technology development."

In other words, cap and trade taxation, and more "green energy" investment. In fact, the influential Third Way is also pushing a "clean energy export coordinator" and the creation of a "one-stop shop for clean energy exporters."

A White House "Consolidation Authority"

Yet another Obama initiative to expand White House control over U.S. trade and industry was reflected in a January 2011 announcement that Obama would call on Congress to give him the same type of "reorganizational power last held by a president when Ronald Reagan was in office." The Obama plan was a "so-called consolidation authority allowing him to propose mergers that promise to save money and help consumers." Reportedly, Obama's first project was to be the combining of "six major operations of the government that focus on business and trade" into a single Department of Industry and Trade. The new agency would consolidate the Office of the U.S. Trade Representative, the Commerce Department's core business and trade functions, the Small Business Administration, the Export-Import Bank, the Overseas Private Investment Corporation, and the Trade and Development Agency.[80] Following ever forward in expanding executive control, three of the six named targets for consolidation—the Export Import Bank, the Overseas Private Investment Corporation, and the Trade and Development Agency—would lose their status as independent agencies. Two years earlier, a similar plan had been proposed by Derek Shearer, a former U.S. ambassador and former Commerce Department deputy under-secretary in the Clinton administration, not to mention a professor of diplomacy at Barack Obama's alma mater, Occidental College.[81]

Buy American . . . or Else

The "Buy American" slogan is another legacy of FDR's New Deal. Roosevelt's 1933 Buy American Act "mandated a purchase preference for domestically produced goods in federal direct procurements." During Obama's 2008 campaign the slogan reemerged and was slated for the 2009 "stimulus" bill. But after threats of a trade war came from both Canada—which threatened its own "Buy Canada" counter-campaign—and from the European Union, the Buy American provision was deleted from the stimulus bill by February 13.[82] Nevertheless, a Buy American provision mandating that all "iron, steel, and manufactured goods" used in a federally funded project must be produced in the United States is a legislative urge that progressive Democrats just can't seem to shake.

We devoted a whole chapter in our previous book—*Red Army*—to "Making It in America," beginning with then Speaker Nancy Pelosi's Making It in America plan. Pelosi had flashed the plan to reporters at a July 14, 2010, press conference, after meeting with President Obama at the White House.[83] Then the re-proposing of Buy American continued, with a number of pieces of legislation introduced in the House during summer of 2010—all to no avail. Again, it was included in the failed American Jobs Act of 2011, and then in the Rebuild America Jobs Act. Now it has resurfaced in the Act for the 99%.[84] And if the Act for the 99%—replete with a Buy American provision—fails to pass, expect to see Buy American attached and reattached to legislation introduced by Democrat progressives until they do somehow get it into law. It simply is not going to go away.

But why is it so important?

The bottom line is this: In the U.S., iron and steel, in particular, are produced by unions. Buy American is pure protectionism for union jobs. Large-scale manufacturing, by and large, is also carried out by union shops. If iron and steel, and large-scale manufacturing, lose out to foreign competitors, there are fewer jobs for unions, and the Democrats lose out, because union dues grease the Democratic Party's money machine.

That is why—as we documented in *Red Army*—groups like the Alliance for American Manufacturing, a union-dominated organization, have played such a prominent role in helping to push for progressive Democrats' manufacturing legislation—including the Buy American provision. But, as we also wrote in *Red Army*, the whole AAM and progressive Democrats' plan for Make It in America and Buy American went up in smoke in May 2011, when President Obama "inserted the new economic slogan, *Win the Future*, into the mix."[85] After the Democrats and their allies had invested a whole year pushing their Make It in America plan, Win the Future came along, only to be made the butt of many jokes ending with exclamations of *WTF?*

Writing in *The Hill*, Russell Berman also pointed out the obvious fact that not much in the Democratic leadership's proposal was actually new, as it included a "raft of legislation party lawmakers have proposed in recent years."[86] But progressives have no choice other than to keep on pushing Buy American—by one name or another. The Democrats' campaign piggy bank depends on it.

7

"EQUAL PAY FOR EQUAL WORK" AND OTHER ACTS OF "FAIRNESS"

A s WITH MANY "skillful politicians," Barack Obama mostly conceals his true intentions and beliefs. But on occasion he makes them perfectly clear. In 2008, Obama's entire presidential campaign had been based on themes of national unity, of transcending partisan differences, on a "red, white, and blue America." Once elected, the unifying Obama seemed to vanish. Overnight, his rhetoric radically changed.

"We're gonna punish our enemies and we're gonna reward our friends," Obama told Latino voters in an interview aired on Spanish TV channel Univision, just a month before the landslide defeat of his political allies—the Reid-Pelosi Democrats—in November 2010.[1] That one sentence "pretty much sums up" Obama's entire presidency, the Heritage Foundation's Conn Carroll later wrote for the *Washington Examiner*.[2]

One of the most deceptive tricks in Obama's rhetorical arsenal is his use of the term *economic fairness*. A prime example of the progressives' use, in general, of harmless-sounding rhetoric in their advancement of radical objectives, this "fairness" derives directly from the Marxist conception of *economic justice*. It is used today with great effect by the many shades of progressives—communists, socialists, Democratic socialists—all over the globe.

MIT economist Lester C. Thurow, who started his career working on President Lyndon Johnson's Great Society welfare programs—and later helped found the socialist-progressive Economic Policy Institute—put it this way in 2003:

> In addition to outlining the process whereby the system of capi-
> talism would end, Marx went on to recommend a new system, com-
> munism, which would, he believed, eliminate the evils of capitalism.
> He never said much about the transformation of capitalism into com-
> munism, but in his vision of communism . . . it would create a new
> society where economic fairness and personal freedom reigned.[3]

It would be a grave error, however, to mistake *Marx's personal freedom*
as in any way similar to the kind of freedom from tyranny of government fought for by America's Founding Fathers and Mothers, who then
enshrined it in the U.S. Constitution, a world-changing advance in human
liberty and self-government. Marx's *personal freedom* would become possible only within the never-realized "higher phase" of communist society.
Marx's *freedom* comes after "all the springs of co-operative wealth flow
more abundantly."

> When the individual liberty of the Founders was transformed into
> the national interest of Teddy Roosevelt and the Progressives, we
> were only one generation away from a major threat to all our personal
> liberties. That threat still exists today.[4]

So wrote Burton W. Folsom Jr., professor of history at Hillsdale College
and senior historian at the Foundation for Economic Education, in October
2010.[5] Folsom was referring to the first President Roosevelt's August 31,
1910, "New Nationalism" speech in Osawatomie, Kansas, urging greater
government control over the economy.[6]

On December 6, 2011, Barack Obama—who well knows the history of
the place—delivered his own speech in Osawatomie.[7] But Obama's speech
contained no mention of the reason for his presidential predecessor's visit
to Osawatomie—the commemoration of revolutionary abolitionist John
Brown—for which Roosevelt had been invited to dedicate the John Brown
Memorial Park. But neither Roosevelt nor Obama had come to Osawatomie

to right a great historic wrong, as had America's most famous, if also notorious, abolitionist.

On August 30, 1856, Brown led the Pottawatomie Massacre, in which five men were killed, at what was named Bleeding Kansas. Brown later led the unsuccessful takeover of the Federal munitions arsenal at Harper's Ferry (later West Virginia) in 1859. The Commonwealth of Virginia tried Brown for treason, for the murder of five more men, and for inciting a slave insurrection. He was found guilty on all counts and hanged. But the controversy about Brown, his persona, his methods, and his secret abolitionist backers, never died.

According to Ken Chowder, author of a documentary about Brown for public television:

> John Brown's soul was already marching on. But the flesh-and-blood John Brown—a tanner, shepherd, and farmer, a simple and innocent man who could kill in cold blood, a mixture of opposite parts who mirrored the paradoxical America of his time—this John Brown had already vanished, and he would rarely appear again. His life instead became the subject for 140 years of spin.[8]

Also not mentioned by Obama, for understandable reasons, was that *Osawatomie* became the name of the newspaper launched by the radical anti-capitalist, domestic terrorist group, the Weather Underground.[9] The Weatherman had been led by two Pentagon-bombing radicals, Bill Ayers and Bernardine Dohrn, who later became Barack Obama's Hyde Park neighbors and close personal and political associates, as we have documented copiously in our previous book, *The Manchurian President*. Each issue of the Weather Underground newspaper included a printed picture of John Brown, with an explanation underneath as to why the publication had been named *Osawatomie*.[10]

In his December 2011 Osawatomie speech, Obama also soundly denounced capitalism, saying it "doesn't work, it has never worked."[11] These words of the president echoed those of Michigan's Marxist congressman, John Conyers Jr., who, a month earlier, had told a gathering of the Democratic Socialists of America, "This system, this capitalist system, is broken and may be un-repairable because the regulatory forces in the government are not willing to step up to the plate."[12]

The meaning of Obama's Osawatomie speech was well explained by Matthew Spalding of *National Review Online*. In his August 1910 speech, Spalding noted, Roosevelt was "at his most progressive"—as was Obama nearly 100 years later:

> If there was any doubt before, it is now clear that [Obama] has given up on the center of American politics and doubled down on his governing model. And this tells us everything about where he is coming from and where he wants to go.[13]

At Osawatomie, Obama repeatedly invoked *fairness*. Fairness, as Obama defined it, is "when everyone engages in fair play, and everybody gets a fair shot, and everybody does their fair share." (The fairness expressed by Karl Marx was, "from each according to his ability, to each according to his need."[14]) Raising taxes on the wealthy would only be fair, Obama said, since *somebody* has to pay for all of his "investments" in infrastructure, education, and "green" projects, not to mention the expansion of unemployment benefits, of government bureaucracy and regulations, and the creation of new jobs programs he is pushing.

In truth, Obama's progressive conception of fairness is not the classic Marxist one, for Marx was the prophet and theoretician of a revolutionary *working class*. But today's neo-socialist progressives have completely abandoned and betrayed the working class, along with small-business owners, in favor of a welfare class, a middle class ever more dependent on government hand-outs, and a progressive, liberal elite. As Spalding puts it:

> Obama has abandoned the "average, middle-class voter and his middle-class values" and "[cobbled] together an alliance of state dependents, government hangers-on, and political elites who claim the capacity to run things." This is the rise of a "new governing class that insists on enforcing political and economic 'fairness' rather than letting us govern ourselves. The managed quest for fairness inevitably leads to bureaucratic favoritism, inequalities based on special interests, and undue political influence."

If not stopped, this corrupt and economically unsustainable *fairness* train will be used to steamroll American citizens for another four years and what will be left of our democracy, at the end of the line, will be unrecognizable.

PAYCHECK FAIRNESS

Progressives such as the Economic Policy Institute almost always include "fair pay" in their credos. Thus, EPI "believes every working person deserves a good job with fair pay, affordable health care, and retirement security."[15]

We should also credit progressive Democrats both for rhetorical consistency, and for persistence. President Obama's January 2012 State of the Union address called for "equal pay for equal work." President Clinton's 1999 State of the Union address had employed identical verbiage—"equal pay for equal work." Clinton's SOTU pronouncement came on the heels of AFL-CIO support for the Paycheck Fairness Act of 1997,[16] a piece of legislation intended to amend and "improve" the Equal Pay Act of 1963.[17] The 1997 legislation has never been passed, but its ultimate adoption remains a prime progressive goal.

Originally, "equal pay" legislation was meant to ensure women would not be paid less for doing the same jobs as men. The 1963 Equal Pay Act addressed pay discrimination claims limited to "the few situations where women and men are doing 'substantially the same' work," while the newer legislation "would allow a broader range of jobs to be evaluated for gender bias" and "toughen the remedies allowed under the Equal Pay Act," as well as "funnel more resources into enforcement."[18]

Sen. Tom Daschle (D-SD) introduced the Paycheck Fairness Act of 1997 in the Senate, along with twenty-three progressive Democrat co-sponsors.[19] A bill of the same name was introduced in the House by Rep. Rosa DeLauro (D-CT), along with ninety-five co-sponsors,[20] and DeLauro has re-introduced the bill in every session of Congress through the most current one.[21] At the time, the likelihood of the bill's passage was considered doubtful, although five state-level "fair pay" laws had been passed and additional laws were being considered in twenty-seven states, "pushed primarily by the state federations of the AFL-CIO."[22] Again in 1999, both the Paycheck Fairness Act and the Equal Pay Initiative were re-introduced in Congress. Opponents claimed the bills not only overlapped with the Equal Pay Act of 1963 but also that:

the new regulations would "create costly litigation and frivolous law-suits. The legislation would allow women to sue their employers for unlimited compensatory and punitive damages in addition to the limited damages and back-pay awards available under federal law."[23]

A National Committee on Pay Equity—which included the working women department of the AFL-CIO—was founded in 1979 as a "coalition of women's groups, civil-rights organizations and unions concerned about the wage gap." Twenty years later, the AFL-CIO's Karen Nussbaum claimed: "The average working family loses more than $4,000 a year because of the wage gap."[24] In 2002, the Economic Policy Institute's Heather Boushey was claiming that "women working full-time earn, on average, 80 cents for every dollar earned by men, they work longer hours for the same paycheck."[25]

Arguing for the opposition were Diana Furchtgott-Roth and Christine Stolba, authors of *Women's Figures*, a book published in 1999 by the American Enterprise Institute. They produced data showing:

> childless women between the ages of 27 and 33 [were making] 98 cents to every man's dollar—a statistic that shatters the glass-ceiling and "pink-ghetto" myths.[26]

Another opponent, Anita K. Blair, who was then vice president of the conservative Independent Women's Forum, claimed in 1999 that the AFL-CIO skewed its numbers in "an attempt to make everything 'unionized.'"[27] The AFL-CIO, Blair said, wants

> our salaries to be decided by government agencies rather than a worker and her boss. Mothers generally make career decisions that result in less hours or wages. That doesn't mean if you're a mother in the workforce that you are being paid less.

In a 1999 article published in the *Civil Rights Journal*, Diana Furchtgott-Roth addressed a joint AFL-CIO/Institute for Women's Policy Research study that "calculated the cost of alleged 'pay inequity' caused by the predominance of women and men in different occupational categories."[28]

The union-financed study, she continued, "compared the wages of workers in female-dominated occupations with those in non-female-dominated occupations. The workers had the same sex, age, race, educational level, marital and parental status, and urban/rural status; they lived in the same part of the country and worked the same number of hours; and they worked in firms of the same size in the same industry." The study "concluded that women were underpaid by $89 billion per year because of occupational segregation. Without sex, race, marital and parental status, and firm and industry variables, this figure rose to $200 billion per year," Furchtgott-Roth wrote.

Although the study boasted "an impressive list of variables," Furchtgott-Roth pointed to two major factors it neglected:

First, it omits the type of job . . . Second, it leaves out the field of education. It is meaningless to say that the earnings of a man or a woman with a B.A. in English should be the same as the earnings of a man or a woman with a B.A. in math. So the study compares workers without regard to education or type of work: secretaries are being compared with loggers, bookkeepers with oil drillers.

Ahead of the 2000 general election, Furchtgott-Roth announced in the *American Spectator* that "comparable work" was back on the table.[29]

It's five months before the November elections, and ultra-liberals Tom Harkin and Ted Kennedy are holding court in Dirksen Senate Office Building [in a hearing] . . . establishing comparable worth–federal wage and salary controls regulating how much employers must pay each male and female worker.

But in 2002 EPI's Heather Boushey was claiming that "comparable worth" would help to eliminate the failure of affirmative action to completely close the wage gap and wage penalty visited upon women for working in a predominantly female occupation like nursing, which requires high levels of education and certification. This was due, she wrote, to the "high degree of segregation of women and men into different types of jobs."[30]

Occupations that have been historically dominated by women are often poorly paid compared to occupations that are dominated by men and that require comparable levels of skill and education.

The proposed comparable-worth legislation, Boushey claimed, "could reduce the wage gap and help low-wage workers without creating an excessive burden for employers."

The above discussion shows the persistence of progressive attempts to socially engineer wages, well beyond the principle of paying women the same as men for doing the same jobs. In 1933, Franklin Roosevelt had called on all employers to sign a Code of Fair Competition agreement as "part of a nationwide plan to raise wages, create employment, and thus increase purchasing power and restore business."[31] It was a detailed code regulating child labor, women's labor, hours of business operation, pay rates, a minimum wage, prices, and more.

Diana Furchtgott-Roth, in her *American Spectator* article, provided a detailed critique of this entire approach. She relies, in part, on former Congressional Budget Office director June O'Neill, in whose view

comparable worth demeaned women because "it conveys the message that women cannot compete in nontraditional jobs and can only be helped through the patronage of a job evaluator."[32]

So now, Furchtgott-Roth pointed out, progressives have simply rebranded *comparable worth* as *pay equity*.

It's a warm, fuzzy concept, designed to lure working women with the promise of potential raises and to discourage political opposition. After all, who could be against equity?

Furchtgott-Roth also explains what passage of the convoluted Fair Pay Act would mean:

The Fair Pay Act would require employers to compensate workers according to an artificial calculation of a job's "value" rather than on what anyone is willing to pay. It would extend the current "equal pay for equal work" doctrine of federal law to equal pay for very different jobs, with the goal of raising the pay of women in female-dominated occupations. In other words, federal bureaucrats would decide which jobs are underpaid and would require employers to raise those wages. . . . It defines discrimination as paying different wages for "equivalent" jobs that are dominated by employees of a particular sex or racial group. In the bill's own words, "The term 'equivalent jobs' means jobs that may be dissimilar, but whose requirements are equivalent, when viewed as a composite of skills, effort, responsibility, and working conditions."[33]

(In a modest progressive compromise—for now—the most recent rendition of the Pay Fairness Act, introduced in April 2011 by Representative DeLauro, does not as specifically stipulate wage controls as did FDR's.)

In 2000, proponents of the Pay Fairness Act were declaring: "The time to pass the bill is now." We are hearing the same thing about much of today's legislation—"We can't wait." While none of the bills were expected to pass in Congress in 2000, Furchtgott-Roth was warning then that "comparable worth and pay equity"—or some other version—could easily become law if then candidate Al Gore were elected president and the Democrats retook Congress. This is the same danger American voters should concern themselves with today. Should Barack Obama be reelected, and/or the Democrats retake control of Congress, find ourselves faced with Depression-era wage and price controls—or worse.

Bear in mind: in June 2000, President Clinton wanted regulations to make it easier to "punish firms for pay equity infractions through denial or withdrawal of federal contracts."[34] In 1997, Vice President Al Gore told the AFL-CIO, "We're going to send a message to companies that want to do business with the federal government: How you treat employees and how you treat unions counts with us."[35] In October 2010, President Obama put it more pithily to Latino voters: "We're gonna punish our enemies and we're gonna reward our friends."

FAIR TAXATION FOR THE RICH—OR CLASS WARFARE?

The progressive Troika—Economic Policy Institute, Demos and the Century Foundation—along with many other progressive groups, have published numerous articles about taxing the rich, all of which predict dire consequences if such taxation is not increased, or if—heaven forbid—it should stop. Case in point, an August 2010 commentary by John Irons, then EPI's research and policy director, and by Andrew Fieldhouse, EPI/ Century Foundation federal budget policy analyst:

> Economist Mark Zandi of Moody's Analytics estimates that every dollar spent making the Bush income tax cuts permanent generates only 32 cents of economic activity. Comparatively, every dollar spent on unemployment assistance generates $1.61 worth of economic activity, a dollar of spending on infrastructure yields $1.57 and a dollar in assistance to states to prevent layoffs of teachers or first responders yields $1.41. Tax cuts for the wealthy are simply not a good way to stimulate the economy....
>
> Simply put, the cost of extending the upper-income Bush tax cuts, in both dollars and lost opportunities, is unacceptably high. . . .
>
> A one- or two-year extension of the cuts for the wealthy is a poorly designed stimulus and would set a fiscally irresponsible precedent for our nation's long-run budgetary planning. Congress should extend permanently reductions for the middle class and let the other provisions expire.
>
> We need to streamline and modernize the tax code, not perpetuate a failed system.[36]

In an August 2011 briefing paper, Fieldhouse and Isaac Shapiro, EPI director of regulatory policy research, claim the top 1 percent of households "benefited disproportionately" from the Bush-era tax cuts. The top 1 percent "received 38% of the total amount of these tax cuts, which is more than the combined amount of the total amount of the tax cuts received by the bottom 80% of tax filers."[37]

The key phrase here is "bottom 80% of tax filers," because now half of all Americans pay no federal income tax at all.

A Heritage Foundation analysis over nearly fifty years—from 1962 to 2009—based on data gleaned from individual income returns, calculated in February 2012 that the "percentage of people who do not pay federal income taxes, and who are not claimed as dependents by someone who does pay them, jumped from 14.8 percent in 1984 to 49.5 percent in 2009. . . . That means 151.7 million Americans paid nothing in 2009. By comparison, 34.8 million tax filers paid no taxes in 1984."[38]

The U.S. Treasury's Office of Tax Analysis reports U.S. individual income tax is "highly progressive," meaning "a small group of higher-income tax- payers [pay] most of the individual income taxes each year."[39] The top 1 percent of taxpayers, for example, "paid 33.7 percent of all individual income taxes in 2002. This group of taxpayers has paid more than 30 percent of individual income taxes since 1995. Moreover, since 1990 this group's tax share has grown faster than their income share."

How about those 151.7 million Americans who pay no federal income taxes?

Annie Lowrey, now an economic policy reporter for the *New York Times*, wrote in *Slate* (October 2011) that "deductions and poverty" are responsible for the 47 percent who pay no federal income tax. They "qualify for enough breaks to cancel their tax obligations out."

> Of that group, 44 percent are claiming tax benefits for the elderly, like an exemption for Social Security payments. And 30.4 percent are claim- ing credits for "children and the working poor," like the child-care tax credit. The remainder gets breaks for investment income, spending on education, itemized deductions, and a mish-mash of other things. When combined, it's all enough to cancel out their income tax requirements.
>
> In short, it is not that they are not paying their taxes. It is that the country's tax structure lets them off the hook.[40]

Lowrey also credits the Bush tax cuts for some of those exemptions.

> For instance, the 2001 cuts, extended under the Obama administra- tion, doubled the child tax credit from $500 to $1,000 and expanded eligibility for the Earned Income Tax Credit among married taxpayers.

Additionally, the Bush tax cuts lowered income taxes in every bracket, making it easier for a household's liability to get fully offset by deductions and credits. And on top of all that, the stimulus bill introduced a host of further tax cuts.

Contrary to the barbed rhetoric coming from progressives, it's not "all Bush's fault." And if tens of millions of Americans are now paying no income tax, the definition "rich Americans" being targeted for big tax increases is being pushed down onto the upper middle class.

In September 2011, Obama started pushing for his $447 billion jobs bill, promising to pay for it by raising taxes on the wealthy and businesses.[41] Jacob "Jack" Lew, then director of the Office of Management and Budget (now Obama's chief of staff), affirmed that proposed tax hikes on the wealthy and businesses would pay for Obama's entire half-trillion-dollar jobs scheme.[42]

Lew stated itemized deductions would be limited for individuals making more than $200,000 a year, and for families making more than $250,000. Lew purported this would raise about $400 billion.[43] Suddenly, the definition of "wealthy" became $200,000.

Obama also proposed raising $18 billion by treating earnings of investment fund managers as "ordinary income" rather than taxing it at lower capital gains rates. Additionally, he would "eliminate many oil and gas industry tax breaks to raise $40 billion and change corporate jet depreciation rules to bring in another $3 billion."[44] All this is in line with Schakowsky's Fairness in Taxation Act, which called for taxation on capital gains and dividend income as "ordinary income" for those taxpayers making over $1 million. If enacted in 2011, Schakowsky wrote, her act would raise more than $78 billion.[45] Although Obama's proposed tax rules would not take effect until January 2013, Obama was "not offering any spending cuts to pay for the jobs plan," Lew said.[46]

"Obama is trying to raise income tax rates without having to admit it," Timothy P. Carney commented in the *Washington Examiner*:

> This is simply a rate hike by another name.... This matters because of the incentive effects. Eliminating tax deductions makes people

poorer, which is bad. Raising rates (explicitly or sneakily) makes people poorer and reduces their incentive to earn—doubly bad.[47]

GOVERNMENT JOBS, RAISING TAXES, CUTTING DEFENSE

The hundreds of billions of dollars to be spent under the EPI's Act for the 99% job-creation measures (see chapter 5 on the WPA) could allegedly be offset by Rep. Jan Schakowsky's Fairness in Taxation Act. EPI projects ten-year savings "which would more than pay for all of the near-term job-creation policies."[48] Schakowsky's act creates new tax brackets for taxpayers earning an income starting at $1 million—taxed at a 45 percent tax rate. It ends with a $1 billion and higher bracket—taxed at a 49 percent tax rate.[49] This revenue "would more than offset costs associated with the major job-creation proposals included in the Act for the 99%, while leaving ample room to apply some of the savings to long-term deficit reduction," EPI claims. Schakowsky introduced her tax act March 16, 2011. Thus far, it has earned no Congressional action.[50]

The Congressional Progressive Caucus, for its part, would pay for its "fairness" agenda by cutting national defense and hiking taxes on U.S. energy producers. CPC defense cuts would include: "unnecessary" defense programs, which the CPC claims would save $280 billion, in addition to approximately $1.2 trillion saved by restricting spending in Afghanistan to planning and executing a "responsible troop withdrawal." Congressional Progressives would raise revenue by targeting the oil and gas industry, from which they project raising over $60 billion by ending "tax giveaways" and requiring polluters "to clean up their mess." They also want to level a 0.03 percent tax to disincentivize "dangerous speculation by slightly raising the cost to trade."

The Demos think tank envisions extending unemployment compensation as a kind of "stimulus" spending. The Act for the 99% would increase spending by extending the Federal Emergency Unemployment Compensation (EUC) program through 2012.[51] In an overview of Obama's September 2011 jobs bill, Demos wrote: "By further extending these benefits, the president's plan would not only sustain a lifeline for unemployed workers, but continue one of the most powerful forms of stimulus available to policymakers."[52] For Demos, the bottom line is redistributing wealth by addressing "economic insecurity and inequality" and tax hikes for the wealthy.[53]

Meanwhile, the progressive think tank—John Podesta's Center for American Progress—the clamor has been for higher tax rates for quite some time.[54] CAP's John Irons was lamenting in April 2007, before Obama's presidency, and the Reid-Pelosi Congress, that "concerns about the federal government's massive fiscal deficit will make it hard for Congress to maintain [the] current level of government services and even harder for them to follow a progressive agenda."

TWO-THIRDS OF INCOME TO TAXES?

Nothing as trivial as a massive federal deficit bothers this president, even running for reelection, nor certainly going on to a possible second term. And in truth, it matters little whether the federal government lives strictly within its means. The real catastrophe would come when progressives lack the money to implement their über-expensive agenda.

Back in April 2011, when President Obama delivered his so-called fiscal plan, he did not even offer a budget. Dan Mitchell, of the Center for Freedom and Prosperity Foundation, was among those who identified Obama's speech as a "set of talking points" for the "opening salvo" of his reelection campaign.

> And it's clear that a central theme of his campaign will be class warfare . . . Obama, for all intents and purposes, has taken the moderately left-wing proposal crafted by his Fiscal Commission and moved it significantly in the wrong direction by adding class-warfare tax policy. As such, he is close to the left end of the line, which represents "Statism."[55]

Mitchell later borrowed a term from the president's rhetorical playbook, and pegged Obama as a "stubborn clinger"—"stubbornly clinging to his ideological agenda of bigger government and class warfare. . . . Wasteful programs magically become 'investments' for growth, and higher tax rates get turned into 'shared sacrifice,'" he noted.

Interestingly, we already know what eventually happens with this approach. Europe's welfare states are now dealing with the wreckage of Obamanomics-type policies and the results are not pretty.[56]

Mitchell further elaborated on the president's new class warfare strategy. In April 2011, while speaking in Annandale, Virginia, Obama had come out for "lifting the cap on income on which the Social Security payroll tax is applied." (During the 2008 presidential campaign, Obama ran on a plan to "raise the 'tax max' by somewhere between two to eight percentage points for the top 3% of earners."[57]) To put these numbers into perspective: during 2011, there was a maximum amount of income subject to the payroll tax—about $107,000. But, Mitchell writes, "it appears that President Obama wants to radically change this system so that it is based on a class-warfare model."

Andrew G. Biggs, of the American Enterprise Institute, explains how the seemingly small measure of hiking the Social Security tax ceiling would very much increase the overall burden on Americans. It "should be seen in the context of other tax increases that are already in the works," Biggs explained. The top federal income tax rate is 35 percent, plus 2.9 percent Medicare tax, and a "typical state income tax rate of around 5.5 percent," equaling an "all-in top marginal tax rate on earned income" at around 43 percent (or as high as 49 percent in some higher-tax states).

At the time, the Obama administration was planning for a top income tax rate of 40.8 percent and an increased Medicare tax rate on high earners of 3.8 percent as of 2013 (due to ObamaCare). If state income tax rates would not change, remaining constant at around 6 percent, the "top marginal tax rate will rise under current plans to 51 percent, with a maximum in high-tax states such as Hawaii and Oregon of around 56 percent," according to Biggs.

If the ceiling on Social Security payroll taxes were to be eliminated, about 24 percent of households "would be affected by higher taxes over their lifetimes," Biggs wrote. "Total maximum marginal tax rates on earned income would range from a low of 57 percent in states with no income tax to a high of 68 percent in Hawaii; the population-weighted average top rate would be almost 63 percent."[58]

An April 2011 *Wall Street Journal* editorial on Obama's "max tax" was equally damning:

> President Obama's deficit pitch is that if only a fraction of the highest income Americans were "asked to pay a little bit more" the fiscal seas would part—but all those little bits are starting to pile up. Speaking Tuesday in Annandale, Virginia, Mr. Obama came out for lifting the cap on income on which the Social Security payroll tax is applied.
>
> Currently, the employer and employee each pay 6.2% up to $106,800, a level that rises with inflation each year. Mr. Obama didn't hint at specifics, though he did run in 2008 on a plan to raise the "tax max" by somewhere between two to eight percentage points for the top 3% of earners. But whatever he means, let's underscore what a dramatic departure from current tax policy Mr. Obama is so casually floating.
>
> For starters, if the White House wants to lift the cap for high earners but doesn't upcap benefits for a corresponding increase, it would change Social Security from a quasi-insurance program, in which there is at least some connection between the taxes paid on wages in return for benefits, into a welfare transfer program.[59]

The *WSJ* editorial also cited a paper by Andrew Biggs:

> Biggs calculates that this and other tax increases Mr. Obama favors would bring the top marginal rate to somewhere between 57% and 68% when factoring in state taxes. Tax levels like these haven't been seen since the 1970s.[60]

Dan Mitchell believes Obama is "cleverly avoiding specifics, largely because the potential tax hike could be enormous." The above focuses mostly on the "employee" side of the payroll tax; the "employer" share of the tax is also 6.2 percent. So an increase in marginal tax rates "for affected workers could be as high as 12.4 percentage points."[61]

* * *

For now, Republicans in Congress are keeping things in check.

In his 2012 State of the Union address, Obama offered his tax plans, "with scant detail," the Associated Press reported. Obama "used the word 'fair' seven times to describe tax increases aimed at groups the Occupy movement has branded as the 'one percent' of Americans who are doing extremely well while the rest of society struggles," the AP wrote. AP also reported at the end of January 2012 that Democrats "immediately made clear that there [would] be Senate votes this year on the subject."[62]

In particular, Sen. Charles Schumer (D-NY) told the AP he was "relishing a push on 'some kind of Romney rule, I mean Buffett rule.'" Obama has "embraced a Buffett rule, named for billionaire Warren Buffett, who has cited the inequity of laws that let him pay a lower tax rate than his secretary," the AP noted:

> Obama's tax proposals could "also be read as an opening gambit in what looms as a titanic partisan struggle to be waged after the November elections, perhaps in a lame duck session of Congress in December."

James Pethokoukis of AEI did a little fact-checking on Obama's SOTU charges:

> we need to change our tax code so that people like me, and an awful lot of members of Congress, pay our fair share of taxes. . . . We don't begrudge financial success in this country. We admire it. When Americans talk about folks like me paying my fair share of taxes, it's not because they envy the rich. . . . Tax reform should follow the Buffett rule: If you make more than a million dollars a year, you should not pay less than 30 percent in taxes.

"Are wealthier Americans really not paying their fair share?" Pethokoukis asked before addressing the president's allegations of inequity:

- The top 1 percent pays 37 percent of federal income taxes (and in 2009 earned 16.9 percent of adjusted gross income). The taxable income of those in the 35 percent bracket was taxed at 49 percent, and Federal income tax revenues would be just $78 billion higher.

- The top 0.1 percent pays 17.1 percent of taxes and earns 7.8 percent of adjusted gross income.
- The average income tax rate for the top 1 percent is 24 percent (while the bottom 50 percent pay just 1.85 percent and only 2.3 percent of income taxes).
- If you took half of the annual income from every person making between $1 million and $10 million, it would only decrease the nation's debt by 1 percent.
- If you took every dollar from everyone making more than $10 million per year, it would only reduce the nation's deficit by 12 percent and the national debt by 2 percent.
- The IRS will give out roughly $110 billion in "refundable" tax credits this year to households that paid zero income taxes.
- In order to get the deficit to 2 percent by 2020—using Obama's budget baseline—it would take a 91 percent top rate by taxing just the rich.

Never mind that Obama and the progressive Democrats had run the national debt, by February 2012, up to $15.4 trillion and mounting—quickly. Statistically speaking, there is no way to make all of this add up—even using a very high-end, government-subsidized calculator.

Writing in late January 2012 in *The Hill*, Bernie Becker reported, "Some Democrats suggest their party will not move away from the new strategy in 2013, when real policymaking is expected to pick up steam, since eliminating tax breaks could be politically painful."[63]

Both the occupant of the White House and the composition of the next Congress will decide in which direction America goes. If Obama is reelected and Democrats control the money, the path is clear.

8

GOVERNMENT HEALTH CARE
FOR ALL

O N THE SECOND anniversary of ObamaCare—"his signature legislative accomplishment"—the president made no mention of it in public. Just three days before the U.S. Supreme Court was to begin its hearing of oral arguments on the constitutionality of the law (March 26, 2012) Obama would not offer a "vigorous public defense of the law, holding events or even making public remarks in the lead-up to the Supreme Court case," according to senior administration officials.[1]

The president's men and women were being less than completely honest. While it is true that Obama himself would not address the persistently unpopular measure, a well-orchestrated plan by high-profile Democratic operatives working in conjunction with the White House had already been launched to save ObamaCare. Under no circumstances would progressives and their fellow travelers ever give up on enacting single-payer health care legislation controlled by the federal government. Ensuring ObamaCare is implemented will be a signature policy effort for a second Obama term regardless of the Supreme Court decision.

The second day of the Supreme Court's review turned out to be surprisingly vigorous. But as former Clinton advisor Dick Morris pointed out on the Fox News Channel, even were ObamaCare to be struck down by the high court—or only the individual mandate be deemed unlawful—Obama and progressives had readied their rejoinder with a "single-payer option." In other words, an unconstitutional mandate that would have forced Americans to buy a product—health insurance—would be superseded by a tax on all Americans, similar to those levied as Social Security and Medicare taxes.[2]

The Center for American Progress, with very close ties to the White House, is the most important of dozens of progressive think tanks, as we mention in our other chapters. CAP has declared the individual mandate an "essential pillar of comprehensive health care reform," though what progressive groups like CAP really mean by "reform" is socialized medicine (i.e., mandatory, government-controlled, single-payer health insurance).[3] In a May 2008 report, CAP explained that socialized medicine is a "concept that has been embraced, demonized, and misunderstood since the early 20th century in the United States." While the U.S. has "stood by and watched the entire industrialized world turn to varying forms of government-supported health care systems for all their citizens," in the U.S., CAP's experts wrote, "similar policy changes" have been blocked because of fear.[4] According to CAP, the U.S. version of Medicare is "best characterized as a single-payer system."

> The government provides Medicare to all citizens over the age of 65 (with various exemptions and exceptions) using public funding that reimburses public and private providers of medical services. Medicare is financed through general tax revenues, a 2.9 percent dedicated payroll tax split evenly between employers and workers, and monthly beneficiary premiums.[5]

What CAP neglected to mention is that Medicare, as it currently operates, has not eliminated private insurers, nor is it truly a single-payer plan. Medicare participants may purchase private insurance, known as Medigap, to take advantage of employer-based plans. Or they may opt into buying Medicare Parts C and/or D (i.e., the Medicare Advantage and Prescription Drug plans, respectively). Medicare Parts C and D are private plans, though contracted through the government's Medicare program, meaning that health care professionals are "paid with government funds that are allocated to private insurance providers."[6]

This is a win-win for health insurers, and fertile ground for government/private sector cronyism. One of the major private-sector beneficiaries of ObamaCare would be the American Association of Retired Persons (AARP), a group of 39 million members, and the nation's largest provider of Medigap. AARP lobbied hard for ObamaCare and now stands to profit from it.[7] A late-March 2011 report by the House Ways & Means Committee exposed AARP's "apparent conflict of interest" and revealed the tradeoff for AARP's support of the law—AARP stands to make $1 billion over ten years "on health insurance plans whose sales [were] expected to pick up under the new law."[8]

A major grouping of socialists within the U.S. Congress—the seventy-five-member Congressional Progressive Caucus—still mostly favors a single-payer plan. The CPC, founded originally by the Democratic Socialists of America, attempted to relaunch single-payer in December 2011 with its Restore the American Dream for the 99% Act. The 99% Act would provide protections for Medicare, Medicaid, and Social Security;[9] hence it is not purely a single-payer plan.

The CPC bill projects $88 billion in "savings" by allowing a "public option" to operate in conjunction with private health insurance in so-called health care exchanges. It also posits an additional $156 billion in savings by allowing Medicare to negotiate drug prices with pharmaceutical companies. The progressive legislation would also reinstate higher federal Medical Assistance Percentage rates, which is the reimbursement formula for federal Medicaid grants to the states. This would purportedly "ease the state budget crises and help states finance health care for disadvantaged children, poor seniors, and the disabled."[10] The CAP called this provision of the 99% Act "the single most important step the federal government could take to provide relief to state and local governments," perhaps boosting employment by 349,000 jobs in fiscal year 2012.[11]

Of course, the key word here is *perhaps*. As you will see, a gigantic coalition of left-wing progressive groups like CAP were not so certain of ObamaCare's future and, in early 2011, launched an all-out campaign to save ObamaCare a year in advance of the bill's scrutiny before the Supreme Court.

SINGLE-PAYER AS TAX PLAN

These chapters are being written immediately following the high court's March 26–28, 2012, hearing of oral arguments on ObamaCare, and before the court hands down its ruling in June. Our analysis is, should the Supreme Court strike the law, or its individual mandate, then the huge messaging efforts now under way to prevent its repeal will immediately shift to pushing for a single-payer health care plan—which will be touted as a legitimate tax—to be implemented before the current Obama administration comes to an end.

Should ObamaCare be repealed or overturned, progressive journalist Ezra Klein prognosticated in his March 30, 2012, *Washington Post* column that neither Democrats nor Republicans would be likely to propose "any big changes" to the current health care system. Klein did suggest how the single-payer health insurance goal could be accomplished piecemeal.[12] Rising health care costs for employers, he opined, would lead Senate Democrats to "begin dipping their toes in the water with a strategy based around incremental expansions" of Medicare, Medicaid, and the Children's Health Insurance Program (CHIP). As this plan inched forward through budget reconciliation in the Senate—where the policies could be passed with only 51 votes—it would lead to "more and more Americans being covered through public insurance" and eventually to "something close to a single-payer system" with a majority of Americans covered by the federal government.[13]

A great majority, perhaps—but not every American. When one recalls that ObamaCare was pitched to the American public as a moral imperative, in order to provide health coverage to 30–40 million Americans who were uninsured, the following should provoke outrage. According to a March 15, 2012, estimate by the Congressional Budget Office and the Joint Committee on Taxation, even if ObamaCare is upheld and fully implemented, there will still be 27 million Americans with no health insurance coverage.[14]

A not-so-surprising development occurred a mere two days after the Supreme Court arguments ended and it was apparent that ObamaCare was in deep trouble. On March 30, CAP and ObamaCare's other progressive supporters were described by Judicial Watch as "apoplectic at how badly the oral arguments went for their side." The groups' first target was Don

Verrilli, Obama's solicitor general, whose embarrassing stumbling performance failed to defend the indefensible before the Court.[15]

Amy Gardner of the leftist-friendly *Washington Post* cautiously characterized the fate of ObamaCare as "uncertain." She also reported that progressives—aghast at the thought of ObamaCare being ruled unconstitutional, and thereby sound its demise—were ready with a second prong of attack. The Obama front group, Know Your Care/Protect Your Care, which we discuss in detail below, planned to "throw out its playbook," Gardner reported, and "would devote its time in the fall to going negative on the court itself—painting the conservative justices as partisan ideologues who robbed Americans of needed benefits."[16]

Ever impatient, President Obama jumped the gun to lead an early attack. In an April 2 speech, Obama had the "unmitigated gall," as *American Thinker* contributor Fay Voshell put it, to warn the "unelected" Supreme Court (Obama's words) that it had better rule in his favor. Obama, Voshell added, "revealed not only his hypocrisy, but the extent [to which] he will go to in order to preserve the key accomplishment of his administration. He seems fully to intend to intimidate the Court into rubber-stamping the Affordable Care Act of 2010 as constitutional."[17]

OBAMACARE RESET VERSION 2.0

While the Center for American Progress has been deeply involved in drafting and promoting all of the legislative efforts by Barack Obama and progressives in Congress, CAP was most staunchly supportive of Obama's health care plan. CAP now is also deeply involved in the campaign to save ObamaCare. At a mid-April 2011 press conference in Washington, D.C., Duval Patrick, the Democratic governor of Massachusetts, CAP's president, Neera Tanden, and Jim Doyle, the former Democratic governor of Wisconsin, jointly announced the launch of the Know Your Care and Protect Your Care (KYC/PYC) public relations efforts.[18] (Recall that Patrick has been a spokesman for Obama's reelection campaign.) Patrick alleged that ObamaCare was "under attack by well-coordinated and well-funded organizations that spread misinformation in order to take away people's benefits by repealing health care." He told reporters:

This campaign will be an aggressive effort designed to explain and promote these rights as well as protect against other attacks such as attempts to privatize Medicare and Medicaid.[19]

Writers at the *Huffington Post* claimed the catalyst for the Patrick-Tanden-Doyle so-called counteroffensive was the 2011 budget proposal of Rep. Paul Ryan (R-WI), which the U.S. House had passed prior to its Easter 2011 recess. According to *Huffington Post's* Michael McAuliff and Sam Stein:

> The Republican Party's endorsement of sharply conservative prescriptions to fix ailing state and federal budgets is threatening to reunite the progressive movement and heal its disillusionment with the Democratic Party.
>
> Over the past week, an informal coalition of non-government groups has plotted ways to make town halls increasingly uncomfortable for Republican lawmakers—a coordination that is more advanced than previously reported.

One of the main groups in this coalition is KYC/PYC. McAuliff and Stein wrote that support for KYC/PYC was "being provided from D.C.-based organizations with an eye towards expanding the echo chamber ... Still, it's difficult to dismiss both the synchronicity and glee with which these groups have operated," the *Huffington Post* writers concluded. In particular, they named the Obama-allied group, Americans United for Change, which, they wrote, "has become the de-facto organizer of the movement." (More on AUC below.) They also reported that CAP had "sent trackers to film various events" such as town hall forums. In addition, they reported that a third entity, a Democrat-oriented consulting firm called New Media Partners, had "pitched these same events to local and national reporters in search of more earned-media." (We did not find New Media Partners named in conjunction with KYC/PYC in any other reports.)

And, of course, Big Labor is involved: the SEIU and the union-affiliated Health Care for America Now (HCAN)—"two entities deeply invested in fighting Ryan's vision of Medicare reform, took the lead on field operations." They were backed by the Soros-funded MoveOn.org, AFSCME, the Social Security Campaign, and "other groups."[20]

A central question is: whence cometh the money for the gigantic Save ObamaCare campaign we are about to describe to you? Aside from pointing out the host of deep-pocketed backers listed above, no one we know of has yet traced the precise money trail. When you read how many high-powered—and high-priced—progressive political operatives are involved in this campaign, you will understand that its price tag runs into many millions of dollars. How many millions it is impossible to know at this juncture, let alone the sources of those millions. But the enormous scope of the progressive effort to save ObamaCare—probably the costliest and most unpopular expansion ever of government power—makes clear that its proponents are sparing no effort or expense to defend it.

All this comprises a major shift towards more offensive tactics. During the 2009 and 2010 sell of ObamaCare to the American public, more subtle messaging had been used. As we wrote in *Red Army*, a major coalition called the Herndon Alliance—whose sole purpose had been to soft-sell a government takeover of American health care (and which is also part of this new effort)—had helped politicians "to sell the American public on ObamaCare by crafting appealing, moderate language to sell a radical plan."[21] Now that ObamaCare is already law—though in a certain amount of legal and political jeopardy—the more aggressive KYC/PYC "will push back against what is expected to be an onslaught of ads financed by the conservative groups and targeting the health care law," wrote Michael D. Shear in the *New York Times*.[22] "Technically," explained Stephen Koff in the Cleveland *Plain Dealer*, the Protect Your Care half of KYC/PYC—which is chartered by the IRS as a 501(c)4 organization—is "all about defending" ObamaCare, and can "participate in political activity to defend the bill." But its sister organization, Know Your Care, is a 501(c)3 group whose "focus is education," Koff added.[23] So PYC is free to work with the Obama administration and members of Congress on "policy issues," especially those connected with Obama's reelection campaign. However, PYC "may not coordinate with the politicians on their elections," Koff wrote. For its part, PYC is clear about its purpose: It "will create the political and media space for elected officials, industry leaders and community advocates to champion the Affordable Care Act and hold accountable those who seek to take those benefits away by repealing or defunding the law."[24]

POWER COALITION

Clearly, the Obama administration, progressives in Congress, and progressive groups and unions are very worried. But they are also stunningly well prepared for a fight. It's all hands on deck with an army of big-name political operatives working overtime. Perhaps not intending to be so revealing, the *New York Times* account reported: "A collection of Democratic and labor operatives have left their organizations to form a pair of independent groups [KYC/PYC] with the mission of defending the health care overhaul championed by President Obama and Congressional Democrats during 2009 and 2010." In fact, this "collection" includes several individuals with close ties to the Obama administration. The number of high-powered political operatives working for KYC/PYC read more like a presidential campaign team than it does any "grassroots" operation:

- KYC/PYC's senior advisor Neera Tanden, according to her CAP bio, served as a senior adviser for health reform at the Department of Health and Human Services. She advised secretary Kathleen Sebelius and worked on Obama's White House health reform team to pass the ObamaCare bill. "In that role she developed policies around reform and worked with Congress on particular provisions of the legislation."[25]

  Tanden served as director of domestic policy for the Obama-Biden presidential campaign, where she managed all domestic policy proposals.

  Tanden is also closely connected with Secretary of State Hillary Clinton. She was policy director for Clinton's presidential campaign and was legislative director for then senator Clinton, "where she oversaw all policy in the Senate office." During her New York senatorial campaign, Tanden was Clinton's deputy campaign manager and issues director. Earlier, during the Clinton administration, Tanden served as associate director for domestic policy and as a senior policy advisor to the first lady.

  Tanden has been with CAP since its launch in 2003. She served as CAP's vice president for academic affairs and joined as its senior vice president for domestic policy.

- KYC/PYC's campaign manager is Tanya Bjork, who most recently served as director of federal affairs for Governor Jim Doyle. Bjork "managed the state's federal priorities" and served as the Doyle administration's "chief liaison with the White House, federal agencies, Congress and other governors."[26]

Bjork also served as the Wisconsin state director for the Obama campaign, regional director for EMILY's List, regional political director for the AFL-CIO, and as a senior campaign staff member for the late senator Paul Wellstone (D-MN) and former senator Russ Feingold (D-WI).[27]

- Senior advisor Paul Tewes is a partner in political consulting firm New Partners. Additionally, Tewes and his partner, Steve Hildebrand, President Obama's deputy campaign manager, operate the Washington, D.C.–based political campaign consulting firm Tewes-Hildebrand. Both are considered among Obama's top advisors.[28]

Tewes worked as coordinated campaign director in 2001–2002 at the Democratic Senatorial Campaign Committee and as its political director in 2003–2004. Eventually, he became political director of the DSCC before moving on to Obama's 2008 presidential campaign.[29] Tewes was Obama's state director for the Iowa caucuses, where Tewes and his team "built the largest grass-roots organization in history, culminating in a win that launched Obama's historic campaign." Obama later appointed him as head of the Democratic National Committee (DNC).[30]

- KYC/PYC's finance adviser is Ami Copeland, also a partner in New Partners.[31] Copeland "managed and helped build the most successful political fundraising operation in history" as deputy national finance director for Obama's presidential campaign during the primary and as senior finance adviser to the DNC.[32]

Previously, in 2001–2002, Copeland worked as a political fundraiser for the successful reelection campaign for Sen. Tom Harkin (D-IO). In 2003, Copeland raised contributions as the

Midwest regional finance director for the DSCC, after which he
was recruited by former majority leader Sen. Tom Daschle (D-SC),
as his deputy national finance director for his reelection campaign,
2003–2004, and by Sen. Bill Nelson (D-FL) as his finance director
in his successful reelection campaign, 2005–2006.[33]

- KYC/PYC's original communications director was Eddie P. Vale,
  who worked for the AFL-CIO as political communications director. Previously, in the 2008 campaign cycle, Vale served as communications director for the IE group, Progressive Media USA, and
  for John Edwards's presidential campaign in New Hampshire.[34]

  Vale told the *Boston Globe* in April 2011 that PYC did not have to
  disclose its donors. Both groups, he said, could "run television and
  radio ads in key races, as well as send out mailings and make phone
  calls to voters." At the time, an "official involved in the groups"
  told the *Globe* a combined $5 million had been raised to date.[35]

Sam Stein noted in the *Huffington Post*: "How the organizations will
structure their operations or spend their money isn't entirely clear. Officials
at the launch were coy with strategy and plans, stressing only that Know
Your Care/Protect Your Care will be informative in nature, will be active in
races and will work through the 2012 election until the major components
of the law are implemented in 2014."[36]

- In September 2011, Darden Rice moved up from communications
  director at Progress Florida for KYC/PYC to become the groups' new
  communications director. At the time, KYC/PYC were in Orlando,
  protesting "threatened cuts to Medicare, Medicaid and Social Security."[37] A well-known Florida political figure, Rice was president of the
  League of Women Voters in the St. Petersburg area, and previously
  served as national field coordinator for the Sierra Club's Cool Cities
  Campaign and as the Florida-based representative at the Sierra Club.[38]
- Jim Margolis, a senior adviser to Obama during his 2008 presidential campaign, is a KYC/PYC media consultant. Currently, Margolis not only represents Majority Leader Harry Reid (D-NV), but
  also "more Democratic senators than any other consultant in the

nation."[39] A senior partner at GMMB, a Washington-based political consulting, advertising, and communications firm, Margolis was a key strategist in Bill Clinton's 1992 presidential campaign.[40]

- David DiMartino, a partner at Blue Line Strategic Communications, is a communications adviser for the groups. He held senior communications positions in national campaign organizations, including the DSCC in 1999–2000 and for the 2003–2004 presidential primary for Sen. John Kerry (D-MA). He also served on Kerry's staff.[41]

- John Anzalone, a partner at Anzalone-Liszt Research, is KYC/PYC's pollster. In 2008, Anzalone "helped build a firm that helped elect Barack Obama as President."[42] Anzalone conducted polling during the health care and financial reform debates for the Common Purpose Project, HCAN, and Americans United for Change. He "works regularly with the DCCC, DSCC and the DGA on their candidate recruitment and independent expenditure programs."[43]

ENTER THE RADICALS

Leading political reporter Ben Smith, then at *Politico*, reported in April 2009 that the Common Purpose Project was meeting quietly every Tuesday afternoon at the Capitol Hilton, bringing together "top officials from a range of left-leaning organizations, from labor groups like Change to Win to activists like MoveOn.org, all in support of the White House's agenda." The group's membership overlapped, Smith wrote, with "a daily 8:45 a.m. call run by the Center for American Progress' and Media Matters' political arms; with the new field-oriented coalition Unity '09; and with the groups that allied to back the budget as the Campaign to Rebuild and Renew America Now."

The Common Purpose Project was founded by political consultant Erik Smith. CPP differed from other groups in one major respect: White House communications director Ellen Moran was included in its meetings, Smith reported. One of Smith's sources stated that the meetings provided a "way for the White House to manage its relationships with some of these independent groups."[44]

The innocuous-sounding official CPP description is that it is a 501(c)(4) "founded to bring together progressive leaders and organizations in an effort to collaborate on effective public policy messaging."[45] The majority of CPP's board members were connected to the 2008 Obama for America campaign.[46]

Each of these individuals is a member of the KYC/PYC advisory board. There are yet still more members to the team, and we discuss them below. First, however, we will take a look at some of the tactics progressives have employed (and will continue using) to salvage ObamaCare from the jaws of possible defeat—or, in that eventuality, to push with all of their considerable resources for an alternate single-payer health care plan.

Campaign of Aggression

While KYC/PYC was announcing its launch in Washington, D.C., on April 14, 2011, the campaign to defend ObamaCare hit the airwaves in Iowa with a commercial defending it as "a boon to small business."[47] Spokesman Eddie Vale said the groups' "five-figure television buy" was "accompanied by 'saturation'-level online ads in Des Moines [and] Ames." The ad featured a "small businessman explaining that 'there's plenty to worry about when you own a small business,' including 'paying for health insurance.' "The messaging shifted the focus to jobs creation. Vale explained that the ad "builds on our educational efforts around the Affordable Care Act and expands the case that it's not just about health care, it's also about jobs."

The following month, the PYC website compared ObamaCare to Mitt Romney's health care plan. A graphic prepared by the Center for American Progress claimed: "Romney's health care plan in Massachusetts was good policy and an important foundation for the Affordable Care Act. The key to success for both is the inclusion of an individual responsibility provision."[48]

On July 13, 2011, the day of the first official Republican debate in Manchester, Nwe Hampshire., PYC launched its first television ad on ABC local WMUR and in the Boston area, as well as online ads. Also, "visibility around town and at the debate" was accompanied by "rapid response and fact checking' on both ObamaCare and Romneycare.[49] The group ran its biggest Internet advertising to date, including a "Google blast" in Manchester and ads run on mobile phones for people on St. Anselm's college campus, where the debate was held, and via Google searches. Also, PYC did "visibilities" in Manchester and at the debate with signs proclaiming "Hands Off My Medicare," "Hands Off My Medicaid," as well as ones "thanking Mitt Romney for his health care plan." (Note that similar signs were carried by demonstrators March 26–28, 2012, outside the Supreme Court building in Washington.)

Immediately after the September 12, 2011, so-called Tea Party GOP presidential debate, PYC carried on as though it had hit the $100 million lottery. Sam Stein gave an abbreviated account of the chain of events at the *Huffington Post*:

> A bit of a startling moment happened near the end of Monday night's CNN debate when a hypothetical question was posed to Rep. Ron Paul (R-TX).
>
> "What do you tell a guy who is sick, goes into a coma and doesn't have health insurance? Who pays for his coverage? Are you saying society should just let him die?" Wolf Blitzer asked.
>
> "Yeah!" several members of the crowd yelled out.
>
> "Paul interjected to offer an explanation for how this was, more-or-less, the root choice of a free society. He added that communities and non-government institutions can fill the void that the public sector is currently playing.
>
> "We never turned anybody away from the hospital," he said of his volunteer work for churches and his career as a doctor. "We have given up on this whole concept that we might take care of ourselves, assume responsibility for ourselves . . . that's the reason the cost is so high."[50]

Eddie Vale immediately went into full propaganda mode, telling the *Los Angeles Times*, "The moment offered 'a disturbing view into the Tea Party's extreme right-wing position on health care when members of the audience clapped and cheered the idea of letting someone without health insurance die.' Even worse," Vale continued, "none of the Republican candidates on stage expressed a word of disapproval as the Tea Party audience literally clapped for blood. This was a spectacle one would have expected back in the gladiatorial combat of ancient Rome, not at a presidential debate.'"[51]

Michael Muskal, writing at the *Los Angeles Times*, provided a different version of the exchange between Blitzer and Paul, which makes clear that it was Blitzer who kept pushing until he got his *gotcha* moment. Mukasy, however, was just as guilty of skewing his own report. Right before reporting Vale's comment, Mukasy inserted: "Still, that some in the audience were willing to let people die became a symptom of the conservatives' disregard for people, at least as far as progressives are concerned."[52] This is a good example of how progressive messaging is predictably exploited by the compliant news media.

Stein reported at the *Huffington Post* that PYC had already launched a new website with a riff on *Let him die?* The LetHimDie.com website asked visitors: "Who will the Republican candidates listen to? The Tea Party or the American people? Watch our ad on the Tea Party's cheering and applauding for letting an uninsured man die."[53]

On September 14, Vale told the *Boston Globe* that PYC was expending $5,000 to test its ads that day and expected to spend between $10,000 and $15,000 for Google ads online, as well as in the early voting states of New Hampshire, Iowa, and Florida, that would run nationwide until the next presidential debate the following week. The total cost, according to Vale, would "depend on how many people click on the ads." Additionally, Vale said PYC was launching an online petition linked to the ads, "urging the Republican candidates to condemn the cheering."[54]

In opposition to the PYC campaign, in a September 16 column at *USA Today*, Katrina Trinko complained:

> As no fan of ObamaCare, I apparently want to see the streets littered with the dead bodies of the uninsured . . . Never mind that the Tea Party mob consisted of two or three loudmouthed jerks in an audience of over a thousand. [Nor is it such a remote possibility that the yellers might actually have been progressive plants.—Ed.]
>
> The disagreement between liberals and conservatives isn't about whether to save the man's life, but how to save his life. Liberals see the ideal solution as government-funded (and mandated) insurance for all, while conservatives see the best way as encouraging personal responsibility, and if that falls through, bringing together family, community, and generous donors to pay the bills.[55]

Also let us note that PYC's website, LetHimDie.com, was actually a joint project with Americans United for Change (AUFC), a group heavily involved in Obama's 2008 campaign. According to *Discover the Networks*, AUFC was founded in 2005 to "fend off" President George W. Bush's "top policy priority at the time: privatizing Social Security." AUFC later advocated for the usual socialist platform, including allowing Medicare to directly negotiate lower prices for prescription drugs and "improving access to affordable healthcare for all Americans [by means of government-controlled, socialized medicine, that is]."[56] While claiming to be a "non-partisan" organization, *DTN* wrote, AUFC's "agendas are entirely consistent with, and supportive of, those of the Democratic Party." In fact, FactCheck .org reported in October 2011 that the AUFC message "closely mirror[ed] that of the Obama White House."[57] In 2009, AUFC, with the financial support of MoveOn.org, SEIU, and AFSCME, backed an advertising campaign to support Obama's massive "stimulus" bill.[58]

AUFC's acting executive director is Tom McMahon, formerly executive director of the DNC and deputy national campaign manager for Howard Dean's 2004 presidential bid. AUFC's deputy executive director is Caren Benjamin, an aide to then House Speaker Nancy Pelosi (D-CA)[59] and a senior media specialist with the AFL-CIO in the D.C. metro area.[60]

What might AUFC have in store for 2012?[61] In a *Washington Post* account headlined "Obama offers 2012 election supporters change they can believe in—next term," AUFC's senior strategist said,

A successful campaign will heavily focus on the radical, do-nothing Republican Congress. That will resonate with people. Most [Americans] believe Obama shares their values and their concerns, and where he has failed them is his effectiveness to improve the economy.

It seems to me the case the campaign needs to make is that that failure is a consequence of the damage created by Republicans and the refusal of Congress to take the necessary steps that he proposed for the economy.[62]

The assessment comes from Robert Creamer, who heads the Strategic Consulting Group and is married to progressive Illinois Rep. Jan

Schakowsky (D-IL). Creamer himself is no newcomer to progressive activism, and illustrates how progressive think tanks and their political cohorts both draft and promote radical legislation. According to his own company bio, Creamer worked with AUFC, "where he helped coordinate the campaign to pass President Obama's landmark jobs and economic recovery legislation."[63] Cut from the left-wing theorist Saul Alinsky's cloth, around 1970, Creamer worked with Heather and Paul Booth, of the radical incubator Midwest Academy, on a project called Campaign Against Pollution. By 1977, then executive director of the Illinois Public Action Council, Creamer was among those invited to attend VISTA roundtable discussions.[64] He also served on Midwest's board of directors (1999–2000).[65] In more modern times, during summer 2007, Creamer was one of the instructors for Camp Obama, a summer training program for campaign interns and volunteers.[66]

Creamer is a "political force in his own right," political blogger John Ruberry wrote in September 2005. Creamer consulted for former Chicago Mayor Richard M. Daley and since-convicted felon Illinois governor Rod Blagojevich on prior political campaigns.[67] In 2009, Creamer was the author of a blueprint for universal health care. Creamer wrote the document while incarcerated in federal prison for five months in 2006, after signing a plea bargain on bank fraud and tax evasion charges while heading Citizen Action of Illinois.[68]

AGIT-PROP FOR THE CAMERAS

Aside from LetHimDie.com, another joint PYC-AUFC operation—this one a progressive reincarnation of old Soviet-style agit-prop—was staged on October 21, 2011, at the Wharton School of Business of the University of Pennsylvania. This incident illustrates two important dimensions of the "save ObamaCare" campaign—the use of 1960s-style radical direct action protests, and the videotaping of same for use as viral propaganda on the Internet.

First, protesters from groups including PYC, AUFC, Occupy Philly, Philadelphia AFL-CIO, Fight for Philly, SEIU PA State Council, Keystone Progress, Moveon.org, NCPSSM, Progress Now, and AFSCME demonstrated at the Philadelphia school following the cancellation of a speech there by U.S. House majority leader Rep. Eric Cantor (R-VA). According to Think Progress, a propaganda website of the Center for American Progress, Cantor was "apparently afraid of dissident audiences."[69] The *Los Angeles Times* and other news media confirmed that Cantor had cancelled a planned speech on income inequality because he feared protestors would "fill the seats," as attendance was not limited to "students and others affiliated with the school."[70]

The day before Cantor was to appear, the unofficial count of tents pitched at Occupy Philly opposite City Hall had reached 304. This did not include protesters simply "hanging out" there during the occupation's third week.[71] By that night, the University of Pennsylvania's Capitol Police had informed Representative Cantor that it was "unable to ensure that the attendance policy [for students, faculty, alumni, and other members of the UPENN community] previously agreed to could be met." So Cantor cancelled, but then approximately five hundred Occupy Philly protesters stormed the campus and, by force, entered Huntsman Hall, where Cantor was to have given his lecture. Protesters chanted "Eric Cantor, come out, come out wherever you are" and "We are the 99 percent."[72]

Think Progress actually watered down its version of the event, reporting merely that "hundreds of protesters entered the Wharton School and chanted about economic justice." A thirty-seven-second video on its website shows protesters shouting inside the hall while students on a balcony inside the building are "chanting in unison, 'Get a job! Get a job!'"[73] Recall here that the *Huffington Post*'s Michael McAuliff and Sam Stein had written in April 2011 that CAP was going to send out "trackers to film various events" at town hall forums.[74] Obviously, CAP's "film trackers" were not confining their activities to formal meetings between the citizenry and their elected representatives.

CAP is not the only group capturing GOP events on video and posting clips on YouTube, on behalf of the high-powered Protect Your Care campaign. The Ramirez Group, which describes itself as a "full-service public affairs, strategic communications and political consulting firm" located in Las Vegas, has also posted several.[75] Group principals include Andres Ramirez, who began his career as a legislative aide to Senate majority Leader Harry Reid, followed by work for Nevada governor Bob Miller in the state's

Washington, D.C. office, Ramirez served most recently as senior vice president of the progressive think tank New Democrat Network. Ramirez also serves as vice chair of the DNC's Hispanic Caucus, "where he is tasked with helping the DNC develop and implement its Hispanic engagement strategy."[76] Andres' wife, Jacqueline (Jacki) Ramirez, who manages client relationships and internal operations for the Ramirez Group, served for nearly a decade as a regional representative to Senator Reid.[77]

Marco Rauda, prior to joining the Ramirez Group, served in 2010 as the deputy political director for the Rory Reid for Governor Campaign in Nevada. Rory is Harry's son. Rauda helped organize the 2008 Nevada Democratic Caucuses on behalf of the Nevada State Democratic Party and later "oversaw successful voter registration and mobilization programs targeting Hispanics."[78]

Lastly, Warren Flood was hired by the Ramirez Group following the 2008 Nevada Democratic Caucuses, when he served as the Obama campaign's western region data director. He served also on the Obama-Biden transition team and, in January 2009, was appointed as director of information systems and technology for the Office of the Vice President. After two years, Flood left to join the DNC's National Targeting team for the 2010 election cycle. Besides his position with the Ramirezes, he is president of the political consulting firm Bright Blue Data.[79]

With regard to the Hispanic vote in the 2012 presidential election, we must mention the role of the mega-ObamaCare coalition, the Herndon Alliance, which continues to be instrumental in shaping the ObamaCare message. In December 2011, PYC and the Herndon Alliance received the results of two polls conducted on their behalf. The research was done by Anzalone Liszt Research, a firm headed by KYC/PYC board member John Anzalone. ALR had also poll-tested messaging with "encouraging results" for advocates of ObamaCare in June 2011.[80] One of the new polls showed that Hispanic voters had a "more positive impression" of ObamaCare "than the population as a whole—a fact that could help the president maintain his strong support among a voting block that backed him by a 36-point spread in 2008."[81] The second poll showed, in the research group's opinion, that "not only do Hispanic voters strongly support" ObamaCare, but they also "offer the law's allies a tremendous opportunity to increase support for the law."[82]

WHAT'S NEXT?

With major legal challenges to ObamaCare before the Supreme Court scheduled for late-March 2012, the White House launched an "aggressive campaign" to "help shape public opinion" for the health care act, according to Robert Pear at the *New York Times*.[83] The new campaign reportedly emerged after months of urging by progressives both inside and outside of Congress, to get the White House "to make a more forceful defense of the health care law." According to the *Times* report:

> White House officials summoned dozens of leaders of nonprofit organizations that strongly back the health law to help them coordinate plans for a prayer vigil, press conferences and other events outside the court when justices hear arguments for three days beginning March 26.[84]

Pear's report also mentioned the names of some of the sixty groups represented at the meeting and working with the White House: PYC, SEIU, AFSCME, HCAN, CAP, Families USA (FUSA), and the National Council of La Raza. What followed was the mapping out of a strategy to "call attention to tangible benefits of the law, like increased insurance coverage for young adults."

Five months after mid-September 2011, when the radical Occupy Wall Street movement had exploded into public consciousness and rapidly spread from New York to hundreds of other locations around the country—and with the endorsement and encouragement of the top Democrat leadership—the White House claimed with the proverbial straight face that it was "sensitive to the idea that they were encouraging demonstrations."[85] A few days later, Robert Bluey of the Heritage Foundation exposed a four-page strategy memo—specifically mentioning Families USA, Know Your Care, and HCAN—that outlined day by day the game plan developed by the White House and progressive advocacy groups for manipulating public discussion during the Supreme Court's hearing of oral arguments on ObamaCare from March 26 to March 28. Advocacy groups were told to frame the debate over two issues:

- Remind people that the law is already benefiting millions of Americans by providing health care coverage, reducing costs and providing access to healthcare coverage. This message will include the ideas that these are benefits that politicans/the Court (are) trying to take away from average Americans.
- Frame the Supreme Court oral arguments in terms of real people and real benefits that would be lost if the law were overturned. While lawyers will be talking about the individual responsibility piece of the law and the legal precedents, organizations on the ground should continue to focus on these more tangible results of the law.[86]

With a straight face of its own, the *New York Times* reported the White House denials that it was "trying to gin up support by encouraging rallies outside the Supreme Court, just a stone's throw from Congress on Capitol Hill."[87]

In truth, rallies and demonstrations were exactly what they planned—as evidenced by national media—and not only outside the Supreme Court.

FUNNY NUMBERS

"The process of finding out just what's in ObamaCare continues!" So wrote Jim Pethokoukis at the *American Enterprise* blog on March 15, 2012. Under one scenario, he wrote, "the gross costs through 2022 could be $2.1 trillion if even more businesses than expected decide not to offer health insurance and more people need government subsidized coverage."[88]

Even a writer at the left-wing msnbc.com admitted:

Figuring out the ten-year cost of the Affordable Care Act is like trying to track a constantly moving target. That's partly because the ten-year forecasting window keeps advancing each year: the new forecasting window covers the years 2012 to 2022.[89]

Those comments were elicited by a stunning revision issued by the Congressional Budget Office two days earlier, to the effect that its cost estimate of $940 billion over ten years—made at the time President Obama signed the bill in March 2010—would actually be nearly double, at $1.76 trillion.[90] How could such a shocking underestimation have occurred? Let's call it Democrat sleight of hand. Philip Klein explained at the *Washington Examiner*:

> Democrats employed many accounting tricks when they were pushing through the national health care legislation, the most egregious of which was to delay full implementation of the law until 2014, so it would appear cheaper under the CBO's standard ten-year budget window and, at least on paper, meet Obama's pledge [in September 2009] that ObamaCare would cost "around $900 billion over 10 years."[91]

Rick Moran stated it more bluntly at the *American Thinker*:

> Being wrong is not the same as lying. Obama wasn't wrong. He knew the funny numbers his administration was putting out. He knew the accounting tricks the Democrats were playing. He knew it all. And he looked the American people in the eye and lied to them.[92]

Klein reminded us that, prior to the bill's passage, critics of the CBO score[93] had predicted "that the true 10 year cost would be far higher than advertised once projections accounted for full implementation."[94]

As of this writing, no one can predict how much—if any—of ObamaCare will remain after the Supreme Court issues its ruling, probably in this summer, on the legal challenges to the law. There is also the prospect that Congress might respond with new legislation if the justices invalidate only parts of the law. With so many variables, we cannot foresee the precise course of events. But one thing is certain. If progressives in Congress have the upper hand after 2012, and Barack Obama is reelected, single-payer health care will have become America's burden.

9

ELECTIONS: STEALING THE FUTURE

A CAMPAIGN IS UNDER way to change the very nature of American presidential elections. In true progressive fashion, its organizers have been working since 2006 to accomplish their goal—to borrow a Fabian Socialist expression—by *stealth*. Under the rubric of a "National Popular Vote," this plan would allow the fourteen most populous American states, mostly majority-Democrat, to determine the outcome of future presidential elections. The voters of the thirty-six less populous states would then effectively be disenfranchised. If successful, this stealth campaign would give Americans less democracy, all in the name of giving us more.

Naturally, most Americans have no concept whatsoever of the existence, import, objectives, financiers, or progress to date of this dangerously anti-democratic initiative. And though its alarming advance would not be in time to influence the result in November 2012 (although we will document other issues for this upcoming election), under a second Obama term its chances for success would be enormously increased. In that case, NPV would forever change the way Americans elect our president, and the American political landscape would be permanently altered in favor of the left.

Aside from this looming danger, though not immediate, of a "National Popular Vote," we discuss here two threats that are very imminent: a foreign-headquartered company that has already been given contracts to conduct "on-line voting" in some nine hundred U.S. jurisdictions, including for overseas U.S. military personnel; and a mysterious ballot initiative, approved already in all fifty states, to put a third (presumably conservative) candidate on the ballot for November 2012, thus splitting the anti-Obama vote.

"POPULAR VOTE" ACTUALLY VOTER FRAUD

Barry F. Fadem is president of the National Popular Vote, based in California. In June 2008, Fadem disingenuously asked, "Why are all the other elections in this country based on the popular vote except for the most important one, the presidency?"[1]

Although only Americans who are up on their civics lessons would know the answer, there is a very good one. The vote for president is the only one in which all Americans vote for a national leader (as well as his or her possible successor, the vice president). In framing the U.S. Constitution, the Founding Fathers displayed their characteristic wisdom and subtlety in firmly rejecting a purely popular vote to elect the president, in order to balance the power of the larger states against the smaller. The Electoral College was fashioned as a compromise between an election of the president by direct popular vote and election by Congress.[2]

William C. Kimberling, deputy director of the Federal Elections Commission, explained in a 1992 paper why a direct popular vote had been rejected by the Founders:

> Direct election was rejected not because the Framers of the Constitution doubted public intelligence but rather because they feared that without sufficient information about candidates from outside their State, people would naturally vote for a "favorite son" from their own State or region. At worst, no president would emerge with a popular majority sufficient to govern the whole country. At best, *the choice of president would always be decided by the largest, most populous States, with little regard for the smaller ones.*[3] [Emphasis added]

The same problem would apply to future presidential elections should a national popular vote ever be enacted. For example, in a hypothetical 2012 election scenario, reaching 270 of a possible 538 electoral votes would only require Barack Obama to retake the majority of the states he won in 2008. It is possible that only fourteen states, those with the largest populations, would decide the presidency for voters in all fifty states.[4]

NPV wants to overturn this compromise in the U.S. Constitution and substitute what they are selling as a logical idea for how a president should be elected—and all with virtually no public knowledge, discussion or debate of what is at stake, let alone a Constitutional amendment. As "Jacquerie" at *Gulag Bound* observed in October 2011:

> This sneaky scheme to upend Constitutional rights and protections of all states and their residents in selecting the nation's leader is underway as an explicit attempt to defeat the careful Constitutional amendment process with *no* public knowledge, *no* voter input, *no* public referendums and *no* input from states which object to this measure. All NPVC takes is a portion of current state houses to make it law for all of *us*—always!
>
> [...]
>
> Akin to ObamaCare, if this National Popular Vote Compact is passed—no matter how wrong and corrupt—it would take massive funding and endless delays to drag through the courts in hopes of any reversal.[5]

While the stated purpose of Fadem's group is "to implement a nationwide popular election of the president of the United States,"[6] what NPV actually aims to pull off is what "Jacquerie" identified as the "ultimate vote fraud."[7] The plan is ingeniously and "intentionally complicated [in order] to keep it obscure until it's too late to stop it."[8]

Innocuously enough, National Popular Vote, or NPV, operates as a 501(c)(4) tax-exempt nonprofit organization committed to promoting social welfare. While the organization's earnings must go toward charitable, education, or recreational purposes, it can also "lobby, campaign, and otherwise participate in elections so long as the activities are in line with the organization's purpose and are not the primary activity for the organization."[9]

ELECTIONS: STEALING THE FUTURE

Who's Behind NPV?

The organization's chairman and alleged major funder is Dr. John R. Koza. He was the cofounder, chairman, and CEO of Scientific Games Inc., where he coinvented the rub-off instant lottery ticket used by state lotteries. In the 1980s, Koza and attorney Barry Fadem promoted the lotteries "by various states through the citizen-initiative process and state legislative action." Fadem "specializes in all aspects of campaign and election law, and provides expert consultation in the area of initiatives and referendums."[10]

In 2006 Koza and Fadem coauthored the book *Every Vote Equal: A State-Based Plan for Electing the President by National Popular Vote* with Mark Grueskin, Michael S. Mandell, Robert Richie, and Joseph F. Zimmerman. Koza has "reportedly pledged $12 million" to NPV, previously gave "tens of thousands of dollars to various Democratic Party committees and liberal candidates; he was an Al Gore elector in 2000," according to Tara Ross and Trent England in the *Weekly Standard*.[11]

Another NPV financier is Tom Golisano, founder and chairman of Paychex, the nation's second largest payroll and human resource company. Golisano cofounded the Independence Party of New York in 1994 and ran as the party's gubernatorial candidate. While Golisano has "also pledged millions to NPV," he is a registered Republican, "even though he supported John Kerry and gave a cool $1 million to the Democratic National Convention in 2008," Ross and England wrote in 2011.

NPV's secretary, Chris Pearson, served in the Vermont House of Representatives in 2006. Prior to that, Pearson was director of the Presidential Election Reform program at FairVote (formerly the Center for Voting and Democracy). Unsurprisingly, NPV is partnered with FairVote, which has received funding from George Soros' Open Society Foundations. One of Soros's sons, Jonathan Soros, is a major FairVote supporter.[12]

Robert Richie has been executive director of FairVote since he cofounded it in 1992.[13] Richie is a member of the civil society committee of the George Soros–led Bretton Woods Committee, which seeks to literally remake the world economy.[14] FairVote supports "universal voter registration" and a "national popular vote" for president, with "instant runoff voting for single-winner offices," and a "more transparent and accountable election

161

administration."[15] In an August 2004 article archived on the FairVote web-site, the organization also stated that its Democracy USA agenda called for the abolition of the Electoral College.[16] In fact, in a December 15, 2008, *Wall Street Journal* opinion piece, Jonathan Soros, a son of George Soros, wrote that it was time to junk the Electoral College.[17]

Who else supports NPV? Again, several organizations, some purpose-fully and some unwittingly. Organizational support comes "almost exclu-sively from left wing groups" such as the American Civil Liberties Union, the League of Women Voters, and the Soros-funded Common Cause and the Demos group (which we describe in detail elsewhere in this book for its heavy influence in framing the policies of Obama and the progressives in Congress). But NPV's army of lobbyists have also been working with the Republican National Committee, the American Legislative Exchange Council, and "conservative think tanks such as the Heartland Institute and the Heritage Foundation," as Ross and England reported in August 2011.[18]

Formal endorsers of the FairVote plan as of July 2010 included the NAACP, the National Institute for Latino Policy, National Latino Congreso, Public Citizen, Sierra Club, and U.S. Public Interest Research Group (PIRG).[19]

NPV MARCHES FORWARD

In 2007, Maryland became the first state to approve a "national popular vote" compact. As a result, in a theoretical winner-take-all contest, Maryland would allocate all of its ten electoral votes to the candidate who won the most votes nationally—even if the same candidate did not win the most votes in Maryland itself.[20]

By March 2012, eight states—California, Hawaii, Illinois, Maryland, Massachusetts, New Jersey, Vermont, Washington, plus the District of Columbia—had enacted the "national popular vote" into law. Two other states, Colorado and Rhode Island, had passed it in both houses but it had not been enacted. Ten more states had passed it in one house, and ten oth-ers had passed it in a committee. Eleven states had held hearings on it, and nine more states had introduced bills.[21]

"These nine states have provided this dangerous and unconstitutional movement 132 of the 270 electoral votes required to win the presidency," observed a South Carolina blogger in August 2011. "Once this group has 270 electoral votes, the Electoral College will be rendered moot, the Constitution will be undermined and the U.S. president will be elected based on popular vote."[22]

There is, however, one hitch in the NPV plan: in order for a "national popular vote" to predominate, the full 270 electoral votes must be based on identical legislation (the "interstate compact") passed by each state. A candidate would still need 270 electoral votes to win the presidency.

WHAT IS THE "INTERSTATE COMPACT"?

Its advocates claim that the "national popular vote" movement is a direct result of the 2000 presidential election. George W. Bush won the Electoral College vote and Al Gore won the popular vote. The progressive left was so infuriated that it went in search of a solution to ensure such a circumstance could not happen again.

It is also claimed that the National Public Vote Compact originated when two East Indian–American law professors, brothers Akhil Reed Amar and Vikram David Amar, responded to a March 2001 proposal[23] by Robert W. Bennett of Northwestern University Law School for a direct popular election of the president without amending the Constitution.[24] In their article, the Amar brothers wrote:

> Imagine this: Americans could pick the President by direct national election, in 2004 and beyond, without formally amending our Constitution.
>
> A small number of key states—eleven, to be precise—would suffice to put a direct election system into effect. Alternatively, an even smaller number of key persons—four, to be exact—could approximate the same result, with a little help from their friends." [The four "key persons" would be the two presidential and two vice presidential candidates, who would commit themselves beforehand to winners-take-all results.]
>
> If the eleven biggest states were to pass our law, an odd theoretical possibility would arise: A candidate could win the presidency, by

winning the national popular vote, even if he or she lost in every one of these big states! (Imagine a scenario where the candidate narrowly loses in each of these states, but wins big most other places.) Should this theoretical possibility deter big states from passing our law?

The Amar brothers noted some flaws in their proposal—one of which hinged on cooperating versus non-cooperating states:

> These questions suggest an even more mind-boggling prospect: our national-vote system need not piggyback on the laws and machinery of non-cooperating states at all! Let these non-cooperating states hold their own elections, but so long as they amount to less than 270 electors, these elections would be sideshows. The cooperating states could define their own rules for a uniform "National Presidential Vote" system.

They then suggested they were just being creative while pursuing a "thought experiment":

> Some will doubtless dismiss all this as mere academic daydreaming, but the daydreams are useful in illustrating how much constitutional creativity is possible within the existing constitutional framework, short of formal amendment.

It appears that Akhil Amar had been working out his national direct vote theories in articles he wrote well before Election 2000. Professor Bennett cited two separate articles Amar wrote in 1994 and 1995.[25]

> Amar had suggested that a majority of American voters could now require Congress to convene a constitutional convention by submitting a petition to that effect "and that an amendment could be lawfully ratified by a simple majority of the American electorate."[26]

Bennett countered that Amar's argument, though skillful, could not be supported by the Constitution. He wrote:

But there is not a word in the Constitution that would support such a procedure. As suggested in the text, moreover, such a procedure is thoroughly at odds with the most fundamental assumptions of our constitutional order, including importantly the role of the states. For instance, qualification to vote in federal elections was originally and remains to a degree within the discretion of the states.

Bennett included Amendment XVII of the Constitution, "so that there are not even uniform national qualifications that would seem necessary to give coherence to the notion of a 'simple' national majority."

In 2000, Akhil Amar noted that just because "the dreaded specter of a clear popular loser becoming the Electoral College winner" had not happened yet, it did not mean "we should wait to fix the system."[27]

Three years prior, in 1997, Amar had testified before a House subcommittee studying the issue of Electoral College reform. Amar told the subcommittee:

A car with a defective airbag might seem to run quite well until there's a collision . . . If "we the people" would want to amend the Constitution after the "loser president" materializes—and I tend to think we would—why are we now just waiting for the inevitable accident to happen?[28]

Amar's concern that the Electoral College would be responsible should the American voters elect a "loser president" is almost laughable in light of the presidency of Barack Obama.[29] Amar also told Congress the "thought of having a president who does not truly represent the people's choice is disturbing." In his opinion, the Electoral College had become "a constitutional accident waiting to happen."[30] Echoing proponents of critical race theory— such as Obama's Harvard Law School professor, Derrick A. Bell—Amar claimed that the Electoral College had only been created to protect slavery.[31] In fact, a law school roommate of Amar's at Yale (1982–83), Michael Stokes Paulsen, wrote in a critical 1997 review of Amar's *The Constitution and Criminal Procedure: First Principles*, that Amar "explicitly embraces critical race theory." Paulsen quotes Amar as saying in 2000:

Without the Electoral College, Northern states that let free blacks vote would have had more votes and more power, and a state wanting to elect a particular candidate could have doubled its clout instantly simply by extending voting rights to women.

Justification for the Electoral College is rooted "in racism and sexism," noting no other political bodies (whether foreign nations or our own states and cities) think enough of the Electoral College system to use it for their elections.[32]

Amar also told New Left activist Todd Gitlin, "There are so many equality problems in our election systems."[33]

In October 2000, Amar came up with a new rationalization for doing away with the Electoral College—it was old-school:

We have the Electoral College for reasons that made sense 200 years ago. The framers of the Constitution were afraid that people across a very broad continent wouldn't have enough knowledge about candidates. That doesn't apply now that we have national media.[34]

For Amar to assert that our legacy news media will keep the voting public sufficiently informed is also almost laughable. Nothing could be further from the truth.

The Amar brothers are a real American success story. Their parents, both physicians, came to the United States in the 1950s to do their residencies.[35] Akhil Reed Amar, a professor of law at Yale University, graduated summa cum laude from Yale in 1980, with a double major in economics and history, received his law degree there in 1984, and served as editor of the *Yale Law Journal*. He clerked for then judge Stephen Breyer.[36] It was noted in 2000 that he would have been listed among the 100 most influential lawyers in America but that he had never taken the bar exam.[37] Akhil's brother, Vikram David Amar, is now a professor of law at the University of California–Davis, and writes in the public law fields, particularly Constitutional law, civil procedure, and remedies. He is a 1988 graduate of the Yale Law School and clerked for Justice Harry Blackmun.[38]

Akhil is considered a liberal Democrat.[39] He gained his first notice in 1993 when he and several other scholars submitted an amicus brief in the Paula Jones sexual harassment case on behalf of President Bill Clinton. In September 1996, Amar was a leading witness for Senate Democrats on the Judiciary subcommittee on the Constitution, Federalism and Property Rights on the issue of "The Indictability of Sitting Presidents."[40] Amar defended Clinton against impeachment in testimony, in writings, and on television, arguing that the Constitution provided a sitting president with immunity from ordinary state or federal criminal prosecution. However, immediately upon a president leaving office, he would be subject to ordinary prosecution.[41]

Commented conservative columnist Ann Coulter at the time:

> The law professor contingent of the Rainbow Coalition have recently repainted their placards "Law Professors Against Paula Jones" to "Law Professors Against Impeachment."
>
> [Amar and one of Obama's Harvard Law School mentors and advisers, Lawrence Tribe, had an] "infinite capacity to interpret the Constitution in a manner that is constantly most convenient for . . . any Democratic President."[42]

Following the O. J. Simpson trial, the Amar brothers refused to blame the jurors for the trial's outcome and, in fact, wanted to empower jurors even more. They argued that jurors need to feel a sense of duty by giving them "more responsibility and independence in determining verdicts." For example, juries could be allowed to take notes and receive reasonable pay for jury duty. Lawyers could be restricted in the number of peremptory challenges allowed in *voir dire*. Trials ending in non-unanimous verdicts could be decided by "majority rule." It was said they believed that "freeing the process of justice from overly rigid rules could produce more faith and trust in the legal system, a primary goal of strengthening democracy."[43]

The Amar brothers had begun to form their concept of what voter rights should be several years before their 2001 paper on a national popular vote. In 1996, they wrote in *Policy Review*:

The founders of our nation understood that no idea was more central to our Bill of Rights—indeed, to government of the people, by the people, and for the people—than the citizen jury. It was cherished not only as a bulwark against tyranny but also as an essential means of educating Americans in the habits and duties of citizenship. . . .

Once we see how juries serve as major avenues for popular education and political participation, the connections early American observers drew between jury service and other means of political participation—especially voting—make more sense.[44]

In the same article, the brothers continued to lay the groundwork by equating jury duty with voting—and, further, with voters being the same as legislators:

We have come to think of voting as the quintessential act of democratic participation. Historically, the role of the people in serving on juries was often likened to the role of voters selecting legislative bodies, and even to the role of legislators themselves.

Taking their argument one step further, they claimed the Supreme Court had "reinforced the linkage of jury service and voting as part of a 'package' of political rights."[45]

Step back another decade, to 1987, and we find Akhil Amar proposing what amounts to the surrender of states' rights, in a nationalist "compact theory." In his article for the *Yale Law Journal*, "Of Sovereignty and Federalism," Amar asserts that "during the process of ratification of the Constitution, 'previously separate state Peoples agreed to *consolidate* themselves into a single continental people.'" Amar's "variant would grant that the compact theory is an accurate description of the United States up until 1789, when the United States became a federal republic."[46]

The flaws in Amar's "compact theory" were explained by Michael Lind, writing in the Winter 2002 *Wilson Quarterly*:

The most interesting part of Amar's theory—the notion that previously distinct state peoples fused during 1787–88 to become a single national people—is contradicted by Madison's statement in *The Federalist* 39 that the federal constitution would be ratified "by the people not as individuals composing one entire nation, but as composing the distinct and independent States to which they respectively belong."[47]

Lind's reference to James Madison's Essay 39 in *The Federalist Papers* is to what scholars esteem as the single most important exposition of the U.S. Constitution. For the layman, a summary and analysis of the essay explains its intent as being to "determine whether or not the framers established a republican form of government. . . . Since the term 'republic' is loosely used, we must look to the theoretical principles of republicanism as they have been defined." Herein we find the perfect Constitutional argument against the use of the interstate compacts for a National Popular Vote to elect a U.S. president.

A republican form of government is one which derives its powers either directly or indirectly from the people and is administered by persons who hold public office for a limited period of time or during good behavior. No government can be called republican that derives its power from a few people or from a favored and wealthy class.[48]

It logically follows that a government that calls itself a republic cannot allow a minority of the states—even if they have larger populations and are more heavily weighted in electoral votes—to use said power to determine the presidency and the future of the United States for all its citizens. (The Amars and others cite as their authority Article II of the Constitution: "Each State shall appoint, in such Manner as the Legislature thereof may direct, a Number of Electors, equal to the whole Number of Senators and Representatives to which the State may be entitled in the Congress. . . .")

Samuel H. Beer, Eaton Professor of the Science of Government Emeritus at Harvard University, amplified on Lind's article by referring to Madison's *Federalist* 46. The issue is the problem of federal-state conflict.

Madison, he wrote, approved of "the rivalry of the two levels [of government] as an example of checks and balances," which he

169

identified as the "common superior"—"the 'great body of citizens of the United States,' of whom 'the federal and state governments are in fact but different agents and trustees' and who, if there were federal-state conflicts, would 'in every case' decide the outcome." Madison concluded, Beer wrote, "that 'the ultimate authority, wherever the derivative may be found, resides in the people alone.'"[49]

Again, we have an argument against the "national popular vote." The "ultimate authority" is all of the people, all of the states, not just a select group of them.

As a South Carolina blogger put it:

> Our founding fathers understood that pure Democracy (majority/mob rules) can lead to the curtailing or elimination of liberty for the minority or stated another way; pure Democracy leads to tyranny of the majority. 50%+1 of the population can impose their will on the remaining 50%-1 of the population. History has shown us that this can lead to, among other things, dictatorships, totalitarianism, discrimination and slavery.[50]

WILL 2012 ELECTIONS BE HACKED?

How future Americans will elect future presidents is only one of several serious concerns for voters.

A more present danger is the scandalous fact that a foreign-based company—Scytl—is implementing or taking over hundreds of new online U.S. voting systems. Scytl has previously faced questions about the security of its electronic voting technologies, which are now set to be deployed in nine hundred U.S. jurisdictions. The firm already provides balloting for overseas U.S. military and civilian voting in nine states, and handles elections technologies in several districts. Concerns have also been raised about Scytl's ties to the Spanish government and to international venture capital firms. Scytl's official press release announcing its acquisition noted that Scytl is a portfolio company of leading international venture capital funds Nauta Capital, Balderton Capital, and Spinnaker SCR.[51] On January 11, 2012, Beverly

Harris of blackboxvoting.org reported that the Barcelona-based U.S. election results reporting firm Scytl had acquired 100 percent of SOE Software, the leading software provider of election management solutions in the United States. SOE Software operates under the name ClarityElections.com.

Harris sounded the alarm that results reporting will now be redirected to Scytl's centralized privately held server, which is "not just USA-based, but global."

"Because most US jurisdictions require posting evidence of results from each voting machine at the precinct, public citizens can organize to examine these results to compare with SOE results," Harris continued. Black Box Voting "spearheaded a national citizen action to videotape / photograph these poll tapes in 2008.... With the merger of SOE and Scytl, that won't work.

"With SCYTL internet voting, there will be no ballots. No physical evidence. No chain of custody. No way for the public to authenticate who actually cast the votes, chain of custody, or the count."[52]

By purchasing SOE Software, Scytl has only increased its involvement in the U.S. electoral process, according to MarketWatch.com:

The integration of these two software companies creates the industry leader in the election software market with a full range of solutions covering from Internet voting to election night reporting and online pollworker training, and a strong market presence worldwide.[53]

In May 2009, Scytl had formally registered with the U.S. Election Assistance Commission (AEC) as the first Internet voting manufacturer in the U.S. under the EAC Voting System Testing and Certification Program.[54] Also in November of that year, Scytl entered into an agreement with another firm, Hart InterCivic, to jointly market a flexible and secure electronic pollbook purportedly to allow U.S. election officials and poll workers to easily manage the electoral roll on Election Day in an efficient and convenient manner.[55]

Scytl's ePollBook had already replaced the paper precinct roster in Washington, D.C., During the November 2010 midterm elections, Scytl successfully carried out electoral modernization projects in fourteen states. The company boasted that a "great variety" of Scytl's technologies were involved in these projects, including an online platform for the delivery of blank ballots to overseas voters, an Internet voting platform and e-pollbook software to manage the electoral roll at the polling stations.[56] The states that used Scytl's technologies during the midterms were New York, Texas, Washington, California, Florida, Alabama, Missouri, Indiana, Kansas, Mississippi, New Mexico, Nebraska, West Virginia, and Washington, D.C.

At least as early as 2008, serious doubts were already being cast upon Scytl's systems. At that time, Project Vote noted that the Florida Department of State commissioned a review of Scytl's remote voting software and concluded, in part:

- The system is vulnerable to attack from insiders.
- In a worst-case scenario, the software could lead to
  1. voters being unable to cast votes;
  2. an election that does not accurately reflect the will of the voters; and
  3. possible disclosure of confidential information, such as the votes cast by individual voters.
- The system may be subject to attacks that could compromise the integrity of the votes cast.

In April 2010, Voter Action, an advocacy group promoting elections integrity in the U.S., sent a lengthy complaint to the U.S. Election Assistance Commission charging that the integration of Scytl systems "raises national security concerns."[57] Voter Action charged that

Foreign governments may also seek to undermine the national security interests of the United States, either directly or through other organizations.

The Voter Action document notes that Scytl was founded in 2001 as a spin-off from a research group at the Universitat Autonoma de Barcelona, which was partially funded by the Spanish government's Ministry of Science and Technology. Scytl's headquarters are in Barcelona, with offices in Washington, D.C.; Singapore; Bratislava; and Athens. And the company provides voter services worldwide, including in France, Norway, Spain, India, the United Arab Emirates, Austria, Australia, Britain, Mexico, Switzerland, the Philippines, and Finland.

Just prior to the November 2010 midterm elections, however, the new Scytl electronic voting system in Washington, D.C., was hacked. The D.C. Board of Elections & Ethics, as a program security trial, reportedly had encouraged outside parties to hack and find flaws in its new online balloting system. A group of University of Michigan students then hacked into the site and commanded it to play the University of Michigan fight song upon casting a vote.[58]

Paul Stenbjorn was the U.S. elections officer who had been deployed in the voting districts that partnered with Scytl during the 2010 midterm elections, and Stenbjorn was directly involved in testing the Scytl system that was hacked. He was executive director of the Board of Elections and Ethics, the independent agency of the district government responsible for the administration of elections, ballot access and voter registration, and he also served as information services manager for the Virginia State Board of Elections.[59]

After the Michigan students infiltrated the system, Stenbjorn told the *Washington Post*: "The integrity of the system had been violated." Stenbjorn said that because of the hack, a portion of the Internet voting pilot was being temporarily scrapped. He told the *Post* the security hole that allowed the playing of the fight song had been identified, but it raised deeper concerns about the system's vulnerabilities. "We've closed the hole they opened, but we want to put it though more robust testing," he said. "I don't want there to be any doubt . . . This is an abundance-of-caution sort of thing."[60]

After the hack, Stenjborn's ethics board decided to relaunch the Internet program under a download-only format, allowing users to access ballots but forcing them to fax or mail them rather than cast a vote online. Still, his D.C. elections board was hailed by the Minority Media and Telecom Council as "[leading] the nation in attempting to overcome the security obstacles and offer e-voting."[61] While on the elections board, Stenjborn had told the Council that e-voting "is many, many years away, more than a decade, possibly more than a generation away."

That, of course, is simply not true. Nor is it true that Scytl can guarantee hacker-free election results.

Meanwhile, after the 2010 elections, Stenbjorn retired from his government position and went to work for Scytl.[62]

WILL THE PRESIDENTIAL ELECTION BE HIJACKED?

Hacking—akin to past election frauds "where the dead cast their votes"—may not be the worst that can happen in November 2012. A mysteriously funded, highly organized effort to secure a place on the 2012 presidential election ballot for a third-party candidate has ties to President Obama and top Democrats.

A group calling itself Americans Elect, or AE, seems designed to appear like a massive, grassroots effort involving millions of citizens acting to draft a third party-candidate. However, the organization's internal voting process has been called into question and there also are concerns AE's by-laws may allow the group's own board members to bypass votes and nominate their own candidate.

AE describes itself as "a non-partisan, non-profit organization founded by Americans from across the political spectrum, who are worried that our nation's deep political divisions keep big problems from being solved."[63] AE sought to hold its own nominating convention on the Internet this June to select an independent presidential and vice-presidential candidate. While it is unclear whether AE will ultimately run an independent candidate in November's election, the organization warrants close observation as it can be called upon in the future to nominate a so-called independent with the intent on splitting the GOP vote. AE is also a case study in how Obama's crafty progressive backers deploy all sorts of electoral schemes to ensure victory at the ballots.

AE reportedly has raised more than $22 million so far and already has been certified to be placed on the ballot in every state in the U.S.[64] To get onto state ballots, AE evidenced mass organizing skills, claiming it collected over two million signatures nationwide in its effort to get on state ballots. Two of AE's board members, Kellen Arno and Michael Arno, were paid by the group for helping to run the massive signature-gathering drive via their firm, Arno Political Consultants.[65]

Arno's firm, APC, has reportedly previously been accused of both forging and fraudulently collecting signatures. In 2004, APC was accused of forging signatures on a petition to legalize slot machines in Miami-Dade and Broward counties.[66] The next year, Boston's Fox 25 News ran a feature interviewing paid signature collectors hired by APC through subcontractors. The interview subjects said they were trained on how to trick people into signing a petition using fraud, including by switching the actual petition text after each signature was collected.[67] In 2007, APC reportedly hired JSM, Inc., which in turn hired independent contractors, who gave snacks and food to homeless people in exchange for signing petitions and registering to vote.[68] Then in 2009, APC gathered signatures to put the Ohio Casino Initiative on the November 3, 2009, ballot, but a subsequent review reportedly found the overall validity of the signatures was certified at just under 51 percent.[69]

Americans Elect, meanwhile, reportedly had earlier been associated with another group that sought an independent candidate. That organization, calling itself Unity08, eventually suspended operations citing organizing and fund-raising issues.[70] Unity08 said it did not back any particular candidate, but two of its founders launched their own national effort to draft New York City mayor Michael Bloomberg to run for president. The *Irregular Times* documented how AE and Unity08 shared the same Washington, D.C., address. Previously, Unity08 had shared an address with the Draft Bloomberg Committee. *Irregular Times* also found that the founders of Unity08 "registered the domain name draftmichaelbloomberg.com in 2007 at a time when Unity08 was insisting that it had no candidates in mind."[71]

AE's funding has been called into question. In late 2010, AE changed its tax status from a tax-exempt group to what is known as a 501(c)(4), or social-welfare organization, which is not required to show its donor list. *Capital Weekly* reported that prior to the change, in the second and third quarters of 2010, AE's more than $1.5 million in funding came from one person—venture capitalist, Unity08 activist and Obama donor Peter Ackerman. Ackerman reportedly gave AE a total of at least $5 million in seed money.[72] Many of AE's other donors are unknown.

AE officials have defended their secretive donor collection practices. "We have to be able to raise significant amounts of money to be able to take on the status quo," Kahlil Byrd, AE's chief executive officer, told *Mother Jones* last November. Byrd said that if his group would be compelled to disclose its donors, there would be "a chilling effect . . . on people's willingness to participate in this process."[73]

Democracy 21 and the Campaign Legal Center, two campaign finance watchdogs, requested in September the IRS investigate Americans Elect, charging it may be violating nonprofit status by function like a political party. But AE's finances are not the only source of controversy.

Mother Jones reported that AE's Internet voting system has been called into question. Pamela Smith, president of VerifiedVoting.org, a voters' advocacy group, argued AE's reliance on Internet voting is insecure and difficult to audit. "If you allow it to be used in public elections without assurance that the results are verifiably accurate, that is an extraordinary and unnecessary risk to democracy," Smith says.

Regardless of any improper voting results, there are also concerns that current guidelines would allow AE to anoint its own candidate. *Salon* reporter Justin Elliott noted that candidates chosen by voters must be approved by a Candidate Certification Committee, which according to the group's bylaws consists of AE's board members.[74] According to the by-laws obtained by *Salon*, this committee will need to certify a "balanced ticket obligation" consisting of candidates who are "responsive to the vast majority of citizens while remaining independent of special interests and the partisan interests of either major political party." AE official Darry Sragow also told Elliot that his group's guidelines are subject to change, and went on to defend AE's board:

> While we don't mean to put the board in the company of the Found-ing Fathers, we'd point out that nobody picked the Founding Fathers, either. They took it upon themselves to turn a popular dream into a shared reality. And they, too, had debates over how much control should be centralized. They knew that too much power in the hands of too few isn't real democracy, but that power too diffuse is anarchy.

AE's board includes multiple ties to Obama, but some Republicans also grace the committee, for example former John McCain aide Mark McKinnon, former New Jersey governor Christine Todd Whitman, Larry Diamond of the

Hoover Institute, and former director of national intelligence Dennis Blair. Besides Peter Ackerman, an Obama donor who gave money to help start AE, the advisory board includes Lawrence Lessig, an Obama technology adviser.[75] Lessig has been mentioned as a future candidate to head the Federal Communications Commission. He is an activist for reduced legal restrictions on copyright material and advised Obama's 2008 presidential campaign.

AE's CEO, Kahlil Byrd, has drawn scrutiny from conservatives because he formerly served as Massachusetts governor Deval Patrick's communications director. Patrick's chief strategist was top Obama strategist David Axelrod.[76] AE board member W. Bowman Cutter is senior adviser to the Podesta Group lobbying and public relations firm, which was founded by John Podesta, who directed Obama's transition into the White House in 2008. Podesta is director of the Center for American Progress, the most important progressive think tank helping to craft White House policy. AE board members Kellen Arno and Michael Arno, noted earlier, are tied to John Podesta. Also on the board is Will Marshall of the Progressive Policy Institute.

AE has ties to Hillary Clinton supporters as well. Lynn Forester de Rothschild, who is a prominent Hillary backer, is on the board, as is Doug Schoen, a former pollster and adviser to Bill Clinton. Schoen recently was in the news after he teamed up with Jimmy Carter's former aide Patrick Caddell to publish an editorial in the *Wall Street Journal*, entitled "The Hillary Moment," in which they called for Clinton to throw her hat into the ring for the presidency.[77] The two wrote another piece at *Politico* calling for Democratic voters nationally—particularly in New Hampshire—to organize a write-in campaign for Clinton.[78]

We conclude by noting that Barack Obama, and the Progressive movement in general, have long specialized in manipulation of the democratic process. Even before his political career, as a Saul Alinsky–style "community organizer" in Chicago, Obama worked closely with groups such as Project Vote and ACORN, which not only focused on voter registration, but was repeatedly found guilty of voter fraud. It is no coincidence that the "progressive tsunami" has brought with it a host of threats to the integrity of the American electoral process. The threat of the "National Popular Vote" may be off in the future, but others, as we have described here, are upon us now, as the Manchurian President battles for his second term.

NOTES

Chapter One: U.S. Armed Forces to Fight "Injustice," Poverty, and "Global Warming"

1. Lawrence Korb, Miriam Pemberton, "A Report of the Task Force on a Unified Security Budget for the United States," Institute for Policy Studies, June 30, 2011.

2. Michael Scherer, "Inside Obama's Idea Factory in Washington," *Time* magazine, November 21, 2008, http://www.time.com/time/politics/article /0,8599,1861305,00.html.

3. Ibid.

4. "Russia and US to Dispose of Tonnes of Surplus Plutonium," *BBC News*, April 13, 2010, http://news.bbc.co.uk/2/hi/8618066.stm.

5. Thomas Omestad, "Nuclear Weapons for All? The Risks of a New Scramble for the Bomb," *US News and World Report*, January 15, 2009, http://www.usnews.com/news/world/articles/2009/01/15 /nuclear-weapons-for-all-the-risks-of-a-new-scramble-for-the-bomb.

6. Charles J. Moxley Jr., "Obama's Nuclear Posture Review: An Ambitious Program for Nuclear Arms Control but a Retreat from the Objective of Nuclear Disarmament," *Fordham International Law Journal* 34, no. 4 (2011), http://ir.lawnet.fordham.edu/cgi/viewcontent .cgi?article=2292&context=ilj.

7. John Feffer, Miriam Pemberton, "The Green Dividend," Institute for Policy Studies report, September 30, 2010, http://www.ips-dc.org/reports /greendividend.

8. "Fact Sheet: U.S. Global Development Policy," The White House Office of the Press Secretary, September 22, 2010. Available at www.whitehouse.gov /the-press-office/2010/09/22/fact-sheet-usglobal-development-policy.

9. Michael Werz, Laura Conley, "Climate Change, Migration, and Conflict: Addressing Complex Crisis Scenarios in the 21st Century," Center for American Progress report, January 2012, http://www.americanprogress .org/issues/2012/01/pdf/climate_migration.pdf.

10. Kim Chipman, "Agencies Urged to Plan for 'Inevitable Effects' of Warming in U.S. Report," Bloomberg News, October 14, 2010, http://www .bloomberg.com/news/2010-10-14/agencies-urged-to-plan-for-inevitable-effects-of-warming-in-u-s-report.html.

11. The White House, "National Security Strategy" (2010), available at, http://www.whitehouse.gov/sites/default/files/rss_viewer/national_ security_strategy.pdf. See also U.S. Department of Defense, "National Security Strategy," Quadrennial Defense Review, 2010, available at http:// www.defense.gov/qdr/. Also the United States Department of State, "Leading Through Civilian Power: The First Quadrennial Diplomacy and Development Review" (2010), available at http://www.state.gov/s/dmr /qddr/. And The White House Office of the Press Secretary, "Remarks by the President to the United Nations General Assembly," press release, September 23, 2010, available at http://www.whitehouse.gov/thepress-office/2010/09/23 /remarks-president-united-nations-generalassembly.

12. Aaron Klein, "Now Obama 'Greening' Hamas?" WND, February 13, 2012, http://www.wnd.com/2012/02/now-obama-greening-hamas/.

13. "About Us: Mission and Vision" section, Connect U.S. Fund website, accessed April 9, 2012, http://www.connectusfund.org/about/mission.

14. Connect U.S. Fund Powerpoint Presentation, www.connectusfund.org/... /Connect%20U.S.%20Fund%20Power%20Point%20Presentation.ppt.

15. Michael Isikoff, "The End of Torture: Obama Banishes Bush's Interrogation Tactics," Newsweek, January 22, 2009, http://www.newsweek .com/2009/01/21/the-end-of-torture.html.

16. "Eric P. Schwartz," Assistant Secretary, Bureau of Population, Refugees, and Migration, U.S. Department of State, http://www.state.gov/r/pa/ei /biog/125768.htm.

17. Cliff Kincaid, "Obama Advisers Demand 'More Blue Helmets on U.S. Troops,'" America's Survival, Inc., http://www.usasurvival.org/docs/ASI_ Rprt_Obama_n_UN.pdf.

18. S. Stephen Powell, Covert Cadre: Inside the Institute for Policy Studies

(Ottawa, IL: Green Hill Publishers, Inc., 1987), 249–50 (quoted from
in "Kerry, the Sandinistas, and the Institute for Policy Studies (IPS),"
FreeRepublic.com, February 11, 2004, http://www.freerepublic.com
/focus/f-news/1076375/posts). Event also reported by Warren Mass, "The
Trouble with Leon Panetta," *New American,* January 7, 2009, http://www
.thenewamerican.com/usnews/election/655.

19. Emerson Vermaat, "Obama's Preferred Future Spy Chief Leon Panetta,"
Free Republic, January 8, 2009.

20. Profile: Institute for Policy Studies, knology.net.

21. S. Stephen Powell, "Moscow's Friends at the Institute for Policy Studies,"
American Opinion, November 1983, quoted in Christian Gomez,
"Leon Panetta and the Institute for Policy Studies," *New American*,
June 11, 2011, http://www.thenewamerican.com/usnews/congress
/7819-panetta-unfit-for-sec-of-defense.

22. "Debt, Deficits, & Defense: A Way Forward," June 11, 2010, Sustainable
Defense Task Force, http://www.comw.org/pda/fulltext/1006SDTFreport
.pdf.

23. "New Era, New Openings: FCNL's 2009 Annual Meeting," Conference
Call Event Summary at Connect Fund website, http://www.connectus
fund.org/events new-era-new-openings-fcnls-2009-annual-meeting.

24. President Barack Obama, "Remarks by the President in Address to the
Nation on Libya," delivered at National Defense University, Washington,
D.C., March 28, 2011, http://www.whitehouse.gov/the-press-office/2011
/03/28/remarks-president-address-nation-libya.

25. International Commission on Intervention and State Sovereignty, *The
Responsibility to Protect*, December 2001, at http://www.iciss.ca/pdf
/Commission-Report.pdf.

26. Peter Beaumont, "Israel May Face War Crimes Trials over Gaza. Court
Looks at Whether Palestinians Can Bring Case. International Pressure
Grows over Conflict," *Guardian* (UK), March 2, 2009, http://www
.guardian.co.uk/world/2009/mar/02/israel-war-crimes-gaza. Daniel
Schwammenthal, "War Crimes: The International Criminal Court
Claims Jurisdiction over U.S. Soldiers in Afghanistan," *Wall Street Journal*,
November 26, 2009, http://online.wsj.com/article/SB1000142405274870
40130045745192530954440312.html.

27. See "Donors" page of Global Center for the Responsibility to Protect
website, accessed July 26, 2011, http://globalr2p.org/whoweare/donors
.php.

28. "Patrons," Global Center for the Responsibility to Protect, http://globalr2p
    .org/whoweare/patrons.php.
29. "About The Elders," The Elders website, http://www.theelders.org/elders.
30. Kofi A. Annan, "Two Concepts of Sovereignty," *The Economist*, September
    18, 1999, http://www.un.org/News/ossg/sg/stories/kaecon.html.
31. "Advisory Board," Responsibility to Protect website, http://www.iciss.ca
    /advisory_board-en.asp.
32. "Annan Calls for Responsibility to Protect," International Commission on
    Intervention and State Sovereignty website, undated, http://www.iciss.ca
    /menu-en.asp.
33. "Advisory Board," International Commission on Intervention and State
    Sovereignty, http://www.iciss.ca/advisory_board-en.asp.
34. George Soros, "The People's Sovereignty: How a New Twist on an Old
    Idea Can Protect the World's Most Vulnerable Populations," *Foreign Policy*
    Magazine, January 1, 2004, http://www.foreignpolicy.com/articles/2004
    /01/01/the_peoples_sovereignty.
35. Ramesh Thakur, "Toward a New World Order," *Ottawa Citizen*, March
    1, 2010, reprinted at http://www.cigionline.org/articles/2010/03
    /toward-new-world-order.

Chapter Two: What Solyndra? New "Green" Stimulus, Federal "Green Bank"

 1. Aaron Klein and Brenda J. Elliott, *Red Army. The Radical Network That Must
    Be Defeated to Save America* (New York: Broadside Books, 2011), 183–204.
 2. "State of the Union 2012: Full Transcript of President Obama's Speech,"
    The Guardian, January 25, 2012, http://www.guardian.co.uk/world/2012
    /jan/25/state-of-the-union-address-full-text.
 3. "Parent of Obama-Backed Battery Maker Goes Bankrupt," *USA Today*,
    January 27, 2012, http://www.usatoday.com/news/washington/story
    /2012-01-27/battery-maker-bankruptcy/52815302/1.
 4. Sharon Terlep, "GM to Idle Chevy Volt Output as Sales Slow," *Wall Street
    Journal*, March 2, 2012, http://online.wsj.com/article/SB10001424052970
    2039866045772576819186031O6.html.
 5. Aaron Klein, "White House Still Listening to Van Jones 'Green' Advice,"
    WND.com, November 30, 2009, http://www.wnd.com/2009/11/117548/.
 6. "2011 Report: Building the Obama Administration's Climate Legacy,"
    Presidential Climate Action Project, January 2011, accessed April 12, 2012,
    http://climateactionproject.com/plan/2011/PCAP_Report_2011.pdf.

7. "About Us" section, Sustainable Communities website, accessed March 12, 2012, http://www.sustainablecommunities.gov/aboutUs.html.

8. Ibid.

9. Bracken Hendricks Lisbeth Kaufman, "Cutting the Cost of Clean Energy 1.0," Center for American Progress report, November 2010, http://www.americanprogress.org/issues/2010/11/pdf/cleanenergycosts.pdf.

10. H.R. 1682: American-Made Energy Act of 2011, 112th Congress, 2011–2012.

11. Kate Gordon, "Enacting President Obama's Manufacturing Blueprint Means Sustained Economic Growth," *Think Progress.com*, January 25, 2012, http://thinkprogress.org/climate/2012/01/25/411594/president-obama-manufacturing-blueprint-economic-growth/.

12. H.R. 487: Manufacture Renewable Energy Systems: Make It in America Act of 2011, 112th Congress, 2011–2012.

13. Solar Energy Regulatory Relief Act of 2011, 112th Congress, 2011–2012.

14. "Climatic Research Unit Email Controversy," *Wikipedia*, http://en.wikipedia.org/wiki/Climatic_Research_Unit_email_controversy.

15. Jonathan Petre, "Climategate U-Turn as Scientist at Centre of Row Admits: There Has Been No Global Warming Since 1995," *The Daily Mail*, February 14, 2010, http://www.dailymail.co.uk/news/article-1250872/Climategate-U-turn-Astonishment-scientist-centre-global-warming-email-row-admits-data-organised.html#ixzz16sZxqEU5.

16. "Report: Antarctic Ice Growing, Not Shrinking," FoxNews.com, April 18, 2009, http://www.foxnews.com/story/0,2933,517035,00.html.

17. Manfred Wenzel, Jens Schröter, "Reconstruction of Regional Mean Sea Level Anomalies from Tide Gauges Using Neural Networks," *Journal of Geophysical Research* 115 (2010), http://www.agu.org/pubs/crossref/2010/2009JC005630.shtml.

18. Cass Sunstein, "Conspiracy Theories," January 25, 2008, Harvard Public Law Working Paper No. 08–03 Abstract, http://papers.ssrn.com/sol3/papers.cfm?abstract_id=1084585.

19. Carol D. Leonnig and Steven Mufson, "Obama Green-Tech Program That Backed Solyndra Struggles to Create Jobs," *Washington Post*, September 14, 2011, http://www.washingtonpost.com/politics/obama-green-tech-program-that-backed-solyndra-struggles-to-create-jobs/2011/09/07/gIQA9Zs3SK_story.html.

20. Ivanpah Solar Generating System website, http://ivanpahsolar.com/.

21. John Upton, "Is Solar Power Too Risky a Bet for the Federal Government? Solyndra's Closure Raises Questions about Multibillion-Dollar Loan Guarantee," *The Bay Citizen*, September 2, 2011, http://www.baycitizen.org/energy/story/solar-power-risky-bet-federal-government/.

22. Scott Martelle, "Utility Infielder. On Obama's Commerce Department Pick, Business and Environmentalists Both Say Meh," *American Prospect*, June 6, 2011, http://prospect.org/cs/articles?article=utility_infielder.

23. T. J. Glauthier, Advisory Board, Lawrence Berkeley National Laboratory, http://www.lbl.gov/LBL-PID/Advisory_Board/members.html.

24. Executive Profile: T. J. Gauthier, Union Drilling, Inc., *BusinessWeek.com*, http://investing.businessweek.com/research/stocks/people/person.asp?personId=22430751&ticker=UDRL:US&previousCapId=7670016&previousTitle=EnerNOC%2C%20Inc.

25. "Deployment, Fueled by $100 Million in Stimulus. Demonstrating Smart Charging 3.0 at Plug-In 2009 Conference," GridPoint.com, August 10, 2009, http://www.gridpoint.com/news/PressReleaseShare/09-08-10/GridPoint%E2%80%99s_Next-Generation_Smart_Charging_Software_to_Support_Largest_U_S_Electric_Vehicle_Deployment_Fueled_by_100_Million_in_Stimulus.aspx.

26. "GridPoint to Provide Solutions for KCP&L's Smart Grid Demonstration Project," GridPoint.com, December 1, 2009, http://www.gridpoint.com/news/PressReleaseShare/09-12-01/GridPoint_to_Provide_Solutions_for_KCP_L_s_Smart_Grid_Demonstration_Project.aspx.

27. "GridPoint to Provide Software Solutions for SMUD's Smart Grid Solar Project," GridPoint.com, November 3, 2009, http://www.gridpoint.com/news/PressReleaseShare/09-11-03/GridPoint_to_Provide_Software_Solutions_for_SMUD%E2%80%99s_Smart_Grid_Solar_Project.aspx.

28. Associated Press, "Argonne National Laboratory Gets $99 Million Boost From Stimulus," *Huffington Post*, May 1, 2009, http://www.huffingtonpost.com/2009/03/31/argonne-national-laborato_n_181483.html.

29. "GridPoint Enables U.S. Postal Service to Reduce Energy Costs in Facilities Nationwide with Energy Management Systems. Supports USPS Goal to Achieve 30 Percent Reduction in Facility Energy Usage," GridPoint.com, May 24, 2010, http://www.gridpoint.com/news/PressReleaseShare/10-05-24/GridPoint_Enables_U_S_Postal_Service_to_Reduce_Energy_Costs_in_Facilities_Nationwide_with_Energy_Management_Systems.aspx.

30. Barack Obama Inauguration Donors 2008 (Top Donors Only), OpenSecrets.org, http://www.opensecrets.org/pres08/inaug_all.php.

31. J. E. Dyer, "Navy Buys Biofuel for $16 a Gallon," *HotAir.com*, December 10, 2011, http://hotair.com/greenroom/archives/2011/12/10/navy -buys -biofuel-for-16-a-gallon/.

32. Edgar A. Gunther, "Top 10 Solar 1603 Treasury Grant Awards," GuntherPortfolio.com, December 10, 2010, http://guntherportfolio.com /2010/12/top-10-solar-1603-treasury-grant-awards/.

33. "New York City Mayor Bloomberg's Live in Girlfriend Owns the Park That Wall Street Protesters Occupy and She Won't Ask Them to Go," Shutking .blogspot.com, October 7, 2011, http://shutking.blogspot.com/2011/10 /new-york-city-mayor-bloombergs-live-in.html.

34. Cassandra Sweet, "DOE Guarantees Loans For Several Renewable-Energy Projects," Dow Jones Newswires, September 23, 2011, http:// www.foxbusiness.com/industries/2011/09/23/doe-guarantees-loans-for -several-renewable-energy-projects/. Editorial: "A NH Solyndra?" *Union Leader* (Manchester, NH), September 28, 2011, http://unionleader.com /article/20110928/OPINION01/709289961.

35. 2011 Lobbying Report: Heather Podesta + Partners, LLC, Senate.gov, http://soprweb.senate.gov/index.cfm?event=getFilingDetails&filingID=C FD1F386-79B8-4CAE-91E0-7DB4F1D82512.

36. Aaron Metha, "Top 5 Lobbyist Bundlers; Power Couple Tony and Heather Podesta Top the List," iWatchNews.org, July 28, 2011, http://www.iwatchnews.org/2011/07/28/5402 /top-5-lobbyist-bundlers-power-couple-tony-and-heather-podesta-top-list.

37. Timothy P. Carver, "Obama's Revolving Door Always Open to Podestas," *Washington Examiner*, November 4, 2009, reported in http://romanticpoet .wordpress.com/tag/podesta-obama-relationship-white-house-visits/.

38. "New York City Mayor Bloomberg's Live in Girlfriend Owns the Park That Wall Street Protesters Occupy and She Won't Ask Them to Go," October 7, 2011.

39. *Blueprint for Legislative Action*, United States Climate Action Partnership, January 2009, http://www.c2es.org/docUploads/USCAP-legislative-blueprint.pdf.

40. Ibid.

41. Ibid.

42. William Greider, "The AIG Bailout Scandal ," *Nation*, August 6, 2010, http://www.thenation.com/article/153929/aig-bailout-scandal.

43. Michael Luo, "In Banking, Emanuel Made Money and Connections," *New York Times*, December 3, 2008, https://www.nytimes.com/2008/12/04/us /politics/04emanuel.html?_r=3&hp=&pagewanted=all.

44. "Barack (Obama) has one of his biggest supporters in terms of funding, the Exelon Corporation, which has spent millions of dollars trying to make Yucca Mountain the waste depository," PolitiFact.com, January 15, 2008, http://www.politifact.com/truth-o-meter/statements/2008/jan/18 /hillary-clinton/exelon-staff-supports-obama/.

45. "Nation's largest nuclear fleet," ExelonCorp.com, http://www.exeloncorp .com/energy/generation/nuclear.aspx.

46. Power Plants, Duke Energy, http://www.duke-energy.com/power-plants /nuclear.asp.

47. Timothy P. Carney, "The power company underwriting the DNC for $10M," *Washington Examiner*, February 20, 2012, http://campaign 2012.washington examiner.com/blogs/beltway-confidential/power-company-underwriting -dnc-10m/384866. Wynton Hall, "DNC Co-Chairman's Company Landed $230.4M in Obama Stimulus Money," *Big Government*, February 21, 2012, http://www.breitbart.com/Big-Government/2012/02/21 /dnc-co-chairmans-company-landed-230-4m-in-obama-stimulus-money.

48. Juliana Goldman and Rachel Layne, "Obama Asks GE's Immelt to Head Economic Advisory Panel, Replacing Volcker," Bloomberg.com, January 21, 2011, http://www.bloomberg.com/news/2011-01-21/obama-taps-ge- s-immelt-for-economy-panel-replace-volcker.html. Shahien Nasiripour, "Obama Picks Jeffrey Immelt, GE CEO, to Run New Jobs-Focused Panel as GE Sends Jobs Overseas, Pays Little In Taxes," *Huffington Post*, January 21, 2011, http://www.huffingtonpost.com/2011/01/21/obama-picks-jeffrey- immel-ge-jobs-overseas_n_812502.html.

49. Chris Woodward, "Ford drops out of USCAP," OneNewsNow.com, January 27, 2012, http://onenewsnow.com/Business/Default.aspx?id=1523872.

50. Free Enterprise Education Institute, "SEC Should Require Companies to Disclose Risk of Global Warming Regulation, Study Says; Companies Risk Earnings While Keeping Shareholders in the Dark, Reports Free Enterprise Education Institute," PRNewswire .com, [date unknown], http://www.prnewswire.com/news-releases /sec-should-require-companies-to-disclose-risk-of-global-warming

-regulation-study-says-companies-risk-earnings-while-keeping-shareholders-in-the-dark-reports-free-enterprise-education-institute-58250537.html.

51. Chris Woodward, "Ford drops out of USCAP," January 27, 2012.

52. "Business Roundtable CEOs Provide Blueprint for U.S. Energy Future," TDWorld.com, June 7, 2007: http://tdworld.com/business/business-roundtable-energy-plan/.

53. Members, Business Roundtable, http://businessroundtable.org/about-us/members/.

54. "Climate Change: Business Roundtable Supports Actions to Address Global Warming," Business Roundtable, September 1, 2007, http://businessroundtable.org/studies-and-reports/climate-change/.

55. "Climate 2030: A National Blueprint for a Clean Energy Economy," Union of Concerned Scientists, May 2009, http://www.pace-cleanenergy.org/articles/climate-2030-report.pdf.

56. Profile: Union of Concerned Scientists, *Discover the Networks*, http://www.discoverthenetworks.org/groupProfile.asp?grpid=6631.

57. Dr. Ileana Johnson Paugh, "Power Grab for Natural Gas – New Executive Order," *Canada Free Press*, April 14, 2012, http://www.canadafreepress.com/index.php/article/45984.

58. "Obama's energy blueprint pushes natural gas to forefront," WordCng.com, March 31, 2011, http://www.worldcng.com/obama%E2%80%99s-energy-blueprint-pushes-natural-gas-to-forefront/.

59. Greg Pollowitz, "How George Soros Profits from Natural Gas Subsidies," *National Review Online*, July 25, 2011, http://www.nationalreview.com/planet-gore/272628 how-george-soros-profits-natural-gas-subsidies-greg-pollowitz.

60. Ibid.

61. Robert Bradley Jr., "A Consumerist, Not 'All of the Above' Energy Policy," Forbes.com, April 9, 2012, http://www.forbes.com/sites/robertbradley/2012/04/09/a-consumerist-not-all-of-the-above-energy-policy/.

62. Ibid.

63. Ibid.

64. Ibid.

65. Brad Johnson, "Greenhouse Goal Has Disappeared From Obama's 'Blueprint for a Secure Energy Future,'" *Think Progress*, March 12, 2012, http://thinkprogress.org/climate/2012/03/12/443112/greenhouse-goal-has-disappeared-from-obamas-blueprint-for-a-secure-energy-future/.

66. Ibid.

67. Ibid.
68. Ibid.
69. Ibid.

Chapter Three: Open Borders, Amnesty for Illegals

1. David Jackson, "Obama: I've Got Five Years to Revamp Immigration," *USA Today*, February 20, 2012, http://content.usatoday.com/communities /theoval/post/2012/02/obama-ive-got-five-years-to-do-immigration -reform/1?csp=34news#.T2tId9lkO1h.
2. Transcript: NPR Democratic Candidates' Debate, npr.org, December 4, 2007, http://www.npr.org/templates/story/story.php?storyId=16898435.
3. NPR, Democratic Candidates' Debate, December 4, 2007. Alex Newman, "Obama's Plan for Immigration 'Reform'," *New American*, December 1, 2008, http://www.thenewamerican.com/index.php/usnews/politics/560.
4. U.S. Immigration and Customs Enforcement Memorandum #306-112 .0026, June 17, 2011, http://www.ice.gov/doclib/secure-communities/pdf /prosecutorial-discretion-memo.pdf.
5. "Immigration Update: Maximizing Public Safety and Better Focusing Resources," The White House blog; August 18, 2011; http://www.white house.gov/blog/2011/08/18/immigration-update-maximizing-public- safety-and-better-focusing-resources.
6. "Obama to Deport Illegals by 'Priority,'" *Washington Times*, August 18, 2011, http://www.washingtontimes.com/news/2011/aug/18/new-dhs -rules-cancel-deportations/?page=all.
7. "Obama Amnesty: Deportations at Record Low," JudicialWatch.org, February 7, 2012, http://www.judicialwatch.org/blog/2012/02/obama -amnesty-deportations-at-record-low/.
8. Aaron Klein, "Obama's New Czar Tied to Occupy, ACORN, MoveOn," WND; January 10, 2012, http://www.wnd.com/2012/01/obamas-new- czar-tied-to-occupy-acorn-moveon/.
9. "Overview—Illegal Aliens in the United States," TheAmericanResistance .com, undated; with up-to-date estimate; http://www.theamericanresistance .com/ref/illegal_alien_numbers.html. Letter from Sen. John McCain can be read here: http://www.theamericanresistance.com/ref/letter_ mccain_2004feb10.html.
10. "A Brief History of Illegal Immigration in the United States," EndIllegalImmigration

.com, http://www.endillegalimmigration.com/History_of_Illegal_Immigration_ in_US/index.shtml.

11. Ibid. Rachel L. Swarns, "Failed Amnesty Legislation of 1986 Haunts the Current Immigration Bills in Congress," *New York Times,* May 23, 2006, http://www.nytimes.com/2006/05/23/washington/23amnesty.html.

12. "A Brief History of Illegal Immigration in the United States," EndIllegalImmigration.com.

13. Ibid.

14. Ibid.

15. "Comprehensive Immigration Reform for America's Security and Prosperity Act of 2009," accessed March 29, 2012, available in full at http:// www.gpo.gov/fdsys/pkg/BILLS-111hr4321ih/pdf/BILLS-111hr4321ih .pdf.

16. Border Patrol Sectors, Customs and Border Patrol, U.S. Department of Homeland Security, http://www.cbp.gov/xp/cgov/border_security /border_patrol/border_patrol_sectors/.

17. "Apprehensions by the U.S. Border Patrol: 2005—2010," *Department of Homeland Security Fact Sheet,* June 2011, http://www.dhs.gov/xlibrary/assets /statistics/publications/ois-apprehensions-fs-2005-2010.pdf.

18. Randal C. Archibold, "Border Plan Will Address Harm Done at Fence Site," *New York Times,* January 16, 2009, http://www.nytimes.com/2009/01/17 /us/17border.html?_r=2.

19. Marshall Fitz, "Immigration for Innovation: How to Attract the World's Best Talent While Ensuring America Remains the Land of Opportunity for All," Center for American Progress, January 2012, http://www.american progress.org/issues/2012/01/pdf/dwwsp_immigration.pdf.

20. "Latinos Pin Hopes of Immigration Reform on Obama. After Helping Barack Obama Win the Election, Latinos Seek to Remind Him to Enact Comprehensive Immigration Reform," McClatchy Newspapers, November 24, 2008, http://www.guardian.co.uk /world/2008/nov/24/latinos-immigration-reform-obama; "Patricia Madrid Named to Obama's National Latino Advisory Council," RootsWire, August 22, 2008, http://rootswire.org/conventionblog /patricia-madrid-named-obamas-national-latino-advisory-council.

21. "Eliseo Medina Speaks on Immigrants for Votes [June 2, 2009]," YouTube, added January 25, 2010, http://www.youtube.com/watch?v=AK7K0itgQt0.

22. Ibid.

23. Tova Andrea Wang, Youjin B. Kim, "From Citizenship to Voting: Improving Registration for New Americans," Demos, December 19, 2011, http://www.demos.org/sites/default/files/publications/fromcitizenshipto voting_demos_2.pdf.

Chapter 4: A Jobs Plan for America

1. Transcript of President Barack Obama's 2012 State of the Union Address, House of Representatives, U.S. Capitol, January 24, 2012, http://www .realclearpolitics.com/articles/2012/01/24/transcript_of_president_ obamas_2012_state_of_the_union_address_112893.html.

2. Mark Landler, "Obama Challenges Congress on Job Plan," *New York Times*, September 8, 2011, https://www.nytimes.com/2011/09/09/us/politics /09payroll.html?_r=1&pagewanted=all.

3. "The Progressive Promise," Congressional Progressive Caucus, http://cpc .grijalva.house.gov/index.cfm?sectionid=63&sectiontree=2,63. Among those principles are: economic justice; access to affordable, high -quality health care for all; guaranteed Social Security benefits for all; and environmental justice, including increasing construction of "green" buildings and renewable and "green" energy, with at least three million new jobs.

4. About, Socialist International, http://www.socialistinternational.org /about.cfm. Members, Socialist International, http://www.socialistinterna tional.org/viewArticle.cfm?ArticlePageID=931.

5. "What is Democratic Socialism? Questions and Answers from the Democratic Socialists of America," Democratic Socialists of America, http://www.dsausa.org/pdf/widemsoc.pdf.

6. "Stand Up to Wall Street. We Want Jobs, Not Budget Cuts," Democratic Socialists of America, 2011, http://www.dsausa.org/docs/Jobs.html.

7. Ibid.

8. Profile: Demos, "Discover the Networks," http://www.discoverthenet works.org/groupProfile.asp?grpid=7690.

9. David Callahan and Tamara Draut, *Help Wanted. America Needs a Better Jobs Plan. A Response to the Obama Jobs Speech*, Demos, September 8, 2011, http://www.demos.org/sites/default/files/publications /HelpWanted_ResponseToObamasJobsPlan_Demos.pdf.

10. Steven Greenhouse, "The Challenge of Creating Good Jobs," *Economix/New York Times*, September 7, 2011, http://economix.blogs.nytimes.com/2011 /09/07/the-challenge-of-creating-good-jobs/.

11. Ibid.

12. Bill Baden, "The Ranks of the Underemployed Continue to Grow," Money /USNews.com, October 19, 2011, http://money.usnews.com/money/careers /articles/2011/10/19/the-ranks-of-the-underemployed-continue-to-grow.

13. Ben Peck and Amy Traub, *Worth Working For: Strategies for Turning Bad Jobs into Quality Employment*, Demos, October 2011, http://www.demos.org/sites /default/files/publications/worthworkingfor_goodjobs_Demos.pdf.

14. H.R.3192 Paid Family and Medical Leave Act of 2005, introduced June 30, 2005, by sponsor Rep. Pete Stark (D-CA), http://www.govtrack.us /congress/bill.xpd?bill=h109-3192.

15. Peck and Traub, *Worth Working For*.

16. Steven Greenhouse, "The Challenge of Creating Good Jobs," September 7, 2011. H.R.283 Living American Wage (LAW) Act of 2011 introduced January 12, 2011, sponsored by Rep. Al Green (D-TX), http://thomas.loc .gov/cgi-bin/query/z?c112:H.R.283. The bill asks for the minimum wage to be calculated based on the federal poverty threshold for a family of 2, as determined by the Census Bureau. At a minimum, the minimum wage would be adjusted every four years "so that a person working for such a wage may earn an annual income that is not less than 15 percent higher than the Federal poverty threshold for a family of 2, as determined by the Census Bureau," and the minimum wage "should be set at a level high enough to allow 2 full-time minimum wage workers to earn an income above the national housing wage."

17. Donald R. Stabile, *The Living Wage: Lessons from the History of Economic Thought* (Northampton, MA.: Edward Elgar Publishing, Inc., 2008), 109.

18. Steven Malanga, "How the 'Living Wage' Sneaks Socialism into Cities," *City Journal*, Winter 2003, http://www.city-journal.org/html/13_1_how_ the_living_wage.html.

19. "ACORN People's Platform," 1990, http://web.archive.org/web /20010615002306/www.acorn.org/people%27s_platform.html.

20. Profile: Wade Rathke, ChiefOrganizer.org, http://chieforganizer.org /biography/.

21. "The Rebranding of ACORN," Judicial Watch, August 22, 2011, http:// www.judicialwatch.org/files/documents/2011/acornspecialreport 08222011.pdf.

22. Malanga, "How the 'Living Wage' Sneaks Socialism into Cities."

23. Callahan and Draut, *Help Wanted*.

24. Peck and Traub, *Worth Working For.*

25. *Labor Board v. General Motors Corp.* 373 U.S. 734 (1963), Certiorari to the United States Court of Appeals for the Sixth Circuit, No. 404, Argued April 18, 1963, Decided June 3, 1963, http://caselaw.lp.findlaw.com/cgi-bin/getcase.pl?court=US&vol=373&invol=734.

26. Sam Hananel, "Obama May Make 'Living Wage' Factor in Contracts," Associated Press/*Washington Post*, February 26, 2010, http://www.washingtonpost.com/wp-dyn/content/article/2010/02/26/AR2010022600092.html.

27. Bruce Western and Jake Rosenfeld, "Unions, Norms, and the Rise in American Wage Inequality," Harvard University, March, 2011, http://www.wjh.harvard.edu/soc/faculty/western/pdfs/Unions_Norms_and_Wage_Inequality.pdf.

28. Brittany Mayer-Schulur, "The Resurgence of Labor Law under the Obama Administration," *The Hennepin Lawyer*, August 25, 2009, http://hennepin.timberlakepublishing.com/article.asp?article=1352&paper=1&cat=147.

29. John Wojcik, "Many Workers to Benefit in 2012 from New Obama Rules," *PeoplesWorld.com*, January 2, 2012, http://peoplesworld.org/many-workers-to-benefit-in-2012-from-new-obama-rules/.

30. Jim Abrams, "Unions Look to Obama to Help Advance Their Agenda," Associated Press, November 10, 2008, http://www.usatoday.com/news/washington/2008-11-10-3562954163_x.htm.

31. Callahan and Draut, *Help Wanted.*

32. Richard Berman, "Employee Free Choice Act May Backfire on Unions," *Washington Examiner*, February 2009, http://washingtonexaminer.com/opinion/2009/02/employee-free-choice-act-may-backfire-unions/104955.

33. Callahan and Draut, *Help Wanted.* On June 7, 2012, several members of the Congressional Black Caucus, led by Rep. Jesse Jackson Jr. (D-IL), introduced the Catching Up to 1968 Act to raise the minimum wage to $10 an hour.

34. Linda Gorman, "Minimum Wages," *The Concise Encyclopedia of Economics*, 2nd ed., http://www.econlib.org/library/Enc/MinimumWages.html.

35. Ed Morrissey, "Unemployment Stays at 8.3%, 227K Jobs Added," *Hot Air*, March 9, 2012, http://hotair.com/archives/2012/03/09/unemployment-stays-at-8-3-227k-jobs-added/?utm_source=co2hog.

36. Employment Situation Summary, Bureau of Labor Statistics, released March 9, 2012, http://bls.gov/news.release/empsit.nr0.htm.

37. Daniel Helper, "Valerie Jarrett: 'People Who Receive That Unemployment Check Go Out and Spend It and Help Stimulate the Economy,'" *Weekly Standard*, February 22, 2012, http://www.weeklystandard.com/blogs/valerie-jarrett-people-who-receive-unemployment-check-go-out-and-spend-it-and-help-stimulate-economy_631716.html?utm_source=co2hog.
38. Alan S. Binder and Mark Zandi, "Stimulus Worked," *Finance & Development*, December 2010, https://www.imf.org/external/pubs/ft/fandd/2010/12/pdf/Blinder.pdf.
39. Alan S. Binder and Mark Zandi, "How the Great Recession Was Brought to an End," July 27, 2010, 16, http://www.economy.com/mark-zandi/documents/End-of-Great-Recession.pdf.
40. Andrew Fieldhouse and Ethan Pollack, "Debt Ceiling Deal Threatens Deep Job Losses and Lower Long-Run Economic Growth," *Economic Policy Institute and The Century Foundation Issue Brief #311*, August 4, 2011, 2–3, http://web.epi-data.org/temp727/EPI-TCF_IssueBrief_311.pdf.
41. "New Developments on Federal Unemployment Extensions," State of California Employment Development Department, updated January 31, 2012, http://edd.ca.gov/Unemployment/Federal_Unemployment_Insurance_Extensions.htm.
42. "Not In Labor Force," Economic Research, Federal Reserve Bank of St. Louis, Updated March 9, 2012, http://research.stlouisfed.org/fred2/series/LNS15000000.
43. Doug Ross, "Lies, Damn Lies, and Obama's Unemployment Numbers," *Doug Ross Journal*, February 3, 2012, http://directorblue.blogspot.com/2012/02/lies-damn-lies-and-obamas-unemployment.html.
44. Tyler Durden, "Implied Unemployment Rate Rises to 11.5%, Spread to Propaganda Number Surges to 30 Year High," ZeroHedge.com, February 3, 2012, http://www.zerohedge.com/news/implied-unemployment-rate-rises-115-spread-propaganda-number-surges-30-year-high.
45. Jim Pethokoukis, "Why the Official 8.3 Percent Unemployment Rate Is a Phony Number—and What It Means for Obama's Reelection," *American Enterprise*/American Enterprise Institute, February 3, 2012, http://blog.american.com/2012/02/why-the-official-8-3-percent-unemployment-rate-is-a-phony-number-and-what-it-means-for-obamas-reelection/; HPS Jobs Fact Sheet 2012, Hamilton Place Strategies, January 2012, http://www.hamiltonplacestrategies.com/.

46. John Crudele, "Rosy Report a Ruse. An 8.3% Jobless Rate?" *New York Post*, February 3, 2012, http://www.nypost.com/p/news/business/rosy_report_ruse_LsXHVA9epmxGzTBHeOW6WP.
47. Callahan and Draut, *Help Wanted*.
48. Seth Harris, "Work Sharing: A Success Story," U.S. Department of Labor blog, September 14, 2011, http://social.dol.gov/blog/work-sharing-a-success-story/.
49. "Work Sharing Should Be Part of the President's Job Program," Center for Economic and Policy Research, September 7, 2011, http://www.cepr.net/index.php/press-releases/press-releases/work-sharing-should-be-part-of-the-presidents-job-program.
50. Profile: Center for Economic and Policy Research, *Discover the Networks*, http://www.discoverthenetworks.org/groupProfile.asp?grpid=7226.
51. Dean Baker, *Work Sharing: The Quick Route Back to Full Employment*, Center for Economic and Policy Research, June 2011, http://www.cepr.net/documents/publications/work-sharing-2011-06.pdf.
52. International Labor Comparisons, U.S. Bureau of Labor Statistics, last updated February 2, 2012, http://www.bls.gov/ilc/intl_unemployment_rates_monthly.htm#Rchart1.
53. Dean Baker, "How Larry Summers' Memo Hobbled Obama's Stimulus Plan. The Obama Administration's Economic Blueprint Was Fatally Flawed: It Led to a Weak Stimulus and Premature Deficit Reduction," *The Guardian* (UK), February 24, 2012, http://www.guardian.co.uk/commentisfree/cifamerica/2012/jan/24/larry-summers-memo-hobbled-obamas-stimulus.
54. Ibid.
55. Callahan and Draut, *Help Wanted*.
56. Ibid.
57. Profile: Center on Budget and Policy Priorities, SorosFiles.com, updated October 2011, http://sorosfiles.com/soros/2011/10/center-on-budget-and-policy-priorities.html.
58. Callahan and Draut, *Help Wanted*.
59. Ibid.
60. Profile: Institute for Policy Studies, "Discover the Networks," http://www.discoverthenetworks.org/groupProfile.asp?grpid=6991.
61. John Cavanagh and David Korten, "A Main Street Jobs Agenda," Institute

for Policy Studies, November 28, 2011, http://www.ips-dc.org/articles
/a_main_street_jobs_agenda.

62. Ibid.

63. Ibid.

64. Ibid.

65. Callahan and Draut, *Help Wanted*.

66. Cavanagh and Korten, "A Main Street Jobs Agenda.

67. The Making Work Pay Tax Credit, Internal Revenue Service, http://www
.irs.gov/newsroom/article/0,,id=204447,00.html.

68. Roberton Williams, "Why Congress Should Bring Back the
Making Work Pay Tax Credit," *Christian Science Monitor,* http://
www.csmonitor.com/Business/Tax-VOX/2011/1206/Why
-Congress-should-bring-back-the-Making-Work-Pay-tax-credit.

69. Adam Weinstein, "'We Are the 99 Percent' Creators Revealed," *Mother
Jones,* October 7, 2011, http://motherjones.com/politics/2011/10
/we-are-the-99-percent-creators.

70. "Wall Street Protests Spread," CBSNews.com (photo gallery), October 17,
2011, http://www.cbsnews.com/2300-201_162-10009481-50.html.

71. Act for the 99% introduced December 13, 2011, sponsored by Raul M.
Grijalva, http://thomas.loc.gov/cgi-bin/bdquery/D?d112:2:./temp
/~bdJicf::|/home/LegislativeData.php|. Andrew Fieldhouse and Rebecca
Thiess, "The Restore the American Dream for the 99% Act: An Analysis of
Job-Creation Provisions," Economic Policy Institute, December 13, 2011,
http://www.epi.org/publication/restore-american-dream-99-act-analysis-
job/. The People's Budget 2012, Congressional Progressive Caucus, http://
grijalva.house.gov/uploads/The_CPC_FY2012_Budget.pdf.
    The CPC's Act for the 99% shadows its own 2012 People's Budget 2012.

72. "Progressive Caucus Restore the American Dream Act Introduction,"
YouTube.com, December 13, 2011, http://www.youtube.com
/watch?v=WXXQjWj15ag.

73. Philip L. Harvey, "Back to Work: A Public Jobs Proposal for Economic
Recovery," Demos, 2011, http://www.demos.org/sites/default/files
/publications/Back_To_Work_Demos.pdf.

74. Mortimer M. Zuckerman, "Why the Jobs Situation Is Worse Than It
Looks. We Now Have More Idle Men and Women Than at Any Time
Since the Great Depression," *U.S. News & World Report,* June 21, 2011,

http://www.usnews.com/opinion/mzuckerman/articles/2011/06/20
/why-the-jobs-situation-is-worse-than-it-looks.

75. Jim Pethokoukis, "The Obama Jobs Gap Is Up to 15 Million Missing Jobs,"
American Enterprise/American Enterprise Institute, April 2, 2012, http://blog
.american.com/2012/04the-obama-jobs-gap-is-up-to-15-million-missing-
jobs/.

76. "20 Ideas for Jobs Creation," Center for American Progress, January 3, 2012,
http://www.americanprogress.org/issues/2012/01/20_job_creation_
ideas.html; David M. Abromowitz, et al., *Meeting the Jobs Challenge*, Center
for American Progress, December 2, 2009, http://www.americanprogress
.org/issues/2009/12/jobs_challenge.html.

77. Caroline Baum, "'Jobs Created or Saved' Is White House Fantasy,"
Bloomberg News, October 27, 2009, http://www.bloomberg.com/apps
/news?pid=newsarchive&sid=aUuHhaDx8Hr8.

78. Ibid.

79. "Adviser: High Unemployment for Years," *Politico*, September 12, 2009,
http://www.politico.com/news/stories/0909/27052.html.

80. "Leaders Urge Congress to Create Green American Dream," PR Newswire,
February 2, 2009.

81. Ibid.

82. David Espo, "AP Sources: Wash. Rep. Inslee to Resign House Seat," *Denver
Post*, March 10, 2012, http://www.denverpost.com/politics/ci_20146560
/ap-sources-wash-rep-inslee-resign-house-seat/.

83. *Jobs21! Good Jobs for the 21st Century. A BlueGreen Alliance Blueprint to Solve
the Jobs Crisis*, BlueGreen Alliance, August 2011, http://www.bluegreen
alliance.org/admin/publications/files/Platform-vFINAL.pdf.

84. American Recovery and Reinvestment Act of 2009: Green Capacity
Building Grants, U.S. Department of Labor, http://www.doleta.gov/pdf
/greenjobs.pdf.

85. Michelle Dunlop, "Green-Job Training Put on Hold after Program
Produces Few Jobs. The Program Has Shown Poor Results, and the
Agency That Oversees Training Has Stopped Referring People," *The
Herald* (Everett, WA.), February 2, 2012, http://heraldnet.com/article
/20120202/BIZ/702029905/1060/COMM0619. Testimony of Elliott
P. Lewis, assistant general for Audit, Office of the Inspector General, U
.S. Department of Labor, at a hearing held by the House Committee
on Oversight and Government Reform Subcommittee on Regulatory
Affairs, Stimulus Oversight, and Government Spending, *The Green Energy*

Debacle: Where has all the taxpayer money gone? November 2, 2011, http://www.oig.dol.gov/public/reports/oa/2012/18-12-900-03-390.pdf.

86. *Jobs21!*

87. Profile: Blue Green Alliance, "Discover the Networks," http://www.disco verthenetworks.org/groupProfile.asp?grpid=7570.

88. Klein and Elliott, *The Manchurian President*, 222.

89. John Podesta and Karen Kornbluh, "The Green Bank. Financing the Transition to a Low-Carbon Economy Requires Targeted Financing to Encourage Private -Sector Participation," Center for American Progress, May 21, 2009, http://www.americanprogress.org/issues/2009/05/green_bank.html.

90. *Jobs21!*

91. Jim Lane, "Bingaman Introduces Clean Energy Standard Bill; Natural Gas, Biomass, Wind, Solar Set to Gain," *BioFuelsDigest.com*, March 2, 2012, http://www.biofuelsdigest.com/bdigest/2012/03/02/bingaman -introduces-clean-energy-standard-bill-natural-gas-biomass-wind-solar -set-to-gain/.

92. Fact Sheet: The Clean Standard Energy Act of 2012, U.S. Senate Committee on Energy & Natural Resources, March 2, 2012, http://www .ascension-publishing.com/BIZ/CESA-2012-2page.pdf.

93. Amy Harder, "Strong RES Would Create 850K Jobs," *National Journal*, September 27, 2010, http://energy.nationaljournal.com/2010/09/can-energy-mandate-muster-supp.php.

94. Fact Sheet: The Clean Standard Energy Act of 2012, U.S. Senate Committee on Energy & Natural Resources, March 2, 2012.

95. *Jobs21!*

96. "20 Ideas for Jobs Creation," Center for American Progress, January 3, 2012.

97. Ibid.

Chapter Five: It's Back! FDR's Works Progress Administration and Other Obama Job Nightmares

1. *The Economic Value of Opportunity Youth*, Corporation for National and Community Service and the White House Council for Community Solutions, January 2012, http://cdn.theatlantic.com/static/mt/assets /business/Economic_Opportunities_of_Youth.pdf.

2. Employment Situation Summary, Bureau of Labor Statistics, released March 9, 2012, http://bls.gov/news.release/empsit.nr0.htm.

3. *20 Ideas for Jobs Creation*, Center for American Progress, January 3, 2012,

http://www.americanprogress.org/issues/2012/01/20_job_creation_
ideas.html.

4. Alana Semuels, "For Many Unemployed Workers, Jobs Aren't Coming
   Back. The U.S. Unemployment Rate Will Remain Elevated for Years,
   Experts Say, a Grim Prospect for Americans Who Have Exhausted
   Their Benefits," *Los Angeles Times*, September 5, 2010, http://www
   .latimes.com/business/la-fi-america-unemployment-mainbar-
   20100905,0,1306277,print.story.

5. *Investing In America's Economy: A Budget Blueprint for Economic Recovery
   and Fiscal Responsibility*, Our Fiscal Security (partnership of Demos,
   Economic Policy Institute, and Century Foundation), November 29, 2010,
   4, http://www.demos.org/sites/default/files/publications/Blueprint_
   OFS_Demos.pdf.

6. Transcript of President Barack Obama's 2012 State of the Union Address,
   House of Representatives, U.S. Capitol, January 24, 2012, http://www
   .realclearpolitics.com/articles/2012/01/24/transcript_of_president_
   obamas_2012_state_of_the_union_address_112893.html.

7. David Muhlhausen in Mike Brownfield, "State of the Union 2012: Heritage
   Reaction Roundup," Heritage Foundation, January 24, 2012, http://blog
   .heritage.org/2012/01/24/state-of-the-union-2012-heritage-reaction-
   roundup/. David Muhlhausen is most likely referring to Peter Z. Schochet,
   John Burghardt, and Sheena McConnell, "Does Job Corps Work? Impact
   Findings from the National Job Corps Study," *American Economic Review*
   98, no. 5 (December 2008), 1864–86.

8. Also see David Muhlhausen, "Job Corps: A Consistent Record of Failure,"
   Heritage Foundation, February 28, 2007, http://www.heritage.org
   /research/reports/2007/02/job-corps-a-consistent-record-of-failure;
   and "Job Corps: An Unfailing Record of Failure," Heritage Foundation,
   May 5, 2009, http://www.heritage.org/research/reports/2009/05/job
   -corps-an-unfailing-record-of-failure#_edn2.

9. *Wall Street Journal* quote in header at JimBrovard.com, http://www
   .jimbovard.com/.

10. James Bovard, "The Failure of Federal Job Training," Cato Policy Analysis
    No. 77, Cato Institute, August 28, 1986, http://www.cato.org/pubs/pas
    /pa077.html.

11. Muhlhausen in Brownfield, "State of the Union 2012: Heritage Reaction
    Roundup," January 24, 2012.

12. Thomas DiLorenzo, *The Myth of Government Job Creation*, Cato Institute Policy Analysis No. 48, Cato Institute, February 19, 1984, http://www.cato .org/pubs/pas/pa048.pdf.

13. *American Jobs Plan: A Five-Point Plan to Stem the U.S. Jobs Crisis*, Economic Policy Institute, December 2009, http://www.epi.org/page/-/american_ jobs_plan/epi_american_jobs_plan.pdf.

14. Philip L. Harvey, *Back to Work: A Public Jobs Proposal for Economic Recovery*, Demos, 2010, http://www.demos.org/sites/default/files/publications /Back_To_Work_Demos.pdf.

15. Scott Wong, "'Rebuild America Jobs' to Be Pushed by Democrats," *Politico*, October 21, 2011, http://www.politico.com/news/stories/1011/66557 .html.

16. S.1660 American Jobs Act of 2011 introduced October 5, 2011, by sponsor Sen. Harry Reid (D-NV), http://thomas.loc.gov/cgi-bin/bdquery /z?d112:SN01660:/home/LegislativeData.php|.

17. Carpentier, "New Jersey Sen. Lautenberg Says It's Time for a New WPA," October 18, 2011. S.1723 Teachers and First Responders Back to Work Act of 2011, introduced October 17, 2011, by sponsor Sen. Robert Menendez (D-NJ), http://thomas.loc.gov/cgi-bin/thomas.

18. Mike Hall, "Republicans Vote to Keep Teachers, First Responders Off the Job," AFL-CIO Blog, October 21, 2011, http://blog.aflcio.org/2011/10/21 /republicans-vote-to-keep-teachers-first-responders-off-the-job/.

19. Wong, "'Rebuild America Jobs' to be Pushed by Democrats."

20. Statement of Administration Policy, S.1769—Rebuild America Jobs Act (Sen. Klobuchar, D-MN, and 20 cosponsors), WhiteHouse.gov, November 3, 2011, http://www.whitehouse.gov/sites/default/files/omb/legislative /sap/112/saps1769s_20111103.pdf.

21. *Jobs21! Good Jobs for the 21st Century. A BlueGreen Alliance Blueprint to Solve the Jobs Crisis*, BlueGreen Alliance, August 2011.

22. Jesse Lee, "A Vision for High Speed Rail," White House Blog, April 16, 2009, http://www.whitehouse.gov/blog/09/04/16/a-vision -for-high-speed-rail.

23. "High-Speed Rail and the Recovery Act," WhiteHouse.gov, circa April 2009, http://www.whitehouse.gov/high-speed-rail.

24. "High Speed Rail: Creating Jobs, Spurring Growth, Providing Needed Capacity," U.S. Department of Transportation, November 16, 2011, http://

fastlane.dot.gov/2011/11/high-speed-rail-improving-the-present-prepar
ing-for-the-future.html.

25. Thomas Sowell, "Getting Nowhere, Very Fast—on High-Speed Rail," *New American*, January 31, 2012, http://thenewamerican.com/opinion/thomas -sowell/10709--getting-nowhere-very-fast-on-high-speed-rail.

26. San Joaquin County, California, U.S. Census Bureau, http://quickfacts .census.gov/qfd/states/06/06077.html.

27. *Jobs21!*

28. H.R.2847 Green Jobs Act of 2007, introduced June 25, 2007, by sponsor Rep. Hilda Solis (D-CA), http://www.govtrack.us/congress/bill .xpd?bill=h110-2847. H.R.6 Energy Independence and Security Act of 2007, introduced January 12, 2007, by sponsor Rep. Nick Rahall (D-WV), http://www.govtrack.us/congress/bill.xpd?bill=h110-6.

29. Wong, "'Rebuild America Jobs' to Be Pushed by Democrats."

30. Mike Hall, "Senate Republicans Kill Rebuild America Act," AFL-CIO Blog, November 3, 2011, http://blog.aflcio.org/2011/11/03/senate -republicans-kill-rebuild-america-act/.

31. James A. Glasscock [retired clergyman], "Obama's Rebuild America Act Ignores History and Is Doomed to Fail," PhillyBurbs.com, December 26, 2011, http://www.phillyburbs.com/news/local /courier_times_news/opinion/guest/obama-s-rebuild-america-act -ignores-history-and-is-doomed/article_ea144830-4c75-59b8-8a80 -98a6c0087e82.html.

32. Press Release: "Lautenberg Introduces 21st Century WPA Job Creation Legislation. Job Creation Must be Top Priority for Economic Recovery," Office of Sen. Frank R. Lautenberg (D-NJ), September 7, 2011, http:// lautenberg.senate.gov/newsroom/record.cfm?id=333977.

33. Ibid.

34. "21st Century WPA Can Create Millions of Jobs," GOIAM.org, January 24, 2012, http://www.goiam.org/index.php/imail/latest /9736-21st-century-wpa-can-create-millions-of-jobs.

35. Board of Directors, Economic Policy Institute, http://www.epi.org /about/board/. R. Thomas Buffenbarger, Our Team, America's Agenda, http://www.americasagenda.org/Background/Our-Team/R--Thomas -Buffenbarger.aspx. Profile: R. Thomas Buffenbarger, *Bloomberg Businessweek*, http://investing.businessweek.com.

36. Tom Buffenbarger, "A New WPA by Next Labor Day," *Talking Union*

/Democratic Socialists of America, September 5, 2011, https://talkingunion
.wordpress.com/2011/09/05/a-new-wpa-by-next-labor-day/.

37. "Paul Krugman—Obama Is a Mistake," YouTube, April 5, 2011. Video
of Krugman speaking before the Carnegie Council was uploaded by
PaulKrugmanBlog.

38. Paul Krugman, "Deep Hole Economics," *New York Times*, January 3, 2012,
https://www.nytimes.com/2011/01/03/opinion/03krugman.html?_r=1.

39. "More about the WPA," The Lilly Library, University of Indiana at
Bloomington, http://www.indiana.edu/~liblilly/wpa/wpa_info.html.
Sources: Jeffrey B. Morris and Richard B. Morris, eds., *Encyclopedia of
American History*, 7th ed., 1996 and Thomas H. Johnson, *The Oxford
Companion to American History*, 1966.

40. Lewis Meriam and Laurence F. Schmeckebier, *Reorganization of the
National Government: What Does It Involve?* (Washington, D.C.: Brookings
Institution, 1939), 98.

41. Ibid., 99.

42. S.1517 21st Century WPA Act introduced September 7, 2011, by sponsor
Sen. Frank R. Lautenberg (D-NJ), http://thomas.loc.gov/cgi-bin/query
/z?c112:S.1517.

43. 21st Century WPA Act introduced September 7, 2011.

44. Megan Carpentier, "New Jersey Sen. Lautenberg Says It's Time for a New
WPA," The Raw Story, October 18, 2011, http://www.rawstory.com/rs
/2011/10/18/new-jersey-sen-lautenberg-says-its-time-for-a-new-wpa/.

45. "Taxpayer's Tab Issue #32," NationalTaxpayers Union Foundation,
September 20, 2011, http://www.ntu.org/ntuf/taxpayerstab/2-32.html.

46. Lawrence Mishel, "Stop Digging Us into an Ever Deeper Hole! Or, How Not to
Argue for the Payroll Tax Holiday," Economic Policy Institute, December 1,
2011, http://www.epi.org/blog/stop-digging-deeper-hole-argue-payroll-tax/.

47. H.R. 494, 21st Century Civilian Conservation Corps Act introduced
January 26, 2011, by sponsor Rep. Marcy Kaptur (D-OH), http://
thomas.loc.gov/cgi-bin/bdquery/D?d112:2:./temp/~bdHqjO::|/home
/LegislativeData.php|.

48. The People's Budget, Budget of the Congressional Progressive Caucus
Fiscal Year 2012, http://cpc.grijalva.house.gov/files/The_CPC_FY2012_
Budget.pdf.

49. "Civilian Conservation Corps (CCC), 1933–1941," u-s-history.com, http://
www.u-s-history.com/pages/h1586.html.

50. "Taxpayer's Tax Vol. 1 Issue 23," December 14, 2010, http://www.ntu.org /ntuf/taxpayerstab/23.html.

51. Presidential Memorandum—America's Great Outdoors for the Secretary of the Interior, the Secretary of Agriculture, the Administrator of the Environmental Protection Agency, and the Chair of the Council on Environmental Quality, Office of the White House Press Secretary, April 16, 2010, http://www.whitehouse.gov/the-press-office /presidential-memorandum-americas-great-outdoors.

52. Ned Sullivan, "The Key to the Success of the America's Great Outdoors Initiative," *Daily Green*, March 8, 2011, http://www.thedailygreen.com /living-green/blogs/easy-tips/land-and-water-conservation-fund. Land and Water Conservation Fund, U.S. Forest Service, http://www.fs.fed.us /land/staff/LWCF/index.shtml.

53. Kurt Repanshek, "Can We Afford the America's Great Outdoors Initiative?" *National Parks Traveler*, February 21, 2011, http://www.nationalparkstrav eler.com/2011/02/can-we-afford-americas-great-outdoors-initiative7654.

54. Ibid.

55. Barack Obama, State of the Union, January 24, 2012.

56. Nick Snow, "White House Retains Oil Tax Increases in Proposed 2013 Budget," *Oil & Gas Journal*, February 13, 2012, http://www.ogj.com /articles/2012/02/white-house-retains-oil-tax-increases-in-proposed- 2013-budget.html.

57. "America's Great Outdoors: Building a Conservation Legacy from the Ground Up," Center for American Progress, February 24, 2011, http:// www.americanprogress.org/events/2011/02/publiclands.html.

58. "Obama 'Youth Corps' to 'Use Crisis as an Opportunity' to 'Transform America'," P/Oed Patriot, March 20, 2011, http://www.poedpatriot.com /2011/03/obama-youth-corps-to-use-crisis-as.html.

59. 21st Century Conservation Service Corps website, http://youthgo.gov /employment-program/21st-century-conservation-service-corps.

60. Partner, 21st Century Conservation Service Corps, http://youthgo.gov /partner.

61. Charles Pekow, "21st Century Conservation Service Corps Committee Seeks Public Ideas," *Examiner.com*, January 25, 2012, http://www.examiner .com/outdoor-recreation-in-washington-dc/21st-century-conservation- service-corps-committee-seeks-public-ideas. Bob Berwin, "New Version of Civilian Conservation Corps Planned," SummitCountyCitizensVoice.com,

December 12, 2011, http://summitcountyvoice.com/2011/12/12/new
-version-civilian-conservation-corps-planned/.

62. Charter, 21st Century Conservation Service Corps Advisory Committee,
Office of the Great Outdoors, U.S. Department of Interior, http://www.doi
.gov/21csc/history/charter.cfm.

63. 21st Century Conservation Service Corps Advisory Committee, U.S.
Department of the Interior, http://www.doi.gov/21CSC/index.cfm.

64. Charter, 21st Century Conservation Service Corps Advisory Committee.

65. "Emergency Jobs to Restore the American Dream Act," Official Website
of Representative Jan Schakowsky, http://schakowsky.house.gov/index
.php?option=com_content&view=article&id=2975&Itemid=8.

66. Jan Schakowsky, "Discover the Networks," http://www.discoverthenet
works.org/individualProfile.asp?indid=1506.

67. H.R., 2914, Emergency Jobs to Restore the American Dream Act
introduced September 14, 2011, by Rep. Janice D. Schakowsky (D-IL),
Thomas.loc.gov, http://thomas.loc.gov/cgi-bin/bdquery/D?d112:1:./temp
/~bduqRL::|/home/LegislativeData.php|.

68. H.R.2855 Emergency Jobs Now Act introduced September 7, 2011, by
Rep. Keith Ellison (D-MN), http://thomas.loc.gov/cgi-bin/bdquery
/D?d112:1:./temp/~bdnPij::|/home/LegislativeData.php|.

69. Fieldhouse and Thiess, "The Restore the American Dream for the 99% Act."

70. "Clean Energy Corps Proposed to Create Jobs, Fight Global Warming,"
Environment News Service, March 2, 2009, http://www.ens-newswire
.com/ens/mar2009/2009-03-02-093.asp.

71. Michelle Chen, "Fixing Schools: A Smart Plan for Jobs," *In These
Times*, August 19, 2011, http://www.inthesetimes.com/working/entry
/11849/fixing_schools_can_be_a_smart_plan_for_jobs/. *FAST! An
infrastructure program to repair public schools*, Economic Policy Institute,
August 11, 2011, http://www.epi.org/publication/fast_an_infrastructure_
program_to_repair_public_schools/.

72. Isaiah J. Poole, "How to Create 5 Million Jobs in Two Years," Campaign for
America's Future, December 14, 2011http://www.ourfuture.org/blog
-entry/2011125014/how-create-5-million-jobs-two-years.

73. Civil Bob, "Schakowsky's Emergency Bill Explains Why We Have No
Jobs," Civil Candor, October 6, 2011, http://civilcandor.com/schako
wsky%E2%80%99s-emergency-bill-explains-why-we-have-no-jobs/.

74. Fieldhouse and Thiess, "The Restore the American Dream for the 99% Act," December 13, 2011.

75. Chen, "Fixing Schools: A Smart Plan for Jobs."

76. Civil Bob, "Schakowsky's Emergency Bill Explains Why We Have No Jobs."

77. Barack Obama, State of the Union, January 24, 2012.

78. Brian Koenig, "Obama Seeks $5 Billion For Veterans Jobs Corps Proposal," *New American*, February 3, 2012, http://thenewamerican.com/usnews /politics/10762-obama-seeks-5-billion-for-veterans-jobs-corps-proposal.

79. Rick Maze, "Post-9/11 Veterans Unemployment Drops in Jan.," *Army Times*, February 3, 2012, http://www.armytimes.com/news/2012/02 /military-post-911-veterans-unemployment-falls-in-january-020312w/.

80. Kevin Freking, "Administration Unveils Veterans Jobs Corps," Associated Press in *Army Times*, February 3, 2012, http://www.armytimes.com/news /2012/02/ap-military-veterans-jobs-corps-unveiled-020312/.

Chapter 6: Blueprint for a New Economy, National Infrastructure Bank

1. Full transcript as prepared for delivery of President Barack Obama's inaugural remarks at the United States Capitol in Washington, D.C., January 20, 2009, http://abcnews.go.com/Politics/Inauguration/president-obama -inauguration-speech-transcript/story?id=6689022&page=1.

2. Jeff Zeleny and David M. Herszenhorn, "Obama Again Raises Estimate of Jobs His Stimulus Plan Will Create or Save," *New York Times*, January 10, 2009, https://www.nytimes.com/2009/01/11/us/politics/11radio.html.

3. William McGurn, "The Media Fall for Phony 'Jobs' Claims. The Obama Numbers Are Pure Fiction," *Wall Street Journal*, http://online.wsj.com /article/SB124451592762396883.html.

4. Ibid.

5. Ibid.

6. Ibid.

7. "Obama Tells Economic Critics to 'Get Out of the Way'," FoxNews.com, August 7, 2009, http://www.foxnews.com/politics/2009/08/07/obama -tells-economic-critics-way/.

8. "Obama: I Don't Want the Folks Who Created the Mess to Do a Lot of Talking," YouTube.com, August 7, 2009, https://www.youtube.com /watch?v=jifjRVLVjzA.

9. Transcript of President Barack Obama's 2012 State Of The Union Address,

House of Representatives, U.S. Capitol, January 24, 2012, http://www
.realclearpolitics.com/articles/2012/01/24/transcript_of_president_
obamas_2012_state_of_the_union_address_112893.html.

10. Chris Edwards, "Infrastructure Projects to Fix the Economy? Don't Bank
on It," *Washington Post*, October 21, 2011, http://www.cato .org/publications
/commentary/infrastructure-projects-fix-economy-dont-bank-it.

11. Chris Edwards and Peter Van Doren, "Jumping off the Government
Bridge," *National Review*, December 9, 2008, http://www.cato.org
/publications/commentary/jumping-government-bridge.

12. "Obama's Speech in Janesville, Wisconsin," Council on Foreign Relations,
February 13, 2008, http://www.cfr.org/us-election-2008/obamas-speech
-janesville-wisconsin/p15492.

13. Ethan Pollack, *Street Smart—Reforming the Transportation Budget Process*,
Economic Policy Institute, December 10, 2009, http://www.epi.org
/publication/bp254/.

14. Herman B. Leonard, *Checks Unbalanced: The Quiet Side of Public Spending*
(New York: Basic Books, 1986), 164.

15. Ibid.

16. Ibid.

17. Ibid.

18. Ibid.

19. Heidi Crebo-Rediker and Douglas Rediker, *Financing America's
Infrastructure: Putting Global Capital to Work*, New American Foundation,
June 2008, http://www.newamerica.net/files/Financing_America_
Infrastructure.PDF.

20. Profile: New America Foundation, *Discover the Networks*, http://discover
thenetworks.org/groupProfile.asp?grpid=7616.

21. Crebo-Rediker and Rediker, *Financing America's Infrastructure*.

22. Press Release: "Infrastructure Bank Legislation Garners Strong Support,"
Official Website of Rep. Rosa L. DeLauro (D-CT), May 20, 2009, http://
delauro.house.gov/release.cfm?id=2553.

23. Crebo-Rediker and Rediker, *Financing America's Infrastructure*.

24. S.1926 National Infrastructure Bank Act of 2007 introduced August 1,
2007, by sponsor Sen. Christopher J. Dodd (D-CT), http://thomas.loc.gov
/cgi-bin/bdquery/z?d110:SN01926:.

25. Ken Orski, "Senate Committee Highlights Dodd-Hagel 'Infrastructure

Bank' Bid," CascadiaProspectus.org, March 25, 2008, http://www.cascadi aprospectus.org/2008/03/dodd_hagel_propose_national_in.php.

26. H.R.3401 National Infrastructure Bank Act of 2007, introduced August 3, 2007, by sponsor Rep. Keith Ellison (D-MN), http://thomas.loc.gov/cgi-bin/bdquery/z?d110:HR03401.

27. Orski, "Senate Committee Highlights Dodd-Hagel 'Infrastructure Bank' Bid."

28. Ibid.

29. "Felix Rohatyn on an Infrastructure Investment Bank," Center for Strategic and International Studies, March 13, 2008, http://csis.org/testimony /felix-rohatyn-infrastructure-investment-bank.

30. Christopher J. Dodd, "Infrastructure and Job Creation—a Priority for Urban America," National Urban League. The State of Black America, 2009, 101+.

31. Press release, Center for Strategic and International Studies, undated 2008, http://www.stanford.edu/~jgrimmer/Website/Joint/File970.txt.

32. Ibid.

33. Keith Laing, "Obama Pushes for Infrastructure Bank Proposal after Debt Deal," *The Hill*, July 11, 2011, http://thehill.com/blogs/transportation -report/highways-bridges-and-roads/170681-obama-pushes-for-infra structure-bank-proposal-after-debt-deal.

34. Press Release: Sen. John Kerry (D-MA) Testimony Before the Banking, Housing, and Urban Affairs Committee, September 10, 2010, http://kerry .senate.gov/press/release/?id=4ecea306-d131-400c-9d96-1227cb356b15.

35. Ed Pilkington, "Obama Enters Mid-Terms Campaign with $50bn Infrastructure Plan. President on the Road to Persuade Voters Economy Is Safe in His Hands, Ahead of Elections Expected to Be Tough on Democrats," *Guardian* (UK), September 6, 2010, http://www.guardian .co.uk/world/2010/sep/06/obama-mid-terms-campaign-economy. Press Release: "Bill Will Boost Obama Infrastructure Plan," Official Website of Sen. John Kerry (D-MA), September 6, 2010, http://kerry.senate.gov/press /release/?id=d2b3c52b-5d59-40ef-abb9-5d0bff5b2e78.

36. About, European Investment Bank, http://www.eib.org/about/index.htm.

37. Ibid.

38. Zachary A. Goldfarb, "S&P Downgrades U.S. Credit Rating for First Time," *Washington Post*, August 5, 2011, http://www.washingtonpost.com / business/economy/sandp-considering-first-downgrade-of-us-credit-rating /2011/08/05/gIQAqKeIxI_story.html.

39. Press Release: "Testifying In Favor of National Infrastructure Bank," Official Website of Sen. John Kerry (D-MA), September 21, 2010, http://kerry.senate.gov/press/release/?id=4ecea306-d131-400c-9d96-1227cb356b15.

40. BUILD ACT, March 15, 2011, http://kerry.senate.gov/work/issues/issue/?id=22C909EF-1B4D-4454-BDBF-257AA80DC02A. "Sen. Kerry Introduces New Infrastructure Bank Bill," DC.StreetsBlog.org, March 15, 2011, http://dc.streetsblog.org/2011/03/15/sen-kerry-introduces-new-infrastructure-bank-bill/. Michael Cooper, "Group Wants New Bank to Finance Infrastructure," New York Times, March 15, 2011, http://www.nytimes.com/2011/03/16/us/politics/16infrastructure.html.

41. Ibid.

42. Vicki Needham, "Kerry to Introduce Bipartisan Infrastructure Bank Bill," The Hill, March 14, 2011, http://thehill.com/blogs/on-the-money/domestic-taxes/149347-kerry-set-to-introduce-bipartisan-infrastructure-bank-bill.

43. "Sen. Kerry Introduces New Infrastructure Bank Bill," March 15, 2011; Michael Cooper, "Group Wants New Bank to Finance Infrastructure," March 15, 2011.

44. S.3938 Export-Import Bank Reauthorization Act of 2006, http://www.congress.gov/cgi-bin/query/D?c109:4:./temp/~c109q6oK37.

45. Timothy P. Carney, "John Kerry's 'Infrastructure Bank': A Corporate Welfare Slush Fund," Washington Examiner, March 15, 2011, http://washingtonexaminer.com/politics/beltway-confidential/2011/03/john-kerry%E2%80%99s-%E2%80%98infrastructure-bank%E2%80%99-corporate-welfare-slush.

46. Deron Lovaas, "An Infrastructure Bank for Transportation," NRDC.org, June 28, 2011, http://switchboard.nrdc.org/blogs/dlovaas/an_infrastructure_bank_for_tra.html.

47. PublicRadio.org, June 16, 2011, http://marketplace.publicradio.org/display/web/2011/06/16/pm-wall-street-washington-talk-nice--for-a-change/.

48. Michael Likosky, "Kerry's American Infrastructure Bank," Huffington Post, http://www.huffingtonpost.com/michael-likosky/kerry-infrastructure-bank_b_836203.html.

49. Glen Ford, "Obama's Phony Infrastructure Bank," Black Agenda Report, September 2010, http://www.blackagendareport.com/?q=content/obamas-phony-infrastructure-bank.

50. Jake Tapper, "Obama's $50 Billion Infrastructure Plan to Create Jobs in 2011," ABC News, September 2010, http://blogs.abcnews.com/political

punch/2010/09/obama-50-billion-infrastructure-plan-to-create
-jobs-in-2011-.html.

51. Ibid.

52. Mike Lillis, "Liberal House Democrats Urge 'Bold Action' from Obama
    on Jobs Issue," *The Hill*, September 1, 2011, http://thehill.com/homenews
    /house/179289-liberal-dems-urge-bold-action-from-obama-on-jobs-.

53. Act for the 99% introduced December 13, 2011, sponsored by Raul M.
    Grijalva, http://thomas.loc.gov/cgi-bin/bdquery/D?d112:2:./temp
    /~bdJicf::|/home/LegislativeData.php|. Part I—American Infrastructure
    Financing Authority, H.R.12 American Jobs Act of 2011 introduced
    September 21, 2011, by sponsor Rep. John B. Larson (D-CT) (by request),
    http://thomas.loc.gov/cgi-bin/bdquery/D?d112:3:./temp/~bdXp2M::|/
    home/LegislativeData.php|.

54. S.1769 Rebuild America Jobs Act introduced October 31, 2011, by sponsor
    Sen. Amy Klobuchar (D-MN), http://thomas.loc.gov/cgi-bin/bdquery
    /D?d112:9:./temp/~bdUN7G::|/home/LegislativeData.php|.

55. Act for the 99% introduced December 13, 2011. Andrew Fieldhouse and
    Rebecca Thiess, "The Restore the American Dream for the 99% Act: An
    Analysis of Job-Creation Provisions," Economic Policy Institute, December
    13, 2011, http://www.epi.org/publication/restore-american-dream-99-act
    -analysis-job/.

56. Transcript: Obama's Speech to Congress on Jobs, *New York Times*,
    September 8, 2011, http://www.nytimes.com/2011/09/09/us/politics
    /09text-obama-jobs-speech.html?_r=1.

57. Stephanie Kirchgaessner, "Obama to Send Jobs Plan to Congress Monday,"
    Financial Times/CNBC.com, September 11, 2011, http://www.cnbc.com
    /id/44480202/.

58. Evan Lehmann and Saqib Rahim, "Obama Skips Clean Energy to Avoid a
    Political Battle on Jobs," ClimateWire/*New York Times*, September 9, 2011,
    http://www.nytimes.com/cwire/2011/09/09/09climatewire-obama-skips
    -clean-energy-to-avoid-a-politica-36928.html.

59. Part I—American Infrastructure Financing Authority, H.R.12 American
    Jobs Act of 2011, introduced September 21, 2011.

60. Ibid.

61. Patrick Wood, "National Infrastructure Bank: Another Trilateral Ripoff?"
    The August Forecast and Review, September 9, 2010, http://www.august
    forecast.com/tag/delauro/.

62. Transcript of President Barack Obama's 2012 State of the Union Address, January 24, 2012.

63. About, Financial Crimes Enforcement Network, http://www.fincen.gov /about_fincen/wwd/.

64. Mike Brownfield, "State of the Union 2012: Heritage Reaction Roundup," Heritage Foundation, January 24, 2012, http://blog.heritage.org/2012/01 /24/state-of-the-union-2012-heritage-reaction-roundup/.

65. Ibid.

66. Edwin Meese III, "Principles for Revising the Criminal Code," Testimony before the House Judiciary Committee, Subcommittee on Crime, Terrorism and Homeland Security, December 13, 2011, http://www.heritage.org/ research/testimony/2011/12/principles-for-revising-the-criminal-code.

67. Reid J. Epstein, "Richard Shelby: Richard Cordray is DOA," *Politico*, July 21, 2011, http://www.politico.com/news/stories/0711/59545 .html#ixzz1qLey4wiW.

68. Ibid.

69. Brownfield, "State of the Union 2012: Heritage Reaction Roundup."

70. Peter Schroeder, "Advocates Explore Constitutional Options to Appoint Consumer Agency Nominee," *The Hill*, December 11, 2011, http://thehill .com/blogs/on-the-money/1007-other/198579-advocates-explore-consti tutional-powers-to-appoint-consumer-nominee.

71. Press Release: Executive Order—Establishment of the Interagency Trade Enforcement Center, Office of the White House Press Secretary, February 28, 2012, http://www.whitehouse.gov/the-press-office/2012/02/28 /executive-order-establishment-interagency-trade-enforcement-center.

72. John Hull, "Obama Issues Another Unconstitutional Edict," Yahoo.com, February 28, 2012, http://news.yahoo.com/obama-issues-another-uncon stitutional-edict-222500519.html.

73. Transcript of President Barack Obama's 2012 State of the Union Address, January 24, 2012.

74. Jordan Wolf, "5 Low Points in Obama's 2012 State of the Union," Polymic .com, January 25, 2012, http://www.policymic.com/articles /3603/5-low -points-in-obama-s-2012-state-of-the-union/category_list.

75. About, Third Way, http://thirdway.org/about_us.

76. Ed Gerwin, Anne Kim, and Josh Freed, "Getting Our Share of Clean Energy Trade," thirdway.org, February 2010, http://content.thirdway.org/publications/264

/Third_Way_Policy_Memo_-_Getting_Our_Share_of_Clean_
Energy_Trade.pdf.

77. S.708 Trade Enforcement Priorities Act introduced March 31, 2011, by
sponsor Sen. Sherrod Brown (D-OH), http://thomas.loc.gov/cgi-bin
/bdquery/D?d112:2:./temp/~bdVcPM::|/home/LegislativeData.php|.

78. H.R.1518 Trade Enforcement Priorities Act introduced April 13, 2011, by
sponsor Rep. Mark S. Critz (D-PA), http://thomas.loc.gov/cgi-bin/bdquery
/D?d112:1:./temp/~bdVcPM::|/home/LegislativeData.php|.

79. S.1827 Trade Prosecutor Act of 2011 introduced November 8, 2011, by
Sen. Debbie Stabenow (D-MI), http://thomas.loc.gov/cgi-bin/bdquery
/D?d112:3:./temp/~bdVcPM::|/home/LegislativeData.php|.

80. Ken Jarboe, "Obama Plans Government Re-Organization," Athena
Alliance, January 26, 2011, http://www.athenaalliance.org/weblog
/archives/2011/01/obama_plans_government_re-organization.html.

81. Derek Shearer, "Advice to the President: Abolish the Commerce Department,"
Huffington Post, February 16, 2009, http://www.huffingtonpost.com/derek-
shearer/advice-to-the-president-a_b_167223.html. Professor of Diplomacy at
Occidental College and former US ambassador.

82. Aaron Klein and Brenda J. Elliott, *Red Army. The Radical Network That
Must Be Defeated to Save America* (New York: HarperCollins, 2011), 102.

83. John Bresnahan and Jonathan Allen, "At White House, Nancy Pelosi
Leverages Tension," *Politico*, July 14, 2010.

84. *Restore the American Dream for the 99% Act*, Congressional Progressive
Caucus, December 13, 2011, http://cpc.grijalva.house.gov/uploads/2One
.Pager.RAD.99%282%29.pdf. The separate Buy American Improvement
Act of 2011, introduced August 1, 2011, by its sponsor, Rep. Daniel
Lipinski, (D-IL), was last referred to the House Committee on Oversight
and Government Reform.

85. Russell Berman, "Hoyer Pushes 'Make It in America,'" *The Hill*, May 4,
2011.

86. Ibid.

Chapter Seven: "Equal Pay for Equal Work" and Other Acts of "Fairness"

1. Ashley Southall, "Obama Vows to Push Immigration Changes," The
Caucus/*New York Times*, October 25, 2010, http://thecaucus.blogs
.nytimes.com/2010/10/25/in-appeal-to-hispanics-obama-promises
-to-push-immigration-reform/. Video: "Obama to Latinos: 'Punish Our
Enemies'," RealClearPolitics.com, October 26, 2010, http://www.realclear

politics.com/video/2010/10/26/obama_to_latinos_punish_our_enemies.html.

2. Conn Carroll, "Obama's Tax Plan: Crony Capitalism at Its Worst," *Washington Examiner*, February 22, 2012, http://campaign2012 washington examiner.com/blogs/beltway-confidential obamas-tax-plan-crony-capitialism-its-worst/389026.

3. Lester C. Thurow, *Fortune Favors the Bold: What We Must Do to Build a New and Lasting Global Prosperity* (New York: HarperCollins, 2003), 134.

4. George G. Brenkert, *Marx's Ethics of Freedom* (Routledge & Kegan Paul, 1983), http://www.marxists.org/reference/subject/philosophy/works/us/brenkert.htm#24.

5. Burton W. Folsom Jr., "Our Economic Past. Teddy Roosevelt and the Progressive Vision of History," *Freeman* 60, No. 8 (October 2010), http://www.thefreemanonline.org/columns/our-economic-past/teddy-roosevelt-and-the-progressive-vision-of-history/.

6. Theodore Roosevelt, "New Nationalism" (speech), Osawatomie, Kansas, August 31, 1910, http://www.theodore-roosevelt.com/images/research/speeches/trnationalismspeech.pdf.

7. Barack Obama, "Remarks by the President on the Economy in Osawatomie, Kansas," WhiteHouse.gov, December 6, 2011, http://www.whitehouse.gov/the-press-office/2011/12/06/remarks-president-economy-osawatomie-kansas.

8. Ken Chowder, "The Father of American Terrorism. Two Hundred Years After His Birth, Americans Still Revere Him as a Martyr and Loathe Him as a Fanatical Murderer. What was he?" *American Heritage* 51, no. 1 (February/March 2000), http://www.americanheritage.com/content/father-american-terrorism.

9. "Osawatomie: the Weather Underground Newspaper," zomblog, November 1, 2008, http://www.zombietime.com/zomblog/?p=70.

10. Zoe Trodd, "Writ In Blood: John Brown's Charter of Humanity, The Tribunal of History, and the Thick Link of American Political Protest," *Journal for the Study of Radicalism* 1, no. 1 (2007), 1–29, http://muse.jhu.edu/login?auth=0&type=summary&url=/journals/journal_for_the_study_of_radicalism/v001/1.1trodd.html.

11. Barack Obama, "Remarks by the President on the Economy in Osawatomie, Kansas," December 6, 2011.

12. "John Conyers on the Occupy Movement," YouTube, November 5, 2011, http://youtu.be/cVqj3AHjKQk . See Aaron Klein and Brenda J. Elliott, *Red

Army. The Radical Network That Must Be Defeated to Save America (New York: HarperCollins, 2011) for background on Conyers, in particular pages 50–53.

13. Matthew Spalding, "The String-Pullers," *National Review Online*, December 31, 2011, http://www.nationalreview.com/articles/286840/string-pullers-matthew-spalding.

14. Karl Marx, *Critique of the Gotha Program*, Part 1 (first published, abridged in the journal *Die Neue Zeit*, Bd. 1, no. 18, 1890–91), http://www.marxists.org/archive/marx/works/1875/gotha/index.htm.

15. About, Economic Policy Institute, http://www.epi.org/about/.

16. S.71 Paycheck Fairness Act, introduced January 21, 1997, by sponsor Sen. Thomas Daschle (D-SD), http://www.govtrack.us/congress/bill.xpd?bill=s105-71.

17. Fiona Colgan and Sue Ledwith, eds., *Gender, Diversity, and Trade Unions: International Perspectives* (London: Routledge, 2002), 239.

18. Ibid.

19. S.71 Paycheck Fairness Act, introduced January 21, 1997, by sponsor Sen. Thomas Daschle (D-SD). On June 5, 2012, Senate Majority Leader Harry Reid put the Paycheck Fairness Act to a vote. It fell eight votes short of the 60 required to forward it to the Senate floor for debate.

20. H.R.2023 Paycheck Fairness Act, introduced June 24, 1997, by sponsor Rep. Rosa DeLauro (D-CT), http://www.govtrack.us/congress/bill.xpd?bill=h105-2023.

21. Paycheck Fairness Act, 105th through 112th Congresses, http://www.govtrack.us/congress/bill.xpd?bill=s105-71&tab=related.

22. Ibid.

23. Jennifer Kabbany and Julie Hyman, "Proponents of Equal Pay Unbalanced? Women's Earnings Continue to Divide Advocacy Groups, Even as Two Bills Intended to Counter Discrimination Wind Their Way Through Congress," *Insight on the News* 15, no. 18 (May 17, 1999), 41.

24. Ibid.

25. Heather Boushey, "Closing the Wage Gap," Economic Policy Institute, March 4, 2002, http://www.epi.org/publication/webfeatures_viewpoints_gender_gap/.

26. Ibid.

27. Kabbany and Hyman, "Proponents of Equal Pay Unbalanced?"

28. Diana Furchtgott-Roth, "The Myth of the Wage Gap," *Civil Rights Journal* 4, no. 1 (1999), 28.4

29. Dianna Furchtgott-Roth, "Comparable Worth Is Back," *American Spectator,* September 1, 2000.
30. Boushey, "Closing the Wage Gap."
31. Franklin D. Roosevelt, "The President's Reemployment Agreement," July 27, 1933. Online by Gerhard Peters and John T. Woolley, The American Presidency Project, http://www.presidency.ucsb.edu/ws/?pid=14492.
32. Furchtgott-Roth, "Comparable Worth Is Back."
33. Ibid.
34. Ibid.
35. Ibid.
36. John Irons and Andrew Fieldhouse, "Let the Tax Cuts for the Rich Expire," Economic Policy Institute, August 17, 2010, http://www.epi.org/publication/let_the_tax_cuts_for_the_rich_expire/.
37. Andrew Fieldhouse and Isaac Shapiro, *The Facts Support Raising Revenues from the Highest-Income Households,* Century Foundation, August 11, 2011, http://tcf.org/publications/2011/publications/pdfs/IssueBrief310.pdf/++atfield++file.
38. "Chart of the Week: Nearly Half of All Americans Don't Pay Income Taxes," Heritage Foundation, February 19, 2012, http://blog.heritage.org/2012/02/19/chart-of-the-week-nearly-half-of-all-americans-dont-pay-income-taxes/.
39. Robert Longley, "Who Pays the Most Income Tax? Higher Income Earners Pay the Most, Treasury says," About.com, undated, http://usgovinfo.about.com/od/incometaxandtheirs/a/whopaysmost.htm.
40. Annie Lowrey, "99 Percenters, Meet the 53 Percenters. In Response to Occupy Wall Street, Some Conservatives Are Blasting the 47 Percent of Americans Who Don't Pay Federal Taxes. Do They Have a Point?" *Slate,* October 11, 2011, http://www.slate.com/articles/business/mon eybox/2011/10/_53_percenters_conservative_campaign_against_americans_who_don_t.html.
41. Sam Youngman, "Obama Proposes Tax Hikes on Wealthy to Pay for $447B Jobs Bill," *The Hill,* September 12, 2011, http://thehill.com/homenews/administration/180927-obama-proposes-tax-hikes-on-wealthy-business-to-pay-for-447b-jobs-bill.
42. Ibid.
43. Steve Holland and Matt Spetalnick, "Obama Wants Tax Breaks Ended to Pay for Jobs Plan," Reuters, September 12, 2011, http://www.reuters.com/article/2011/09/12/us-obama-jobs-plan-idUSTRE78B31M20110912.

44. Ibid.

45. "Schakowsky Introduces Bill to Tax Millionaires and Billionaires."

46. Zeke Miller, "REVEALED: Obama's Jobs Plan to Raise $400 Billion in Taxes," BusinessInsider.com, September 12, 2011, http://www.businessin sider.com/obama-jobs-plan-would-raise-400b-in-taxes-cut-subsidies-2011-9.

47. Timothy P. Carney, "Obama's Backdoor Rate Hike," *Washington Examiner*, September 12, 2011, http://campaign2012.washingtonexaminer.com /blogs/beltway-confidential/obamas-backdoor-rate-hike.

48. Andrew Fieldhouse and Rebecca Thiess, *The Restore the American Dream for the 99% Act: An Analysis of Job-Creation Provisions*, Economic Policy Institute, December 13, 2011, http://www.epi.org/publication/restore -american-dream-99-act-analysis-job/.

49. "Schakowsky Introduces Bill to Tax Millionaires and Billionaires," Official website of Rep. Janice D. Schakowsky (D-IL), March 16, 2011, http://scha kowsky.house.gov/index.php?option=com_content&view=article&id=28 77&catid=22.

50. H.R.1124 Fairness in Taxation Act of 2011 introduced March 16, 2011, by Rep. Janice D. Schakowsky (D-IL), OpenCongress.org, http://www.open congress.org/bill/112-h1124/show.

51. Ibid.

52. David Callahan and Tamara Draut, "Help Wanted: America Needs a Better Jobs Plan. A Response to the Obama Jobs Speech," Demos, September 8, 2011, http://www.demos.org/sites/default/files/publications /HelpWanted_ResponseToObamasJobsPlan_Demos.pdf.

53. Profile: Demos, *Discover the Networks*, http://www.discoverthenetworks .org/groupProfile.asp?grpid=7690.

54. John S. Irons, "No Alternative: Time to Fix the Tax Code," Center for American Progress, April 23, 2007, http://www.americanprogress.org /issues/2007/04/tax_code.html.

55. Dan Mitchell, "Obama's Budget Plan: Class-Warfare Tax Policy and Bureaucrat-Controlled Health Care," Center for Freedom and Prosperity Foundation, April 14, 2011, http://freedomandprosperity.org/2011/blog /big-government/obama%E2%80%99s-budget-plan-class-warfare-tax -policy-and-bureaucrat-controlled-health-care/.

56. Dan Mitchell, "Even the Europeans Are Trying to Undo the Mistakes of Obama-Style Class Warfare," Center for Freedom and Prosperity Foundation, July 9, 2011, http://freedomandprosperity.org/2011/blog

/big-government/even-the-europeans-are-trying-to-undo-the-mistakes-of
-obama-style-class-warfare/.

57. Dan Mitchell, "Obama Embraces Another Class Warfare Proposal—'Tax
the Rich' Is the Universal Cure!" Center for Freedom and Prosperity
Foundation, April 22, 2011, http://freedomandprosperity.org/2011/blog
/big-government/obama-embraces-another-class-warfare -proposal-%E2%
80%93-%E2%80%9Ctax-the-rich%E2%80%9D-is-the-universal-cure/.

58. Andrew G. Biggs, "The Case Against Raising the Social Security Tax Max,"
American Enterprise Institute, March 22, 2011, http:// www.aei.org/article
/economics/fiscal-policy/taxes/the -case-against-raising-the-social
-security-tax-max/.

59. Editorial: "Obama's Tax Max. The President Floats Another Payroll
Tax Hike," *Wall Street Journal*, April 22, 2011, http://online.wsj.com
/article/SB10001424052748704071704576277133474338552
.html?mod=djemEditorialPage_h.

60. Mitchell, "Obama Embraces Another Class Warfare Proposal—'Tax the
Rich' Is the Universal Cure!"

61. Ibid.

62. "Obama Tax Plan Indicates Theme of Re-Election Campaign, Despite
Improbability It Will Pass Congress," Associated Press, January 30, 2012,
http://www.foxnews.com/politics/2012/01/30/obama-tax-plan-indicates
-theme-re-election-campaign-despite-improbability-it/.

63. Bernie Becker, "Dems Embrace New Strategy on Taxes," *The Hill*, January
27, 2012, http://thehill.com/blogs/on-the-money/domestic-taxes
/206971-dems-embrace-new-strategy-on-taxes.

Chapter Eight: Government Health Care for All

1. Amie Parnes, "Obama Will Avoid Healthcare Defense During Court
Review," *The Hill*, March 21, 2012, http://thehill.com/blogs/healthwatch
/politics-elections/217197-president-will-avoid-high-profile-defense
-during-court-review.

2. Dick Morris on *Fox & Friends*, Fox News Channel, March 28, 2012.

3. Neera Tanden and Topher Spiro, *The Case for the Individual Mandate in
Health Care Reform. A Comprehensive Review of the Evidence*, Center for
American Progress, February 2012, http://www.americanprogress.org
/issues/2012/02/pdf/individual_mandate_execsumm.pdf.

4. Marla Bizzle, Denise Fraga, Laurie Seremetis, and Jeanne Lambrew,

The Specter of Socialized Medicine. What Is It and Is It Invading Our Country? Center for American Progress, May 14, 2008, http://www .americanprogress.org/issues/2008/05/socialized_medicine.html.

5. Ibid.

6. Ibid.

7. Kevin Smith, "AARP Profits from ObamaCare at the Expense of American Seniors, New Report Shows," House Speaker John Boehner's blog, March 30, 2011, http://www.speaker.gov/Blog/?postid=232516.

8. Reps. Wally Herger (R-CA) and Dave Reichert (R-WA), "Behind the Veil: The AARP America Doesn't Know," House Ways & Means Committee, March 30, 2011, http://waysandmeans.house.gov/UploadedFiles/AARP_ REPORT_FINAL_PDF_3_29_11.pdf.

9. Act for the 99% introduced December 13, 2011, sponsored by Raul M. Grijalva, http://thomas.loc.gov/cgi-bin/bdquery/D?d112:2:./temp /~bdJicf::|/home/LegislativeData.php|.

10. Andrew Fieldhouse and Rebecca Thiess, "The Restore the American Dream for the 99% Act: An Analysis of Job-Creation Provisions," Economic Policy Institute, December 13, 2011, http://www.epi.org/publication /restore-american-dream-99-act-analysis-job/.

11. Isaiah J. Poole, "How to Create 5 Million Jobs in Two Years," Campaign for America's Future, December 14, 2011, http://www.ourfuture.org/blog -entry/2011125014/how-create-5-million-jobs-two-years.

12. Ezra Klein, "If ObamaCare Is Overturned, Will That Lead to Single Payer? And Would That Be a Good Thing?" *Washington Post*, March 30, 2012, http://www.washingtonpost.com/blogs/ezra-klein/post/if-obamacare-is -overturned-will-that-lead-to-single-payer-and-would-that-be-a-good-thing /2012/03/29/gIQAQwypiS_blog.html.

13. Ibid.

14. "CBO and JCT's Estimates of the Effects of the Affordable Care Act on the Number of People Obtaining Employment-Based Health Insurance," Congressional Budget Office, March 15, 2012, https://www.cbo.gov /publication/43082.

15. "Weekly Update: ObamaCare on the Ropes," JudicialWatch.org, March 30, 2012, http://www.judicialwatch.org/press-room/weekly-updates/weekly -update-obamacare-on-the-ropes/.

16. Amy Gardner, "Supreme Court's Health-Care Ruling Could Deal Dramatic Blow to Obama Presidency," *Washington Post*, March 30, 2012, http://www

.washingtonpost.com/politics/supreme-courts-health-care-ruling-could-deal
-dramatic-blow-to-obama-presidency/2012/03/28/gIQAfpBYhS_story.html.

17. Fay Voshell, "FDR Redux: Obama Challenges SCOTUS," *American
Thinker*, April 4, 2012, http://www.americanthinker.com/2012/04/fdr_
redux_obama_challenges_scotus.html.

18. "Governor Deval Patrick, Governor Jim Doyle and Neera Tanden
Announce new health care organization," WisconsinHealthNews.com,
April 14, 2011, http://wisconsinhealthnews.com/press-releases/governor
-deval-patrick-governor-jim-doyle-and-neera-tanden-announce-new-health
-care-organization.

19. Michael Levenson, "Patrick Helps Kick Off Twin Efforts to Defend US Health
Care Law," *Boston Globe*, April 11, 2011, http://articles.boston.com/2011-04
-15/news/29422332_1_health-care-law-governor-romney-mitt-romney.

20. Michael McAuliff and Sam Stein, "Paul Ryan's Budget Becomes Bogeyman
Uniting Progressives, Democrats," *Huffington Post*, April 25, 2011, http://
www.huffingtonpost.com/2011/04/25/paul-ryans-budget-angry
-democrats-town-halls_n_853553.html.

21. Aaron Klein and Brenda J. Elliott, *Red Army. The Radical Network That
Must Be Defeated to Save America* (New York: Broadside Books, 2011), 77.

22. Michael D. Shear, "New Groups Form to Raise Millions for Democrats,"
New York Times, April 14, 2011, http://thecaucus.blogs.nytimes.com/2011
/04/15/new-groups-form-to-raise-millions-for-democrats/.

23. Stephen Koff, "Group with Obama Ties Will Fight Repeal of Health Reform
in Ohio," *Plain Dealer* (Cleveland), July 12, 2011, http://www.cleveland.com
/open/index.ssf/2011/07/national_political_group_will.html.

24. About, Protect Your Care, http://www.protectyourcare.org/about/.

25. Profile: Neera Tanden, Center for American Progress, http://www
.americanprogress.org/experts/TandenNeera.html.

26. "Governor Deval Patrick, Governor Jim Doyle and Neera Tanden
Announce New Health Care Organization."

27. Ibid.

28. Profile: Paul Tewes, NewPartners.com, http://www.newpartners.com/meet
-our-partners/paul-tewes.php. "Governor Deval Patrick, Governor Jim Doyle
and Neera Tanden Announce New Health Care Organization."

29. Ibid.

30. Ibid.

31. Profile: Ami Copeland, NewPartners.com, http://www.newpartners.com
/meet-our-partners/ami-copeland.php.

32. "Governor Deval Patrick, Governor Jim Doyle and Neera Tanden Announce New Health Care Organization."

33. Profile: Ami Copeland, http://amicopeland.com/.

34. "Governor Deval Patrick, Governor Jim Doyle and Neera Tanden Announce New Health Care Organization."

35. Levenson, "Patrick Helps Kick Off Twin Efforts to Defend US Health Care Law," April 11, 2011.

36. Sam Stein, "New Health Care Advocacy Group Launches With $5 Million in the Bank (EXCLUSIVE)," *Huffington Post*, April 14, 2011, http://www.huffington post.com/2011/04/14/new-health-care-advocacy-group_n_849391.html.

37. Lisa Marzilli and Beth Bell, "'Protect Your Care' Protests GOP Plans to Cut to Medicare, Medicaid," WMNF.org, September 23, 2011, http://www.wmnf.org/news_stories protect-your-care-protests-gop-plans-to-cut-to-medicare-medicaid.

38. Profile: Darden Rice, LinkedIn, http://www.linkedin.com/pub/darden-rice/8/973/857.

39. "Governor Deval Patrick, Governor Jim Doyle and Neera Tanden Announce New Health Care Organization."

40. Profile: Jim Margolis (2007), http://www.buyingofthepresident.org/index.php/interviews/jim_margolis/.

41. "Governor Deval Patrick, Governor Jim Doyle and Neera Tanden Announce New Health Care Organization."

42. Ibid.

43. Profile: John Anzalone, *Politico*, http://www.politico.com/arena/bio/john_anzalone.html.

44. Ben Smith, "Common Purpose," *Politico*, April 8, 2009, http://www.politico.com/blogs/bensmith/0409/Common_Purpose.html.

45. Mission Statement, Common Purpose Project, http://www.commonpurpose project.org/.

46. Meet the Team, Common Purpose Project, http://www.commonpurpose project.org/team/.

47. Alexander Burns, "Defending Health Care Reform in Iowa," *Politico*, April 14, 2011, http://www.politico.com/news/stories/0811/61005.html.

48. "HCAN, PLAN and Protect Your Care Rally Outside the Office of US Senator Dean Heller (NV)," YouTube, July 29, 2011, https://www.youtube.com/watch?v=v1hJCEXZmJc.

49. Press Release: "Protect Your Care Launches First TV Ad. At First Republican

Presidential Debate Will Be Defending Medicare and Medicaid, Romneycare and the Affordable Care Act," p2012.org, July 13, 2011, http://www.p2012 .org/chrnprep/pyc061311pr.html.

50. Sam Stein, "GOP Tea Party Debate: Audience Cheers, Says Society Should Let Uninsured Patient Die," *Huffington Post*, September 12, 2011, http://www.huffingtonpost.com/2011/09/12/tea-party-debate-health -care_n_959354.html?1315931933.

51. "Protect Your Care Targets Republicans with 'Let Him Die?' Campaign," *Huffington Post*, September 14, 2011, http://www.huffingtonpost.com/2011 /09/14/protect-your-care-campaign-uninsured_n_962115.html.

52. Michael Muskal, "Support at GOP Debate for Letting the Uninsured Die," *Los Angeles Times*, September 13, 2011, http://articles.latimes.com/2011 /sep/13/news/la-pn-ron-paul-gop-debate-20110913.

53. "LetHimDie.com, http://www.lethimdie.com/.

54. Shira Schoenberg, "Advocacy Group Challenges GOP Candidates on 'Let Him Die' Question," *Boston Globe*, September 14, 2011, http://www.boston .com/Boston/politicalintelligence/2011/09/advocacy-group-challenges -gop-candidates-let-him-die-question/mZYv67JNKnzMlnysx73WBL /index.html.

55. Katrina Trinko, "Column: The Truth Behind the 'Let Him Die' Nonsense," *USA Today*, September 16, 2011, http://www.usatoday.com/news/opinion /forum/story/2011-09-16/health-care-tea-party-conservatives-die /50433598/1.

56. Profile: Americans United for Change, "Discover the Networks," http:// www.discoverthenetworks.org/groupProfile.asp?grpid=7475.

57. Robert Farley, [Profile] Americans United for Change, FactCheck.org, October 20, 2011, http://www.factcheck.org/2011/10/americans-united -for-change-2/.

58. Profile: Americans United for Change, "Discover the Networks."

59. Farley, [Profile] Americans United for Change.

60. Profile: Caren Benjamin, LinkedIn, http://www.linkedin.com/pub/dir /Caren/Benjamin.

61. Farley, [Profile] Americans United for Change, October 20, 2011.

62. David Nakamura, "Obama Offers 2012 Election Supporters Change They Can Believe in—Next Term," *Washington Post*, August 26, 2011, http://www .washingtonpost.com/politics/obama-offers-2012-election-supporters -change-they-can-believe-in--next-term/2011/08/25/gIQAJz9AhJ_story.html.

63. Profile: Robert Creamer, Strategic Consulting Group, http://www
    .stratcongroup.com/publication/about.php.
64. Klein and Elliott, *Red Army*, 319, 327.
65. Profile: Midwest Academy, *Undue Influence*, http://www.undueinfluence
    .com/midwest_academy.htm.
66. "Creamer Curdles 'Obama Camp'," *IllinoisReview*, July 13, 2007, http://
    illinoisreview.typepad.com/illinoisreview/2007/07/creamer-curdles.html.
    Credit goes to Tom Roeser for the discovery.
67. John Ruberry, "Fundraiser Tonight for Admitted Check-Kiter and Tax Cheat
    Robert Creamer (Husband of Congresswoman Jan Schakowsky)," *Marathon
    Pundit*, September 14, 2005, http://marathonpundit.blogspot.com/2005/09
    /fundraiser-tonight-for-admitted-check.html.
68. Klein and Elliott, *Red Army*, 327.
69. Zaid Jilani, "VIDEO: Students at Elite Wharton Business School Mock
    99 Percent Movement: 'Get a Job! Get a Job!'" Think Progress, October
    21, 2011, http://thinkprogress.org/special/2011/10/21/350747/video
    -students-at-elite-wharton-business-school-mock-99-percent-movement
    -get-a-job-get-a-job/.
70. Kathleen Hennessey, "Eric Cantor Cancels Wharton Speech After Protests
    Planned," *Los Angeles Times*, October 21, 2011, http://articles.latimes.com
    /2011/oct/21/news/la-pn-cantor-cancels-speech-20111021.
71. Quan Nguye, "'Occupy Philadelphia' Keeps Growing as Move Looms,"
    Philly.com, October 20, 2011, http://articles.philly.com/2011-10-20/news
    /30301755_1_protesters-tents-encampment.
72. Jennifer Sun and Kelsey Matevish, "Protesters Storm Campus After Cantor
    Cancels Visit. Cantor's Office Was Told Thursday That Penn Could Not
    Ensure 'Attendance Policy'," *The Daily Pennsylvanian*, http://thedp.com
    /index.php/article/2011/10/cantor_cancels_huntsman_hall_visit.
73. Jilani, "Students at Elite Wharton Business School Mock 99 Percent
    Movement."
74. McAuliff and Stein, "Paul Ryan's Budget Becomes Bogeyman Uniting
    Progressives, Democrats."
75. Profile: Ramirez Group, http://ramirezgroup.com/.
76. Profile: Andres Ramirez, President, Ramirez Group.com, http://ramirez
    group.com/pr/andres-ramirez.
77. Profile: Jacqueline Ramirez, Principal, Ramirez Group, http://ramirez
    group.com/pr/jacqueline-ramirez.

78. Marco Rauda, Associate, Ramirez Group, http://ramirezgroup.com/pr /marco-rauda.

79. Profile: Warren Flood, Principal, Ramirez Group, http://ramirezgroup.com /pr/warren-flood.

80. John Anzalone, Jeff Liszt, and Matt Hogan, "Key Findings and Message Recommendations from Latest Herndon/Know Your Care Poll," Herndon Alliance, June 6, 2011, http://www.anzaloneresearch.com /Symba/UploadedMedia/SUMMARY%20MEMO%20--%20MAY%20 2011%20HERNDON--KYC%20POLL.pdf.

81. Byron Tau, "Health Care Law Popular Among Hispanics," *Politico*, December 14, 2011, http://www.politico.com/politico44/2011/12/health -care-law-popular-among-hispanics-107416.html.

82. John Anzalone, Jeff Liszt, and Matt Hogan, "Hispanic Voters and the ACA—Key Findings and Message Recommendations," Herndon Alliance, December 20, 2011, http://www.familiesusa.org/conference/health -action-2012/conference-materials/SAT-AM-PLENARY-Herndon-Latinos -Summary.pdf.

83. Robert Pear, "White House Works to Shape Debate over Health Law," *New York Times*, March 9, 2012, https://www.nytimes.com/2012/03/09/us /politics/white-house-works-to-shape-debate-over-health-law.html.

84. Ibid.

85. Ibid.

86. Robert Bluey, "Strategy Memo Details Liberal PR Plan to Promote ObamaCare," Heritage Foundation, March 13, 2012, http://blog.heritage .org/2012/03/13/strategy-memo-details-liberal-pr-plan-to-promote -obamacare/.

87. Pear, "White House Works to Shape Debate Over Health Law."

88. Jim Pethokoukis, "CBO: ObamaCare Could Cost $2.1 Trillion Through 2022," *The Enterprise* blog/American Enterprise, March 15, 2012, http:// blog.american.com/2012/03/cbo-obamcare-could-cost-2-1-trillion- through-2022/.

89. Tom Curry, "Why the Health Care Cost Estimate Keeps Changing," msnbc .com, March 14, 2012, http://nbcpolitics.msnbc.msn.com/_news/2012/03 /14/10689322-why-the-health-care-cost-estimate-keeps-changing.

90. "Updated Estimates for the Insurance Coverage Provisions of the Affordable Care Act," Congressional Budget Office, March 13, 2012, https://www.cbo.gov/publication/43076.

91. Philip Klein, "CBO: ObamaCare to Cost $1.76 Trillion over 10 Yrs," *Washington Examiner*, March 13, 2012, http://campaign2012 .washingtonexaminer.com/blogs/beltway-confidential/cbo-obamacare -cost-176-trillion-over-10-yrs/425831. Remarks by the President to a Joint Session of Congress on Health Care, Office of the White House Press Secretary, September 9, 2009, http://www.whitehouse.gov/the_press_ office/Remarks-by-the-President-to-a-Joint-Session-of-Congress-on -Health-Care.

92. Rick Moran, "Obama's Lies on ObamaCare Catching Up to Him," *American Thinker*, March 14, 2012, http://www.americanthinker.com /blog/2012/03/obamas_lies_on_obamacare_catching_up_to_him.html.

93. H.R. 4872, Reconciliation Act of 2010, March 18, 2010, Congressional Budget Office, https://www.cbo.gov/publication/21327.

94. Klein, "CBO: ObamaCare to Cost $1.76 Trillion over 10 Yrs."

Chapter Nine: Elections: Stealing the Future

1. Pamela M. Prah, "Will States Topple Electoral College?" Stateline.org, June 9, 2008, http://www.stateline.org/live/details/story?contentId=316080.

2. U.S. Electoral College, National Archives and Records Administration, http://www.archives.gov/federal-register/electoral-college/about.html.

3. William C. Kimberling, "The Electoral College," Federal Elections Commission, revised May 1992, http://www.fec.gov/pdf/eleccoll.pdf.

4. The Electoral College, National Popular Vote, http://nationalpopularvote .com/pages/electoralcollege.php. Election Results 2008, President Map, *New York Times*, http://elections.nytimes.com/2008/results/president/map .html. In the 2008 election, Obama won Calif. 55, N.Y. 31, Fla. 27, Ill. 21, Pa. 21, Ohio 20, Wash. 17, N.C. 15, N.J. 15, Va. 13, Mass. 12, Ind. 11, Minn. 10, and Wis. 10, which would put him over the required 270 electoral votes. He also won several smaller states with fewer Electoral Votes each.

5. Jacquerie, "Warning! Progressives' NPV Plan for White House Control, 2012 and Permanently," October 21, 2011.

6. About, National Popular Vote, http://www.nationalpopularvote.com /pages/about.php.

7. Jacquerie, "Warning!"

8. Ibid.

9. Neetal Parekh, "What Is a 501(c)(4) Non Profit Organization?" Free *Enterprise* blog/Findlaw.com, September 23, 2009, http://blogs.findlaw

.com/free_enterprise/2009/09/what-is-a-501c4-non-profit-organization
.html.

10. About, http://www.nationalpopularvote.com/pages/about.php.

11. Tara Ross and Trent England, "George Soros Supports the Tea Party? What
the National Popular Vote Wants You to Believe," *Weekly Standard*, August
16, 2011, http://www.weeklystandard.com/blogs/george-soros-supports
-tea-party_590271.html.

12. Joan, "NPV and the Battle for Michigan," GrassrootsMichigan.com,
November 3, 2011, http://grassrootsmichigan.com/?p=1161. Eliza Newlin
Carney, "GOP Nonprofit Backs Electoral College," *Roll Call*, December
7, 2011, http://www.rollcall.com/issues/57_71/GOP-Nonprofit-Backs
-Electoral-College-210872-1.html?zkMobileView=true.

13. Staff: Robert Ritchie, FairVote.org, http://www.fairvote.org/staff/.

14. Members, Bretton Woods Committee, http://www.brettonwoods.org
/members/.

15. Overview, FairVote.org, http://www.fairvote.org/overview.

16. Steven Hill, "Beyond the 2004 Elections: Democracy, Anyone?" FairVote
.org, August 2004, http://archive.fairvote.org/articles/progpopaug04.htm.

17. Jonathan Soros, "It's Time to Junk the Electoral College," *Wall Street Journal*,
December 15, 2008, http://online.wsj.com/article/SB122930124441705413
.html.

18. Ross and England, "George Soros Supports the Tea Party?

19. Endorsers, FairVote.org, http://www.fairvote.org/endorsers
-of-the-npv-plan.

20. Prah, "Will States Topple Electoral College?"

21. Progress by State, National Popular Vote, accessed March 11, 2012, http://
www.nationalpopularvote.com/map.php.

22. Scott, "Progressives Attempt to Destroy Our Republic with Soros Funded
Popular Vote Group," UpstateVoice.com (S.C.), August 9, 2011, http://
upstatevoice.com/progressives-attempt-to-destroy-our-republic-with
-soros-funded-popular-vote-group/.

23. Robert Bennett, "Popular Election of the President Without a Constitutional
Amendment" (Abstract), Social Science Research Network, March 27, 2001,
http://papers.ssrn.com/sol3/papers.cfm?abstract_id=261057.

24. Akhil Reed Amar and Vikram David Amar, "How to Achieve Direct
National Election of the President Without Amending the Constitution.
Part Three of a Three-Part Series on the 2000 Election and the Electoral

College," FindLaw.com, December 28, 2001, http://writ.lp.findlaw.com/amar/20011228.html.

25. See footnote 28 in Robert W. Bennett, "Democracy as a Meaningful Conversation," *Constitutional Commentary* 14, no. 3 (1997), 481–533.

26. Ibid.

27. "Fix System Before We Elect 'Loser President'," *Daily Herald* (Arlington Heights, IL), October 26, 2000, http://www.highbeam.com/doc/1G1-66477727.html.

28. Ibid.

29. Ibid.

30. Staff Editorial, "Electoral Votes Must Go," University Wire/*Independent Florida Gator*, October 31, 2000, http://www.highbeam.com/doc/1P1-36089171.html.

31. "Fix System Before We Elect 'Loser President.'"

32. Michael Stokes Paulsen, "Dirty Harry and the Real Constitution," *The University of Chicago Law Review* 64, no. 4 (Autumn, 1997), 1457–91, http://www.jstor.org/discover/10.2307/1600223?uid=3739800&uid=2&uid=4&uid=3739256&sid=55874682723.

33. Todd Gitlin, "A Principled Ruling to Some, a Disaster to Others. Legal Experts and Cultural Critics Debate the Supreme Court's Decisive Findings," *Salon.com*, December 14, 2000, http://www.salon.com/2000/12/14/reacts_17/.

34. Cathy Newman, "Keeping an Eye on the Votes That Count; Federal Monitor Ready If Snags Hit Electoral College," *Washington Post*, October 27, 2000, http://www.highbeam.com/doc/1P2-561513.html.

35. "Indian American Aids White House defense," *India Abroad*, February 12, 1999, http://www.highbeam.com/doc/1P1-23055548.html.

36. Ibid.

37. "The National Law Journal Names 100 Most Influential Lawyers in America," PRNewswire, June 5, 2000, http://www.highbeam.com/doc/1G1-62499003.html.

38. Profile: Vikram David Amar, http://writ.news.findlaw.com/amar/index.html.

39. Michael Stokes Paulsen, "How to Interpret the Constitution," *Yale Law Journal* 115, no. 8 (2006), 2037ff.

40. Profile: Vikram David Amar.

41. Ibid.

42. Ann Coulter, "The Professorial Contingent of the Rainbow Coalition," *Human Events* 54, no. 43 (November 13, 1998), 6.

43. "Empowering Jurists: Democratizing the Judicial System" in Karl G. Trautman, ed., *The New Populist Reader* (Westport, CT: Praeger, 1997), 196.

44. Akhil Reed Amar and Vikram David Amar, "Unlocking the Jury Box," *Policy Review,* May/ June 1996, reprinted with permission in Karl G. Trautman, ed., *The New Populist Reader,* 197.

45. Ibid., 199.

46. Michael Lind, "Do the People Rule?" *Wilson Quarterly* 26, no. 1 (Winter 2002), 40ff.

47. Ibid.

48. Study Guide: Summary and Analysis of Essay 39, Alexander Hamilton, John Jay, and James Madison, *The Federalist Papers*, Gradesaver.com, http://www.gradesaver.com/the-federalist-papers/study-guide /section39/.

49. Samuel H. Beer, "[On] Who Rules?" *Wilson Quarterly* 26, No. 2 (Spring 2002) 3ff.

50. Scott, "Progressives Attempt to Destroy Our Republic With Soros Funded Popular Vote Group."

51. "CYTL Acquires SOE Software, Becoming the Leading Election Software Provider," *Market Watch*, January 11, 2012, http://www.marketwatch .com/story/scytl-acquires-soe-software-becoming-the-leading-election -software-provider-2012-01-11.

52. Beverly Harris, "Foreign Company Buys U.S. Election Results Reporting Firm," blackboxvoting.org, January 11, 2012, http://www.drudgereport .com/flash1.htm.

53. Ibid.

54. "Scytl Becomes the first Internet Voting Vendor to Register with the U.S. EAC," SCYTL, May 11, 2009, http://www.scytl.com/en /news_2009.html.

55. "Scytl Partners with Hart InterCivic to Enter the E-Pollbook Market in the United States," SCYTL, November 9, 2009, http://www.scytl.com/en /news_2009.html.

56. "Scytl Carries Out Electoral Modernization Projects in 14 States During the U.S. General Election," SCYTL, November 8, 2010, http://www.scytl .com/en/news_2010.html.

FOOL ME TWICE

57. Cory Way, "Voter Action Comments Regarding Proposed Pilot Program Certification Testing Requirements & Manual," Voter Action, May 26, 2010, http://www.eac.gov/assets/1/AssetManager/Voter%20 Action%20-%20Comments%20Regarding%20Proposed%20Pilot%20 Program%20Certification%20Testing%20Requirements%20&%20 Manual.pdf.

58. Steven Hoffer, "DC Electronic Voting Site Hacked by Iran, China, University of Michigan," *Huffington Post*, October 11, 2010, http://www.aolnews.com /2010/10/11/dc-electronic-voting-site-hacked-by-iran-china-university-of-m/.

59. "BOEE Executive Director Paul Stenbjorn Resigning," DCist.com, October 20, 2011, http://dcist.com/2011/10/breaking_boee_executive_director_ re.php.

60. Hoffer, "DC Electronic Voting Site Hacked by Iran, China, University of Michigan."

61. Janis D. Hazel, "What Will Happen to Minorities When the Only Way to Vote Is Online?" Minority Media and Telecom Council, November 2, 2010, http://broadbandandsocialjustice.org/2010/11 /what-will-happen-to-minorities-when-the-only-way-to-vote-is-online/.

62. Mike DeBonis, "Hacker Infiltration Ends D.C. Online Voting Trial," *Washington Post*, October 4, 2010, http://voices.washingtonpost.com /debonis/2010/10/hacker_infiltration_ends_dc_on.html.

63. Aaron Klein, "Is This How Obama Win Will Be Guaranteed?" WND, January 5, 2012 http://www.wnd.com/2012/01/is-this-how-obama-win -will-be-guaranteed/.

64. Kymberly Bays, "Growing Skepticism Surrounds Americans Elect," *U.S. Independent Voter Network*, March 30, 2012, http://ivn.us/2012/03/30 /growing-skepticism-surrounds-americans-elect/.

65. "Americans Elect Board of Advisors," *Irregular Times*, accessed July 27, 2011, http://irregulartimes.com/index.php/...-july-26-2011/.

66. Steve Benen, "Americans Elect's Dubious New Poll," *Washington Monthly*, January 23, 2012 http://www.washingtonmonthly.com/political-animal /2012_01/americans_elects_dubious_new_p034940.php.

67. "Fox25 Undercover" Fox 25 News at 10, November 6, 2005, Available on YouTube at http://www.youtube.com/watch?v=SMGUaCpmEPU.

68. Jennifer Steinhauer, "Opponents of California Ballot Initiative Seek Inquiry," *New York Times*, November 21, 2007 http://www.nytimes.com /2007/11/21/us/21calif.html?_r=1.

69. Reginald Fields, "Ohio Casino Backers Hire Troubled California Firm Arno Political Consultants," *Plain Dealer*, April 28, 2009 http://blog .cleveland.com/metro/2009/04/ohio_casino_backers_hire_troub.html.

70. Greg Lucas, "Americans Elect: A New Political Party That Isn't," *Capital Weekly*, April 21, 2011, http://capitolweekly.net/article.php?xid =znc6uo0z1a56ld.

71. Ibid.

72. Ibid.

73. Siddhartha Mahanta, "Meet the Political Reform Group That's Fueled by Dark Money," *Mother Jones*, November 18, 2011, http://motherjones.com /politics/2011/11/americans-elect-dark-money-campaign-finance.

74. Justin Elliott, "The Slick Shtick of Americans Elect. Just What Americans Yearn for: A High-Tech Presidential Ticket Funded by Secret Wall Street money," *Salon*, December 9, 2011, http://www.salon.com/2011/12/09 /the_slick_schtick_of_americans_elect/.

75. Ibid.

76. Klein, "Is This How Obama Win Will Be Guaranteed?"

77. Patrick Caddell and Douglas Schoen, "The Hillary Moment," *Wall Street Journal*, November 21, 2011, http://online.wsj.com/article/SB1000142405 2970203611404577041950781477944.html.

78. Patrick Caddell and Douglas Schoen, "New Hampshire Voters Should Draft Hillary," *Politico.com*, December 18, 2011, http://www.politico.com /news/stories/1211/70623.html.

GLOSSARY
OF ACRONYMS

21CSC   21st Century Conservation Service Corps

AARP   American Association of Retired Persons

ACORN   Association of Community Organizations for Reform Now

AIFA   American Infrastructure Financing Authority

AE   Americans Elect

AUC   Americans United for Change

AUFC   Americans United for Change

BGA   BlueGreen Alliance

CAP   Center for American Progress

CBPP   Center for Budget and Policy Priorities

CFPB   Consumer Financial Protection Bureau

CHIP   Children's Health Insurance Program

COWS   Center for Wisconsin Strategy

CPC   Congressional Progressive Caucus

CRU   Climatic Research Unit

CSIS   Center for Strategic and International Studies

DOE   Department of Energy

DOT   Department of Transportation

EAC   Election Assistance Commission

EFCA   Employee Free Choice Act

EPA	Environmental Protection Agency
eTec	Electric Transportation Engineering Corporation
EUC	Emergency Unemployment Compensation
EVs	Electric Vehicles
FAST!	Fix America's Schools Today
FCC	Federal Communications Commission
FEEI	Free Enterprise Education Institute
GHG	Greenhouse Gas
GJA	Green Jobs Act
HCAN	Health Care for America Now
HUD	Department of Housing and Urban Development
ICC	International Criminal Court
ICE	Immigration and Customs Enforcement
IPS	Institute for Policy Studies
KYC	Know Your Care
MWP	Making Work Pay
NAF	New America Foundation
NEERS	National Energy Efficiency Resource Standard
NIB	National Infrastructure Bank
NPV	National Popular Vote
PYC	Protect Your Care
R2P	Responsibility to Protect
SDTF	Sustainable Defense Task Force
SEIU	Service Employees International Union
SERRA	Solar Energy Regulatory Relief Act
START	Strategic Arms Reduction Treaty
TRAC	Transactional Records Access Clearinghouse
USB	Unified Security Budget
USCAP	United States Climate Action Partnership
USCIS	United States Citizenship and Immigrant Services
WAP	Weatherization Assistance Program
WPA	Works Progress Administration

INDEX

Conyers Jr., John: 121
Corsell, Peter L.: 29
Coulter, Ann: 167
Covert Cadre: 14
Creamer, Robert: 151–152
Crebo–Rediker, Heidi: 101
Critz, Mark: 115
Crockett, George: 14
Crudele, John: 63
Cutter, W. Bowman: 177

D
Daley, Richard: 152
Damascus: 5
Daschle, Tom: 123, 145
Deeds, Creigh: 97
DeLauro, Rosa: 101, 123, 127
Democracy 21: 176
Demos: 48, 50–53, 56–57, 59–61,
    64–70, 77, 80, 128, 131–132,
    162
Department of Energy (DOE): 22,
    27, 29
Department of Housing and Urban
    Development (HUD): 22
Department of Transportation
    (DOT): 22, 82
Diamond, Larry: 176
DiLorenzo, Thomas: 79
DiMartino, David: 147
Discover the Networks: 34, 151
Dodd, Christopher: 14, 102,
    111–112
Dohrn, Bernardine: 55, 121
Donohue, Thomas: 105
Draut, Tamara: 51, 53, 56, 65–67
Duke Energy: 31–33

Dunkelberg, Bill: 71
Dunn, Anita: ix
Duvall, Cathy: 72

E
Economic Policy Institute: viii, 57,
    59, 62, 67, 69 77, 79, 82, 85, 88,
    93, 100, 120, 123–124, 128
Edwards, Chris: 98
Elders, The: 16
Election Assistance Commission
    (EAC): 171–172
Electric Transportation Engineer-
    ing Corporation (eTec): 29
Electric Vehicles (EVs): 29
Ellison, Keith: 69, 92, 102, 108
Emanuel, Rahm: 31, 107
Emergency Unemployment Com-
    pensation (EUC): 131
EMILY'S List: 145
Employee Free Choice Act
    (EFCA): 60
Energy Independence Trust: 22
England, Trent: 161–162
Environmental Protection Agency
    (EPA): 22, 37
Equal Pay Initiative: 123
Exelon: 31–32
Export Import Bank: 105–106, 116
Extension Amnesty: 41

F
F–35 Joint Strike Fighter: 6
Fadem, Barry: 159–161
Fair Labor Standards Act: 52
Fairness Doctrine: 25
FairVote: 161–62

Just the Facts

Ecstasy

Sean Connolly

Heinemann Library
Chicago, Illinois

Designed by M2 Graphic Design
Printed in Hong Kong / China
Originated by Ambassador Litho Ltd.

05 04 03 02 01
10 9 8 7 6 5 4 3 2

Library of Congress Cataloging-in-Publication Data
Connolly, Sean, 1956-
     Ecstasy / Sean Connolly.
       p. cm. – (Just the facts)
     Includes bibliographical references and index.
     Summary: Explains the nature, development, addictive qualities, consequences, and legal
     aspects of the drug MDMA, commonly known as ecstasy.
     ISBN 1-57572-256-9 (library)
     1. Methamphetamine abuse—Prevention—Juvenile literature. 2. Methamphetamine abuse—United States—
prevention—Juvenile literature. 3. MDMA (Drug)—Juvenile literature. [1. MDMA (Drug) 2. Drug abuse.] I. Title. II.
Series.

HV5822.M38 C65 2000
362.29'9—dc21
                                         00-024347

Acknowledgments
The Publishers would like to thank the following for permission to reproduce photographs: Advertising Archive: pg.49;
Camera Press: pg.4, pg.10, pg.11, pg.17, pg.22, pg.38, pg.39; Format: pg.26, pg.29, pg.50; Magnum Photos: pg.6, pg.8;
Mary Evans Picture Library: pg.15; Pa Photos: pg.32, pg.36; Photofusion: Mark Campbell pg.19; Retna: pg.12, pg.34,
pg.35, pg.47; Rex Features: pg.5, pg.21, pg.23, pg.25, pg.27, pg.31, pg.43, pg.45; Science Photo Library: pg.6, pg.30,
pg.37; Telegraph Colour Library: pg.41.

Cover photograph reproduced with permission of Science Photo Library.

Every effort has been made to contact copyright holders of any material reproduced in this book.
Any omissions will be rectified in subsequent printings if notice is given to the publisher.

Our special thanks to Pamela G. Richards, M.Ed., for her help in the preparation of the book.

Some words are shown in bold, **like this.** You can find out what they mean by looking in the
glossary.

Contents

Introduction

Ecstasy is a drug that has been used widely for hardly more than a decade, but during that time it has generated an enormous amount of publicity. Some people see it as a harmless element of a good time, a substance that helps make people feel happy and energetic enough to dance the night away. Other people see it as a worrying new addition to a drug industry that is already bursting with ways to avoid reality and ruin lives.

The controversy surrounding ecstasy is made worse because it has revived the idea of the *generation gap*, the unbridgeable gulf between young people and their parents. Ecstasy represents an unknown for parents, since it has become popular in the period since their own teenage years. They cannot be sure whether what they know about the dangers of other drugs, such as alcohol, marijuana, and tobacco, applies to ecstasy.

A way of life that includes taking ecstasy has grown in many vacation resorts popular with young people.

Weighing the evidence

In order for young people and their parents to understand ecstasy, it is important to gather some facts. It is also vital to accept that at this point, there is much that medical professionals just do not know, such as the lasting effects of repeated use. We can say, however, that ecstasy use has increased because users enjoy the experience. Taking ecstasy does not make people violent or aggressive. However, there is mounting evidence that the drug can cause death.

Despite its carefree reputation, ecstasy *has* killed people who take it. Moreover, using ecstasy leads to a number of serious problems, most of which stem from the way it heats the body and encourages people to dance for hours. Some ecstasy users leave the dance floor on a stretcher. Even more frightening is the lack of knowledge about how long-term use of ecstasy might harm people. These concerns themselves should make people think twice before calling ecstasy the *happy drug.*

What Is Ecstasy?

Ecstasy, *e,* or XTC, is a drug that combines some of the effects of such **hallucinogens** as LSD with those of such **stimulants** as amphetamines. The result is a distortion of the user's outlook as well as the energy to go without sleep or food.

A large family

The chemical name for ecstasy is MDMA, which is short for methylene-dioxymethamphetamine. MDMA is just one of 179 members of a family of drugs known as MDA, which are derived from the oils of nutmeg, sassafras, saffron, and crocus. Scientists are able to restructure the molecules of MDA elements to create a dramatic array of drugs. Depending on how these molecules are arranged, the effects of the drug created vary from user confidence and a general energy boost to hallucination.

The effects

The initial effects of ecstasy begin about twenty minutes to an hour after the user swallows a pill. These effects are like those of amphetamines: the user feels more energetic and less inclined to hunger or fatigue. At the same time, the drug raises the blood pressure, heart rate, and body temperature. Ecstasy users sometimes describe sensations associated with nervousness, such as butterflies in the stomach and tingling.

These reactions soon fade and the user begins to feel happy and confident. This comfortable feeling can border on **euphoria** as well as a sense of serenity and closeness to people around them. The effects peak at about two hours and slowly wind down for another two to four hours. Although ecstasy is sometimes described as a mild hallucinogen, it is very rare for a user to hallucinate. Sometimes, however, users tend to exhibit repetitive behavior, such as shaking the head over and over. The setting in which ecstasy is usually taken, a loud dance floor, can encourage such impulses.

The allure of ecstasy

In some circles, ecstasy is called *the love drug.* This nickname reflects one of the main attractions of ecstasy, the way it seems linked to feeling good and a sense of shared purpose. Many ecstasy users refer to being *loved-up* when describing the effects of the drug.

An important clue about the popularity of ecstasy is that it is a drug that people prefer to take together. The word *inclusiveness* is sometimes used to describe ecstasy, referring to the feeling that everyone in a large group is somehow part of a team. The sense of well-being produced by the drug is often strengthened by the sight of dozens of other young people sharing the same experience.

It is this feeling of togetherness and shared sensations that makes dance clubs such popular venues for taking ecstasy. Whereas a similar number of people drinking alcohol could turn aggressive or violent, an ecstasy crowd is more likely to bask in a collective sense of affection. For this reason, women tend to feel less threatened in an ecstasy setting.

The dangers

As with some other drugs, the user's experience with ecstacy depends on his or her frame of mind before taking the drug. An unsettled mood or a sense of anxiety about the surroundings can lead to a *bad trip,* an experience in which the user feels panicky and out of control. In addition, people who use ecstacy only during weekends report feeling down in the middle of the week.

The other negative effects of ecstasy include medical complications. There is mounting evidence that regular use of the drug can cause liver damage. And if a dose of ecstasy makes the user's blood pressure skyrocket, the heart can be strained to the point of failure. Most importantly, **dehydration** associated with ecstasy can lead to **heatstroke, respiratory** collapse, and kidney failure.

The Social Mix

The most widely known aspect of the ecstasy high is the feeling of empathy it creates among its users. However, there are a few other patterns that are immediately obvious. One of the most apparent is the overwhelming proportion of young users. Other drugs entice young people, but few are so closely linked to the young and to contemporary youth culture.

Weekend routine

Some of the statistics available underline ecstasy's popularity with the young. Eight percent of U.S. high school seniors say they have tried it at least once. Half-way through the year 2000, U.S. customs officials had seized more than 5.4 million hits of *e*. By contrast, in all of 1998 they seized just 750,000 hits.

E culture

While the typical ecstasy user has one or two tablets each weekend, there are a few settings that have become part of the *e* culture, as it is known. Across the country, young people are dancing the night away at raves, or all-night parties at which electronic music is played. A whole way of life has evolved around the rave scene, which, despite what some club-owners might say, depends on the reputation for ecstasy-friendly activities. Night after night of dancing reinforces the slightly skewed view of the world that is common with ecstasy. That view lingers long after clubbers have returned to their homes. Ravers often wear loose, wide-legged jeans. Common fashion accessories are trinkets such as suckers, pacifiers, and dolls. Sweating dancers carry bottles of water to battle **dehydration,** a common ecstasy side effect.

❝[In 1998] An estimated 1.5 percent (3.4 million) of Americans at least 12 years old had used MDA at least once in their lifetime. . . . The heaviest use was reported for those between 18 and 25 years old.❞

(National Institute on Drug Abuse 2000)

Ecstasy is commonly taken within a group setting, either on a crowded dance-floor with a powerful sound system, or in an outdoor gathering.

Ecstasy and Addiction

The word **addictive** triggers concern in many people, especially parents who think their children might be involved with ecstasy. It represents the ultimate danger of drug abuse, of being drawn into a spiral of increased use, craving, desperation, criminal activity, and possible **overdose.**

Clearer definitions

Doctors and drug counselors, however, prefer to use the term **dependence** when discussing the regular use of a drug. A number of different factors can contribute to either a physical or **psychological** dependence. Physical dependence is usually linked to the idea of **tolerance,** meaning that the body needs to have increasing amounts of a drug for it to have the same effect. The body begins to expect this increased amount and goes through **withdrawal** if supplies stop. Alcohol and heroin are good examples of drugs that promote physical dependence. Psychological dependence, as the name suggests, has to do with the user's perceived need for the drug to cope with stress or difficult situations. Alcohol also produces a psychological dependence, as do cocaine and amphetamines.

Ecstasy withdrawal

Dependence on ecstasy does not jibe with these textbook examples. It does, however, lead to a certain amount of tolerance. Although ecstasy withdrawal cannot compare with that of heroin or alcohol, there are some symptoms of depression and anxiety that can emerge when people stop using ecstasy.

Some of these psychological reactions relate to what doctors call the *rebound effect* of drugs, meaning that they eventually lead to sensations that are exactly opposite to those they first provided. Heroin, which first-time users experience as a stress-free comfort blanket, eventually leads to panic and near-desperation. Amphetamines, which are noted for supplying energy, can end up draining a user of all energy reserves. Ecstasy, too, eventually produces anxiety, fatigue, and depression in the person who at first found care-free excitement and energy.

The trancelike state that ecstasy induces, with its heightened sense of color and sound, causes some people to take the drug regularly.

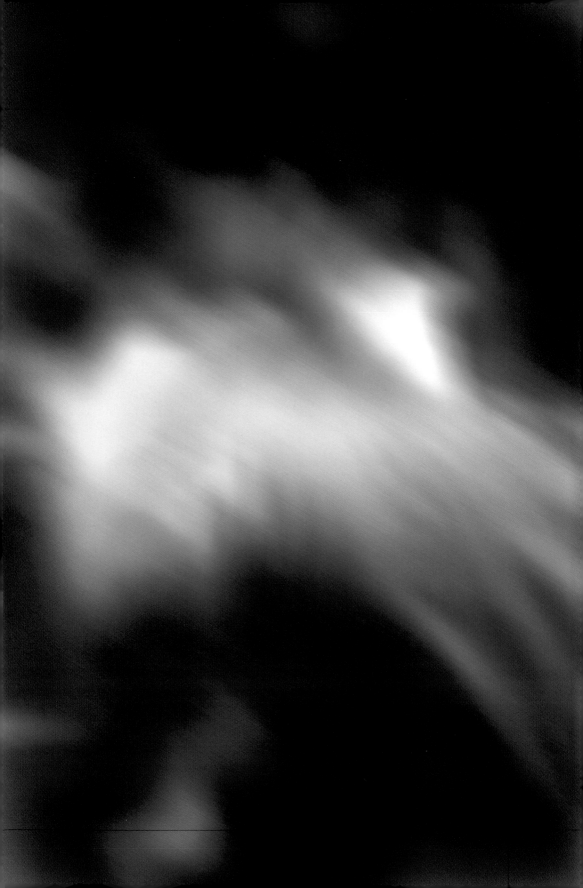

Ecstasy's History

Although it appears very much in the headlines these days, ecstasy has had a checkered history in the nine decades of its existence. It surfaces as a publicized drug, and then drifts back into relative obscurity. Its up-and-down history is partly due to the very mixture of effects that makes it so popular among ravers. It increases sensations of color and sound but cannot be described as a true **hallucinogen,** and it provides energy without the sense of edginess associated with amphetamines.

German research

German **pharmacologists** at the beginning of the twentieth century were involved in intense research to produce new drugs for the public. Many of today's drugs of abuse were developed at around that time, in the flurry of medical research. Cocaine, morphine, and heroin were seen as so-called medical breakthrough drugs when these chemists developed them, towards the end of the nineteenth century. However, by the early 1900s their true effects were emerging.

LSD, which was developed in neighboring Switzerland during the 1930s and 1940s, was also produced as a **therapeutic** drug. Such research was often very hit-or-miss. A basic drug would be isolated from a natural source, such as a plant, and then it would undergo a number of alterations as scientists tested for positive effects. Along the way, some drugs were produced that were not intended to be used on their own, but were useful stepping stones in the production of other **pharmaceuticals.**

MDMA, which we now know as ecstasy, was one such stepping stone. It was first **synthesized** by chemists working for the Merck pharmaceutical company in Darmstadt, Germany, in 1912, and **patented** in 1914. Despite widespread stories today that the drug was developed as an appetite **suppressant,** MDMA was simply a useful tool for producing other drugs. The upheavals of **World War I** caused MDMA to be largely forgotten as chemists turned their attention to wartime efforts.

Fresh attempts

MDMA remained virtually unknown until 1939, when researchers began a series of tests to see if it would work as an appetite **suppressant** or as a **synthetic** version of adrenaline, the hormone that the body produces to deal with stress. Wartime activity during **World War II** put an end to these tests, and it was only after the war that reports about the drug began to appear in Polish scientific papers.

The post-war period ushered in the tense **Cold-War** era, and the **intelligence** departments of many countries began experimenting with drugs to see if they could be used as weapons. One of the drugs that seemed promising in this area was LSD, and military scientists tried similar experiments with MDMA. Unlike LSD, which began to filter onto the streets because of its obvious power, MDMA once more faded into the background because it was less effective in research. The military also abandoned research on MDA, the more powerful parent drug of MDMA.

The *love drug*

During the 1960s, a chemist named Alexander Shulgin began **synthesizing** large quantities of **hallucinogens** and spreading the word about MDA and MDMA. Dubbed the *love drug* by California drug takers, MDA was soon made illegal because its effects resembled those of LSD. In 1972, MDMA, or ecstasy, arrived on the scene as a legal alternative.

California, during the early 1970s, provided fertile territory for the introduction of a legal drug that promised to make people feel happy, energetic, and friendly toward each other. Marriage counselors and therapists recommended ecstasy to the public. It seemed as though the drug provided a way of making people feel better about themselves while drawing others into the sense of friendship and well-being.

In California during the 1970s, many young people celebrated the *love drug.*

"What I found was a lot of people waiting for me to come down from the clouds and begin sharing in the good and bad of being a real person again. What seemed like a gift was just another shortcut that eventually led to nowhere of importance."

(From an anonymous former user of ecstasy)

The Final Dance

Even during the 1970s, when ecstasy was building a reputation for producing happiness and contentment, it was still dispensed mainly by doctors and psychiatrists. The drug was banned in Britain in 1977, but remained legal in the United States until 1985. The legality of ecstasy concerned some people who had been involved with LSD for twenty years. Some researchers continued to believe that LSD could have been a useful, legal **psychological** tool, if only its use had not become so widespread during the 1960s. They believed that ecstasy would suffer the same fate if it became a popular street drug.

The beat goes on

In the United States, many legal manufacturers of the drug clung to the notion that they were benefiting science and society in general. They issued instructions on how to take the drug and what effects to look for. By the mid-1980s, however, their voices were lost in the loud public outcry against the drug that seemed to be taking young people by storm. Much of the reaction was not just to the drug but to the throbbing, rhythmic beat of the dance music.

Young people had realized that ecstasy improved their ability to appreciate sounds, especially rhythmic sounds. Recording companies moved to cash in on this revelation by producing dance music that would energize a large group of people high on ecstasy. In 1985, the real breakthrough came when House music was developed in a Chicago club called the Warehouse (which gave the music its name). House music, and its vital ecstasy element, took the world by storm. However, that same year the U.S. government made ecstasy illegal.

"The party's over. Ecstasy hurts the brain. It is no longer a hypothesis. The drug is toxic. It is no longer appropriate to consider it a recreational drug."

(Alex Stalcup, a physician who runs a drug treatment center in Concord, Calif.)

Who Takes Ecstasy?

Many illegal drugs are popular within a certain social group, or with those taking part in a certain activity. For many people, the path to using ecstasy lies through the world of all-night dancing at raves. Ecstasy, like amphetamines, lets people manage with less sleep (at least for the short term) and allows them to carry on for hours.

All night long

The link between **stimulant** drug use and all-night dancing is not exactly new. Even before **World War II,** people in clubs around the world would take cocaine to stay up dancing until dawn. The rave scene achieves the same result. However, unlike the cocaine experience, which was pursued only by a relatively few people, ecstasy use seems to have reached a greater portion of the population.

Ecstasy has been the power behind the new dance culture because it promotes **empathy** among users. This good-time feeling contrasts strongly with the aggression that had long been associated with bars, discos, and alcohol.

Brief heyday, long-term damage?

Use of ecstasy escalates among people in their mid-teens, many of whom have achieved just enough independence to stay out late. It usually ends when people reach their twenties, or even sooner. Few people in their twenties can afford to lose a night's sleep without suffering negative effects in their studies or work. The experience of ecstasy and raves has not been proven to lead people to use heavier drugs so, for most people, their last *e* tablet is also their last illegal drug. However, by that time, damage may have already been done. According to the National Institute on Drug Abuse, a study showed that monkeys exposed to MDMA for just four days experienced brain damage that was evident 6 to 7 years later.

Using Ecstasy

Use of ecstasy has become much more widespread during the last decade. Its price has dropped, which is part of the reason for this spread. Ecstasy is no longer reserved for special occasions. Ecstasy use is creeping into more everyday settings and situations. In fact, one British commentator suggested that ecstasy is becoming a "Tuesday night playing darts at the pub" type of drug. In other words, ecstasy is becoming an accompaniment to all sorts of activities. It is becoming harder to consider any single user as a *typical ecstasy user.*

The ecstasy scene

However, the overall majority of ecstasy users share some characteristics. People might be attracted to ecstasy for all sorts of reasons, ranging from previous experience with **hallucinogens** and **stimulants** to simple curiosity. People who continue to use the drug regularly do so because they identify with the ecstasy scene.

Many people who use ecstasy have no idea of the price they could pay for the extra energy boost that *e* seems to provide. The body of a repeat ecstasy user is slowly worn out with each sleepless night, and the way that ecstasy suppresses the appetite harms its system. As a result, frequent ecstasy users often feel listless or frazzled during the day.

Raving all night

In the early evening, the ravers assemble. The night's rave might have been planned much earlier in the week, although some still occur at a moment's notice, with carloads of teenagers descending on a deserted barn or warehouse. Just before arriving at the rave, the group takes their *e* tablets. Within an hour, the effects have taken hold and the ravers begin to respond to the music's rhythm. The effects of the drug wear off after about four hours, but by that point the rave has a momentum of its own, carrying the dancers on to daybreak.

Who Sells Ecstasy?

In many ways, the distribution network for ecstasy is different from those for other illegal drugs. Obtaining supplies of drugs that produce a strong physical **dependence** often means approaching unknown dealers. Many dealers fit the image of the shady character offering something from the inside pocket of a raincoat.

Casual exchanges

Getting ahold of ecstasy is a more informal affair. People often buy ecstasy from close friends or people they have seen repeatedly at raves. The nearest comparison is with marijuana, which people often obtain from friends whom they trust. Typically, a friend or fellow raver will ask if someone is carrying, or has the pill they want. Very few people, however, actually make ecstasy. Therein lies the danger.

A leap of faith

Because the production and sale of ecstasy is illegal, its distribution operates outside any type of legal guidelines or regulations. In any *e* transaction, the buyer is never sure of what he or she is actually buying. Some ecstasy tablets have no trace of the drug in them at all, although most samples contain varying amounts of MDMA or related drugs. There is also a risk that an *e* tablet contains animal tranquilizers, amphetamines, caffeine, or LSD. Drugs experts warn that ecstasy capsules are particularly risky since they can easily be opened and altered.

"The majority of people who end up in the E.R. after taking ecstasy are almost certainly not taking MDMA but something masquerading under its name. "

(from "Happiness is . . . a Pill?," *Time*, June 5, 2000)

Wider Effects

Any widespread use of an illegal drug among young people is bound to cause confusion and conflict within the family, and with non-using friends. Although some estimates suggest that more than a million young people are using ecstasy regularly, often every weekend, there are still many more who do not. Many of these people are friends of ecstasy users, and the relationship between the two groups often becomes strained. The same is true among families.

Parental dilemma

Most parents of people who take ecstasy were in their late teens about thirty years ago. The late 1960s was a time of intense drug use, coupled with parental conflict and a general sense of rebellion against traditional values. It is somewhat ironic for many parents, some of whom have their own histories of drug use, to face the same behavior in their own children. Apart from the issue of staying out late, the dance scene itself does not prove to be a terrible threat to family

life. Parents know that they must separate their disapproval of drug use from other feelings about raves themselves. In fact, a large number of ravers don't participate in the drug scene. Ben Wilke, a Houston raver, says, "Real party kids don't do drugs. We go to dance and have a good time."

❝After talking to [Sara's friends], I know if they have concerns about a friend, they don't know whom to talk to. . . . If only they had some sort of third party, a minister, a school counselor, a place where they can go to tell someone. I think things would have been different if I had been told.❞

(Janice Aeschlimann of Naperville, Illinois, whose 18-year-old daughter Sara died in May of 2000 after overdosing on ecstasy)

A test of relationships

Until the drug-use question becomes highly charged, or deadly, most ecstasy users do not think that their drug use threatens their family relationships. For their part, they do not expect their parents to know about—or condone—the use of ecstasy. Tragically, as in the case of Sara Aeschlimann of Naperville, Illinois, parents don't know about their children's *e* use until it's too late. Sara died of an ecstasy overdose during her senior year of high school.

Friendships, however, are a different matter. A drug user's regular habit puts a strain on friendships with non-users. Non-users worry about their friends' drug habit and wonder whether the friend's quest to be "cool" overshadows common sense. Second, a change of attitude can take place in the ecstasy user. Ecstasy makes it hard to take many things seriously, and such activities as studying or playing sports might lose their appeal.

Supply and demand

Supply of ecstasy has managed to keep up with the growing demand for the drug. Because each pill costs only pennies to make but sells for $20 to $40 per tablet on the street, dealers have an incentive to keep pushing it.

Many people can get the sense of shared experience and good feelings through activities in which drugs play no part.

"In Windsor [Ontario] in the late 1970s, it was known as 'Death.' You know why from recent history."

(A drug science expert at the DEA's Drug and Chemical Evaluation Section)

Life with Ecstasy

Using ecstasy involves running risks that many ravers choose to ignore or to play down. These risks are not just confined to regular users; even a single ecstasy tablet can lead to death. While it is very uncertain whether anyone has died directly from the **toxic** effects of the drug, fatalities have occurred from other complications.

Overheating **(far right)** is a common problem among ecstasy users. Users with even minor heart conditions can face risks usually associated with older patients **(below).**

Heatstroke

Dozens of ecstasy deaths have resulted from overheating. Ecstasy raises the body temperature and encourages repeated behavior like frantic dancing, which also raises temperatures. Added to this is the hot environment of most dance floors. Body temperature can exceed the danger limit of 110°F (43°C). Symptoms then include **convulsions,** very low blood pressure, and highly increased heart rate. MDMA seems to interfere with the way blood **coagulates** in the body. If it coagulates in the lungs, the person dies of suffocation.

Too much fluid

Most ravers realize that they need to replace the fluids they lose through sweating and increased body temperature. Drinking too much, however, can lead to trouble. Again, the problem seems to relate to signals that MDMA sends within the body. It prevents the kidneys from expelling excess fluids from the body. Water is retained in the body, especially in brain cells that regulate bodily functions such as breathing and heart rate. Symptoms include dizziness and confusion. In serious cases, the person lapses into a **coma**.

Heart failure

The third major cause of ecstasy-related death comes from the rise in heart rate and blood pressure during an ecstasy high. Although many young people are fit enough to cope with this increased pressure on the circulatory system, others might have even minor heart conditions that had previously been unnoticed. Faced with such a sudden rise in blood pressure, a faulty **coronary** system might fail, causing death.

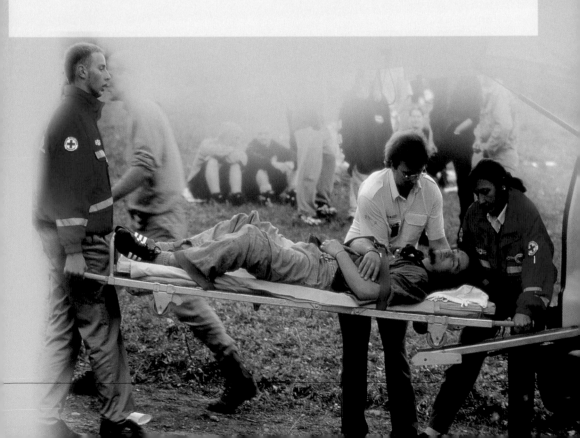

The case of Sara Aeschlimann

On May 13, 2000, Sara and her friends were watching movies in an affluent suburb of Chicago. Police say they took some altered ecstasy tablets there. She died the next day, Mother's Day, of an overdose of paramethoxyamphetamine, a substance some mistake for *e*.

Sara's mother Janice believes that pressure to succeed sent Sara down the treacherous path to her death. "These kids are not bad kids—sports players, pompom girls, smart kids . . . There is the pressure of trying to succeed like your parents or an older sibling. There's a lot of pressure in that."

Sara's mother believes that if she had known about her daughter's ecstasy use she could have prevented the tragedy.

"When [Sara] was lying in the hospital bed and the doctor said there wouldn't be much time, I prayed that this wouldn't be for nothing."

(Janice Aeschlimann, mother of 18-year-old Sara, who died of an ecstasy overdose)

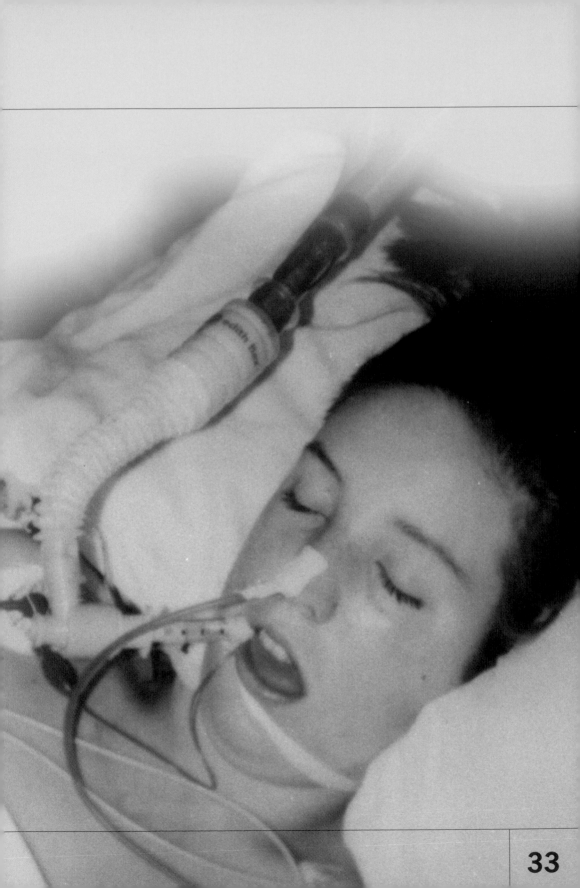

Rave Risks

Although ecstasy is not extremely bad in terms of **dependence,** repeated use can lead to a range of problems—some minor and others more serious. People do build up **tolerance,** and the higher dose that they end up taking can open them up to some **toxic** side effects. Among these are nausea, dizziness, jaw tension, and **heatstroke**.

The heat is on

Although ecstasy is nearly a century old, it has only made headlines for about a decade. It may be too soon to tell how many medical complications might arise from repeated use of the drug, although researchers are beginning to gather evidence that it might cause long-term liver damage in some people.

The issue that has caught the public imagination is the problem of overheating and heatstroke. Both of these problems can arise in a first-time experience, but they are more likely to occur when someone has been taking relatively high doses over a long time. Basically, ecstasy is a **stimulant;** it makes users able to dance longer, which in turn makes them hot.

The drug also raises the body temperature, which makes the user hotter still. These two factors, coupled with the hot and crowded conditions on most dance floors, mean that quarts of water are sweated out. The result can lead to **dehydration** and heatstroke.

Other concerns

This principle of tolerance to the drug increases the problem of overheating and is also linked to other negative side effects. Research into this matter is sometimes **contradictory,** but serious concerns have been raised. For example, four Scottish ravers died in 1992 of **brain hemorrhages,** although three of them had also been using amphetamines. Equally troubling is the suggestion that ecstasy might damage brain cells. Ecstasy is believed to damage the cells that produce and transmit a chemical known as serotonin. Serotonin is said to control sleep, appetite, and mood; however, knowledge about the chemical is limited. It is difficult to prove with certainty what harm ecstasy might do.

The Ecstasy Industry

Ecstasy has evolved from being a drug used in the preparation of other drugs to become a popular drug in its own right. Despite its illegal status in nearly every country, it continues to be produced in vast quantities. Some of the production is due to the many chemical **formulae** that Alexander Shulgin and other chemists have put in the public domain over the years. These formulae offer virtual step-by-step instructions on how to produce ecstasy and other **derivatives** of its parent drug, MDA.

Return to research

News reporters must sift through rumor, hearsay, and conflicting medical reports to try to present a clear picture of ecstasy to their readers.

Even if ecstasy is nowhere near as powerful as LSD, their histories and the industry surrounding them have run parallel. Many of the same people who, during the time when ecstasy was still legal in the United States, argued for a pause before letting it go public are now pressing for further research.

Ecstasy was banned in 1985 in the United States specifically because of the fears that it would damage brain cells. At the time, the evidence leading to this conclusion was based on animal experiments that used much higher doses of MDMA than those taken by humans. The drug was **injected** into rats and monkeys, rather than being taken orally, which is the way most ecstasy users take it. For these reasons, the evidence was discounted; however, studies show that the doses ingested by *e* users today parallel those in the experiments.

❝I think it is important to recognize that, particularly in the rave situation, there are individuals taking six, eight, or ten tablets over a twenty-four to forty-eight hour period. So some of the more recent patterns of human MDMA use in the rave setting are beginning to mimic the regimen of drug administration that we employed in our monkeys.❞

(Doctor George Ricaurte, defending his 1980s animal research on MDMA)

The unknown purpose of serotonin has meant that claims that ecstasy *can* cause brain damage are not the last word. One important question has remained unanswered: just how *does* ecstasy affect people? The beginnings of an answer emerged in California in May 1994, when Doctor Charles Grobb became the first doctor to legally give ecstasy to a human being since its **criminalization.** Grobb's findings confirmed several points that had been observed on dance floors. First, ecstasy does cause an increase in core body temperature, even in the people who had remained in bed throughout the testing period. Second, there is a mild but persistent raising of blood pressure.

Both of these findings fit in with what is described as **anecdotal** research— the first-hand accounts of ecstasy users. They also highlight the dangers of overheating and heart-related problems. What none of the research has discovered, however, is just how ecstasy produces its unique sense of **empathy** among those who take it.

Altered ecstasy

These American researchers, and others studying ecstasy, stress that their work is done with pure MDMA. What people actually buy on the street or in clubs is a different matter, since it can easily be mixed with other drugs. Drug agencies have become particularly concerned by the risk associated with this type of ecstasy. They note that there are two types of ecstasy being sold on the street. The first is actually MDMA, but is very closely linked to the powerful MDA. The second is entirely fake, comprising aspirin, amphetamines, LSD, or other drugs.

A California organization called *DanceSafe* sets up tables at raves, where users can get information and have *e* pills tested. The group has found that as much as 20 percent of the so-called ecstasy sold at raves contains something other than MDMA, and that 40 percent of the pills are fake.

Seemingly identical, a selection of ecstasy tablets can easily contain a number of altered doses.

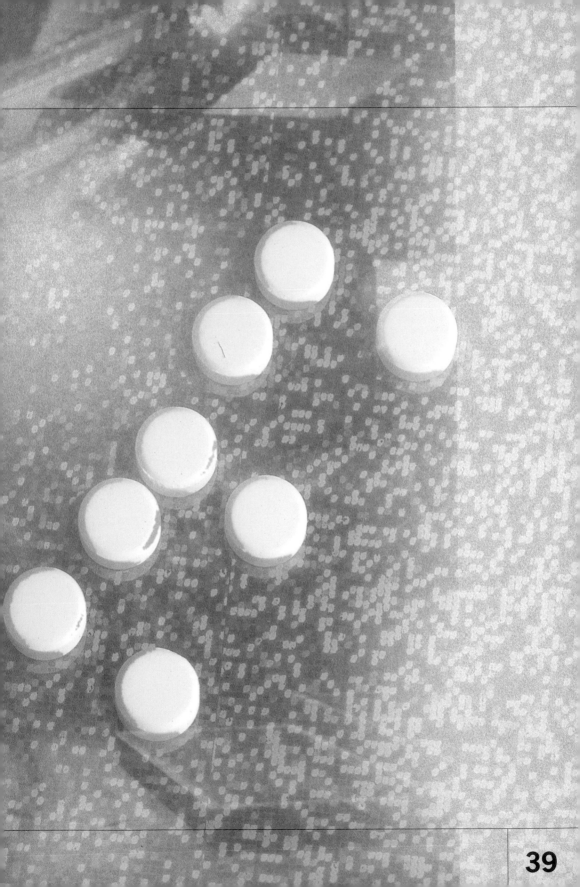

Cashing In

While researchers have been occupied by trying to get to the truth about ecstasy and its effects, the drug itself has continued to enjoy widespread popularity. As a result, the ecstasy scene, sometimes described as *e culture,* generates huge amounts of money. Some of this money finds its way into the hands of drug dealers and **traffickers,** but ecstasy trafficking does not have the same sense of international intrigue, profits, and violence that accompanies the trade in heroin or cocaine.

The rave economy

There is, however, a vast area of economic activity that has benefited directly from the whole club culture. The late 1990s saw a move away from the massive, unplanned raves in abandoned warehouses and toward more commercial clubs. Entrance fees of $10 a head can still generate a good profit for a nightclub.

The whole culture surrounding the dance scene, with which ecstasy is so closely linked, has led to many developments in the wider world of business.

While raves have existed for a decade, the rituals, visuals, fashion, and sounds associated with raves have recently started influencing pop music, advertising, and computer games. The electronic art inspired by the rave scene has influenced a new graphic sensibility, with vivid typography and science-fiction inspired imagery popping up in advertisements for products ranging from cologne to automobiles. Companies with no obvious link to drugs or ecstasy generally have seen the potential for generating more sales among young people. Products such as soft drinks, convenience foods, and even banking services are advertised in a way that reminds ecstasy users of the wacky point of view that the drug produces. In some cases, the packaging of familiar products has been redesigned to be brighter and more carefree in their design.

Growing Concern among Law-Enforcement Officials

Because ecstasy users tend to keep to themselves at dance parties, there was no violence or theft tied to the drugs, as there is with much more widely known drugs such as cocaine or heroin. Therefore, many drug agencies focused their efforts on the more "dangerous" drugs. The ecstasy scene is becoming more dangerous, however, as the lure of outrageous profits attracts organized crime. In 1999, U.S. authorities arrested Sammy Gravano, a former mafia member, for allegedly running an ecstasy ring in Arizona. According to authorities, Gravano's ring distributed 25,000 pills each week, worth $500,000 on the street.

The music industry has also benefited from the rave scene. Deejays associated with the rave scene have become celebrities in their own right. Such performers as Van Dyk, Armand Van Helden, Keoki, and BT are considered artists and superstars. American deejay-composer Moby, whose 1995 album *Everything is Wrong* sold about 125,000 copies, says the rave scene offers a popular alternative to today's bubblegum pop.

"Club culture used to talk a lot about *freedom*. It's turning out to be the freedom to be farmed."

(Journalist Stephen Kingston, quoted in *Altered State* about the "business boom" in rave culture)

Legal Matters

In the United States ecstasy is controlled under the Comprehensive Drug Abuse Prevention and Control Act of 1970. It is illegal to possess or supply it to other people. It is also illegal to produce, import, or export ecstasy, or to allow premises to be used for its production or supply. The U.S. Drug Enforcement Agency (DEA) lists ecstasy among the most serious drugs of abuse in Schedule 1 of its drugs classification.

Heavier penalties

Anti-drug laws in most countries have more severe penalties for drug production and trafficking than for possession of drugs for personal use. In the United States, for example, the maximum sentence for trafficking ecstasy is 20 years in prison and a $1 million fine.

Zero tolerance policies

Many schools throughout the United States have devised their own policies to control drug use on their premises. Under their so-called zero tolerance policies, any student caught possessing or selling any illegal drug can be immediately expelled from school. Such zero-tolerance policies exist in many U.S. workplaces and sports organizations as well.

Controlled Substance Act

The Controlled Substances Act (CSA), Title II of the Comprehensive Drug Abuse Prevention and Control Act of 1970, is the legal foundation of the United States government's fight against the abuse of drugs and other substances. This law is a consolidation of many laws regulating the manufacture and distribution of narcotics, stimulants, depressants, hallucinogens, steroids, and chemicals used in the unlawful production of controlled substances.

Organizers of many public events mount
their own drug checks to make sure no one
with drugs is admitted.

Treatment and Counseling

When people talk about the need for drug treatment and counseling, they are usually referring to the large group of drugs that lead to **dependence,** especially physical dependence. Some form of outside help, in the form of therapy sessions or private counseling, is often necessary to overcome the compulsive desire to have more of the drug. Ecstasy is different. Although repeated exposure to the rave setting might make people more inclined to become regular users, the problem does not lie in the area of dependence. Instead, awareness of the risks of ecstasy is the key to preventing ecstasy abuse or even overdose.

Reasons to say *no*

The best course of action at a rave, of course, is not to take any drugs. However, because ecstasy is so common in this setting, it is important to review the dangers of taking ecstasy.

The following points might help you make the right choice in such a situation.

- Ecstasy users risk severe dehydration unless they have regular intakes of drinks such as water and fruit juices. This risk is significantly increased for ecstasy users who also drink alcohol; alcohol **dehydrates** the body further.

- The frenetic dancing that takes place at raves puts the ecstasy user at an increased risk for dehydration and overheating.

- Ecstasy users are often tempted to take a higher dose to repeat the experience of that first high. This behavior increases the risk of overheating, dehydration, and overdose.

Dehydration alert

Remember that a person who fails to sweat despite frenetic dancing, and who suffers from cramps, dizziness, and nausea, shows an immediate risk of **dehydration.** If you see a friend dehydrating, remember to get help immediately by calling an ambulance. Get the person somewhere cool and splash him or her with cold water.

Raving in New Jersey

According to drug officials, New Jersey and New York are the ecstasy hubs of the United States. A rave in North Bergen, New Jersey, is typical of the rave scene in New York, Florida, and California.

The crowd is mostly middle class, overwhelmingly white, and exceedingly polite. Most are teenagers or people in their early 20s. They had paid $20 to get in, but only $15 if they brought the science-fiction-influenced flyer advertising the event. Many ravers on the scene say they don't take drugs themselves but like the atmosphere of acceptance at raves that they can't find at school. "It's all about the music, the love, the vibe," says Sunny, a history major. Even the people who avoid drugs say that an ecstasy-influenced undercurrent defines the party, the music, and even the clothes. The concession stand caters to ecstasy users, with such items as pacifiers and lollipops to lubricate mouths, and bottles of fruit juice or water to prevent dehydration.

As the night wears on, teenagers huddle cross-legged in clumps. Many are intertwined like nesting kittens. New acquaintances kiss or rub each other's shoulders.

Possessing and taking ecstasy are illegal, but until recently, the police have rarely raided these well-publicized raves. They preferred to focus on major violent crimes and serious drugs. However, concern about altered ecstasy pills and new research about the brain damage that the drug can cause have attracted the attention of law enforcement officials across the country.

Public health publications like this poster in Europe publicize the facts about ecstasy and its many side effects.

ecstasy
know the score

Take E now and you might feel fine. But if you take E you're a human guinea-pig because no-one knows what the long term effects are. Unlike other pills you can buy, E hasn't been medically tested.

What we do know about E is that some people have suffered from strokes, depression, mental illness and even fallen into comas.

There's also some indication that taking E might lead to brain damage. Nobody can be 100% sure, but it's some gamble for a night out.

There's some confusion about how much water to drink on E. When dancing, you need to sip about a pint of non-alcoholic liquid an hour to replace lost fluids. Also remember to wear loose, light clothes and just chill out regularly.

You sweat a lot when you dance, so it's not just the water you've got to replace, there's sodium too. Fruit juice or an energy drink should do the job. It works for marathon runners.

If you'd like more information about drugs or just a talk, give us a call free and in total confidence.

49

People to Talk To

Ecstasy has swept into the public consciousness generally because of its rapid rise in popularity. Although it has become incredibly popular with a certain segment of society, the overall effects of the drug remain unknown. Its reputation as a *happy drug* that draws people together, as well as pressure from drug-using friends, might tempt many young people to try it. While such **peer pressure** is not helpful, it is a strong and persuasive force in the world of young people.

Find a voice of reason

There are people to talk to who can put things in a different perspective, either by giving first-hand accounts of their own drug experiences or by outlining the clear dangers of ecstasy abuse. It is best to turn to parents and older family members first. Unfortunately, many young people feel that they have little in common with their parents. Even sympathetic teachers and other local authorities, such as clergy or law enforcement officials, might seem too close to home.

In the United States, young people can call a wide range of telephone numbers to find out more about ecstasy. Many of the numbers are toll-free, and most are anonymous. Whether you approach one of these organizations, a family member, a youth leader, or a teacher, the important thing is to be able to talk— and listen—openly about your drug concerns. Sharing a problem or worry is the first step towards solving it.

A school setting can provide an informative, yet informal, opportunity to share knowledge about ecstasy.

Information and Advice

The United States is well served by organizations providing advice, counseling, and other information relating to drug use. All of the contacts listed on these pages are helpful springboards for obtaining such advice or for providing confidential information over the telephone or by mail.

Contacts in the United States

**American Council for Drug Education
164 West 74th Street
New York, NY 10023
1-800-488-DRUG**

**Child Welfare League of America
440 First Street N.W.
Washington, DC 20001
(202) 638–2952**
The Child Welfare League of America, based in Washington, provides useful contacts across the country in most areas relating to young people's problems, including drug involvement.

**DARE America
P.O. Box 775
Dumfries, VA 22026
(703) 860–3273**
Drug Abuse Resistance and Education (DARE) America is a national organization that links law-enforcement and educational resources to provide up-to-date and comprehensive information about all aspects of drug use.

**National Clearinghouse for Alcohol and Drug Information (NCADI)
P.O. Box 2345
Rockville, MD 20847
1-800-729-6686**

**Narcotics Anonymous
P.O. Box 9999
Van Nuys, CA 91409
1-800-467-7314**

**Partnership for a Drug-Free America
405 Lexington Ave., 16th Floor
New York, NY 10174
(212) 922-1560**
A private, nonprofit, nonpartisan group of professionals from the communications industry working to inform young people about the dangers of drugs.

**Youth Power
300 Lakeside Drive
Oakland, CA 94612
(510) 451–6666, Ext. 24**
Youth Power is a nationwide organization involved in widening awareness of drug-related problems. It sponsors clubs and local affiliates across the country in an effort to help young people make their own sensible choices about drugs, and to work against the negative effects of peer pressure.

More Books to Read

Alvergue, Anne. *Ecstasy: The Danger of False Euphoria.* New York, N.Y.: Rosen Publishing Group, 1997.

Jaffe, Steven L., ed. Introduction by Barry R. McCaffrey. *How to Get Help.* Broomall, Pa.: Chelsea House Publishers, 1999.

Jaffe, Steven L. *Ecstasy and Other Designer Drugs.* Broomall, Pa.: Chelsea House Publishers, 1999.

Mass, Wendy. *Teen Drug Abuse.* San Diego, Calif.: Lucent Books, 1997.

Robbins, Paul R. *Designer Drugs.* Berkeley Heights, N.J.: Enslow Publishers, Inc., 1995.

Salak, John. *Drugs in Society: Are They Our Suicide Pill?* Brookfield, Conn.: Twenty-First Century Books, Inc., 1995.

Weatherly, Myra. *Ecstasy and Other Designer Drug Dangers.* Berkeley Heights, N.J.: Enslow Publishers, Inc., 2000.

Glossary

addictive leading to dependence

anecdotal based on personal experience

brain hemorrhage bursting of a blood vessel in the brain

brewer company that produces beer

catalyze cause something to develop

coagulate turn from a liquid into a solid

Cold War period in history after World War II during which the United States and its capitalist Western allies competed with the Soviet Union and its Communist allies for world influence

coma state of prolonged unconsciousness during which a person does not respond to sights or sounds

compound combination of one or more chemical substances

contradictory offering two opposing conclusions

convulsion uncontrolled shaking of the body

coronary relating to the heart

criminalization being made illegal

dehydrate, dehydration lose essential fluids from the body

dependence physical or psychological craving or need for something

derivative drug or other substance that has been produced from a different original source

empathy understanding of how others feel

euphoria feeling of great happiness or well-being

formula chemical code for producing a substance

hallucinogens substances that produce hallucinations (seeing things that are not really there)

heatstroke possible suffocation because of overheating of the body

injected pumped into the veins, usually with a type of needle and syringe

intelligence governmental department dealing with spying and information about possible enemies

overdose dose of a drug that is too much for the body to absorb or cope with

paramedic person with expert first-aid training

patent gain the legal right to be the only person or company to manufacture a product for sale

peer pressure pressure from friends of the same age to behave in a certain way

pharmaceutical medical use of chemical sciences

pharmacologist chemist who studies the production of medicines

prescribe order the use of a medicine

psychological relating to the mind and behavior

regimen set routine in an experiment

respiratory relating to the lungs or to breathing

stimulant drug that makes people more alert or energetic

suppressant substance that decreases a desire, such as the urge to eat

synthesize produce through chemical processes

synthetic produced by chemical processes

therapeutic medically useful

tolerance way in which the body learns to deal with or expect more of a substance

toxic poisonous

trafficker person who deals with the distribution of drugs, often across international borders

underground hidden from view of the police or other law-enforcement groups

withdrawal negative physical effects of giving up a substance

World War I war (1914–1918) between Germany, Austria, and their allies against Britain, France, and their allies

World War II war (1939–1945) between Germany, Japan, and their allies against Britain, the United States, and their allies

Index